# THE METHODS OF ETHICS

## Gerard J. Dalcourt

UNIVERSITY
PRESS OF
AMERICA

LANHAM • NEW YORK • LONDON

**Copyright © 1983 by**

**University Press of America,™ Inc.**

4720 Boston Way
Lanham, MD 20706

3 Henrietta Street
London WC2E 8LU England

ISBN (Perfect): 0-8191-3550-X
ISBN   (Cloth): 0-8191-3549-6

All University Press of America books are produced on acid-free
paper which exceeds the minimum standards set by the National
Historical Publications and Records Commission.

TO CATHERINE AND ALBERT

# PREFACE

This book is the result of two decades of off and on work. Its roots go back even further. My interest in ethics started when I was a sophomore in high school and one of my teachers loaned me a short text on it. This led to further reading. Later, when I was at the University of Montreal, the variety of moral philosophies aroused a concern about the methods involved. For, it seemed to me then as it still does, that these various conflicting moral theories could not all be correct and that the erroneous ones had to be the result, at least in part, of an inadequate method. I also became convinced that an adequate moral methodology would have to be multifaceted, open to a consideration of whatever kinds of factors that are relevant, be they metaphysicsal, historical, biological or whatever.

My purpose here is to study some of the main issues of ethical methodology. Historically, there have been many different approaches used for working out ethics. So, for the most part I try to analyze and evaluate the more interesting and influential ones, in order to be able to eventually establish what a valid and proper method for developing ethics would have to consist of.

Accordingly, in the first chapter I have dealt with some crucial aspects of philosophical methodology. In the second, I have sketched out the ethical methods used from the Greeks up to the nineteenth century. In the third through the ninth, I have discussed in detail a variety of contemporary approaches. In the last, I have tried to show what an adequate ethical methodology would involve.

Some of this material has previously appeared in somewhat modified form in various journals: "The Evolutionary Approach to Ethics" in The Thomist 23 (1973): 341-365; "The Sociological Approach to Ethics" in Metaphilosophy 4 (1973): 298-320; "The Pragmatist and Situationist Approaches to Ethics" in Thought 51, no. 201 (June, 1976): 135-136, published in New York by the Fordham University Press; and "A Methodology for Moralists" in Philosophica 16 (1975):65-84. I am grateful to the publishers for permission to use them here.

I also want to express my appreciation and thanks to Mrs. Margaret Chiang for her expert and diligent typing of the initial manuscripts and to my son Albert whose knowledge of and help with the word processing equipment were indispensable in the final stages of the work.

G. J. D.

# TABLE OF CONTENTS

## Chapter Three: The Evolutionary Approach to Ethics

## Chapter Four: The Psychological Approach to ethics

## Chapter Five: The Sociological Approach to Ethics

tics of the moral is counterfactual and inadequate 100. His view of freedom is contrary to experience 102, just as his treatment of "soul" is misleading 102. His positivist metaphysics is the source of his whole theory and of its inadequacy 102. <u>The use of the sociological method and of the social sciences</u>. Moral sociology is not ethics but is of some value to it 103. Sociologists like Durkheim, Weber, Gorer and Moynihan have provided moralists with useful information and insights 103 but there are many other areas they could investigate 104. The kinds of facts moral sociology may uncover 105, and the kinds of theories 105. Areas of cooperation between moralists and sociologists 106. Sociology as a check to ethics 107. Conclusions 107.

## Chapter Six: Analytic Approaches to Ethics

Initially, the analysts rejected a normative function for ethics,while now they tend to a more traditional and even Aristotelian view 109. We shall sketch and evaluate the development of analytic methods in ethics 110. <u>Intuitionism</u>. Moore helped initiate the analytic movement by his insistence on clarity and method 110, especially in ethics 110, which led him to the view that goodness is a non-natural property 111, and that good acts are known as such only empirically 111. Few accepted his conclusions 112. <u>Emotivism</u>. It is an outgrowth of positivism 112. Stevenson, its main proponent, held that moral statements could be true or false 113, that ethical disagreements involve both beliefs and attitudes 113, that meaning is a dispositional property 114, that moral statements are complex 114, that they can be supported or attacked either rationally or emotively 114. But, Stevenson's analysis of types of disagreements results in reducing ethics to psychology 115; his theory of meaning is questionable 115; and he makes ethics to be ultimately nonrational 116. <u>Prescriptivism</u>. Hare's criticisms of Stevenson 117. He wants to show that ethics is a rational discipline 117, by an analysis of the language of morals 117, which however also fails in its goals 118. <u>Good reasons approach</u>. Toulmin rejects other approaches as unhelpful and false 119. His consists of analyzing moral reasoning itself 119, and accepting an harmonious social life as the basic ethical criterion 120. But his approach, though better than Stevenson's and Hare's, also has ethics to be ultimately arational 120. P. Taylor seeks to remedy this by establishing rational criteria for life styles 122, which are too abstractly formal 122. J. Wilson proposes a teleological approach 122, which though superior lacks an adequate psychological foundation and criteria to rank ends 123. Critique. As analytic ethics developed, internal criticism produced a remarkable evolution 124, which can be described as going from a Humean to a more Aristotelian outlook 124. But, language analysis remains insufficient as an ethical method 125; it needs a metaphysics compatible with our moral experience 127; it has failed to make clear the meaning of goodness 127; though useful, its value is mainly propaedeutic 128, since it is mainly metaethical 129. A proper ethical method will be realist, teleological and empirical 130.


## Chapter Seven: The Pragmatic and Situationist Approaches to Ethics


The unity of these methods 131. The pragmatic method in ethics. Originated with Peirce 131, continued by James 132, but mainly developed by Dewey 133, along positivist lines 134; he held a scientific ethics to be verifiable through a pragmatic and concrete testing 134, on the levels of needs and ends 135, so that means determine ends 135, which have no hierarchy 136, and the quest for ultimate ends is harmful 136. Fletcher combines pragmatism and moral theology 136, rejects any moral system 136, holds love to be the only absolute 137, points out his four basic presuppositions 137, and reduces situationism to six propositions 137. Comparison of Fletcher with Peirce and Dewey 138. Critique. Concern with the concrete situation is valid 140, but any pragmatic testing involves some sort of world-view 140, as Dewey's and Fletcher's views on scientific ethics make clear 141. Dewey's notion of method is univocal 142. Growth and love do not really work as ultimate moral criteria 142. Thus, pragmatic ethics is not pragmatic 144. Fletcher's views are an inconsistent combination of traditional and Deweyite ideas 145. The main reason for his difficulties is his nominalism 146, which produces problems that are linguistic 146, and metaphysical 147. His "positivism" also involves him in inconsistency and arbitrariness 147. Conclusions. The theories of the pragmatists result more from their metaphysics than from their method 148. Fletcher is right in rejecting Dewey's view of the continuity of means and ends 148. Neither of them provide a workable hierarchy of ends 149. A pragmatic test is of value for means, but not for ends 149. Thus, pragmatism has validity as a secondary method 149.

# Chapter Eight: The Idealist Approach to Ethics

While some idealists follow an Aristotelian method, more typically they employ a Kantian-like one 151, as does our paradigm here, G. Bastide 151. Bastide's methodology. He sees ethics as a dynamic and reflexive critique 152, whose method is the contrary of the realist one 152, and which creates its own values 153. He distinguishes four ethical methods: doctrinal edification 154, mystical exaltation 155, technological intervention 156, and reflexive provocation 158 which is the source of moral authenticity 159, spiritual conversion 160, the transfiguration of values 161 and criteria for an authentic conscience 162. Characteristics of his method 163. Application of it to the family 164. Critique. Despite his synoptic grandeur, his method is defective 168. It is not necessarily idealist 168; it results from a misinterpretation of realism 169, and from a faulty metaphysics 170 and epistemology 171. He is inconsistent in regard to the objectivity of values 172. His moral criteria are too broad and formal 173 and insufficiently concrete and objective 173. His treatment of retrospection is inconsistent 174, as is also his treatment of natural structure and functions 174. His notion of reflexive provocation is unworkable, mystical and unSocratic 176. His power as a moralist does not derive from his proclaimed method 177, which is helpful mainly in clarifying certain aspects of morality 177.

# Chapter Nine: The Neo-Thomistic Approach to Ethics

The development of neo-Thomism 179. Thomistic theory. The method of ethics is a combination of analysis and synthesis 179. Its basis in Aquinas 180. Its exposition by Sortais 181. Critique. We must be careful not to read too much into Aquinas' texts 183. His practice shows that his approach was dialectical 183, and consciously so 185. Neo-Thomists are overly abstract 185, insufficiently empirical 185, and imprecise 188. Why they disregard dialectics 188. Conclusions 189.

# Chapter Ten: The Method for Ethics

# CHAPTER ONE

# THE PROBLEM OF PHILOSOPHICAL METHODOLOGY

## Notion of Method

The notion of method is one that has allured thinking men at least since the time of the Greeks. The dream of discovering <u>the</u> method, the approach that would enable us to effectively and confidently resolve every sort of philosophical issue, has especially in the modern era raised excited expectations.

Although much has been written about the nature and varieties of method, nevertheless it may be helpful if we would try to determine how the notion itself of method arose. Without doubt it is one that goes far back into the prehistory of man. Despite this, we can still see how it was first arrived at. There are four main sorts of activities that men naturally and necessarily perform: knowing, loving, doing and making. They can perform each of these in a multitude of ways and have been doing so for centuries. Now it seems most likely that the notion of method arose initially in the third kind of activity, doing. Even earliest man engaged in a wide variety: hunting, dancing, praying, collecting, playing games, etc. It was certainly not long before he noticed that there were two quite different ways of performing them. He could proceed in a haphazard way, without much thought or planning or, conversely, he could proceed methodically, that is, with knowledge of what he wanted to do, with a plan of how he wanted to do it and with a step by step implementation of that plan. Once the notion of methodical working or doing was developed, it was natural to extend it to the making of things. For, to effectively produce any artifact he had to do so methodically. It certainly was then a short step, too, to extend the notion further to the act of knowing. One could methodically seek out knowledge, e.g., of when and where game was to be found. And it sooner or later likewise became obvious that even in loving, one could be methodical. Too much method here, one could argue, would be the death of love, but that is another matter. The Greek philosophers gave the notion an explicit formulation and development. We continue trying to

1

improve on them.

In this way we can discern what in general we mean by "method". It is a set of means which we adopt to obtain an end. More specifically, it is a plan of how we shall use certain actions and things to achieve a given end. We may note further that it is a set of means that has not only a unity of a temporal sort, but, what is more important, a teleological unity. Every step of a methodic procedure is there because it helps us, or at least because we believe that it will help us, to achieve a given end. Every step is ordered to this end and thus they together have and constitute a teleological unity. Another characteristic of a methodic procedure is what we may call its universality. A method, that is, can be used repeatedly as long as its practitioners are seeking the same kind of end and doing so within a similar set of conditions.

A point that should be stressed here is that "method" is an analogous term. Unlike a univocal term such as, say, "typist", which means only one particular kind of person, "method" encompasses various means of quite different sorts. Thus, for instance, we may speak of the method of baking bread, of the scientific method, of Hemingway's method of writing, of the method of listening to music and even of a method of resting. The methodical baking of bread involves carefully and precisely following a given sort of recipe, if one is to end up with a product that one could call bread. In employing the scientific method, on the other hand, a person follows certain general canons but he must work out his own "recipe" for each type of problem. What we call the method by which a novelist produces a story will ordinarily be the setting up of a certain number of working conditions that are highly individualized and effective only for psychological reasons and for this particular writer. One writer might stay in bed all morning, musing, then dictate a whole chapter, while another may be able to produce only if he sits at his typewriter on a hard chair with classical music in the background. From the point of view of method, listening to a symphony is in part active and in part passive; you expect and look for diverse sorts of patterns in the music, but you have to leave yourself open to the orchestra so that it can manifest them to you. Resting methodically though does not involve passivity so much as inactivity: one avoids any activity, or at least any activity that produces tension. Thus, in each of these cases "method" means a quite different kind of activity but this diversity of activities warrants a

2

common name because all these activities are similar in certain ways: they are all means to ends and they are means that we may consciously intend to use repeatedly, as often as the situation may warrant it.

The point that "method" is not a univocal term but an analogous one is of some importance. It is clear that it is at least usually far preferable to be methodical. However, should one think that "method" is a univocal term, then he will say that all activities, if they are to be methodical, must follow the same patterns. This is a fairly common error. To illustrate, this mistake seems to be at least a part of what is behind the claim that one should always be scientific, i. e., that one should always use the scientific method. Because the method scientists have developed in the last four hundred years has proven so effective in their endeavors, many people have concluded that only the scientists have method and that to be methodical and therefore effective, we should all adapt to our activities the patterns developed by the scientists. To do this is to maintain that "method" is and can only be univocal. But this clearly does not work. For, mathematicians could never develop geometries through the scientific method. The activities that men engage in are of such fundamentally diverse sorts that success can come only through using radically different kinds of procedures, which have just an analogical sameness. These procedures are all, though different from each other, methodical. So, what will be a good method in one situation will not necessarily be so in another.

Method involves, we may also note, an imposition of rationality into our activities. Even in the case of behavior that is unthinking and habitual, there was necessarily, at the beginning of it, some insight into different ends one could choose between and a reasoned choice of which means one would use. On an automotive assembly line a man may be so used to putting certain parts together that he can do so practically without thinking, and, indeed, he may even be ignorant of the name, nature and function of those parts. But his activity is, despite his subjective incomprehension, methodical and eminently rational, because of the insightful directions of the plant engineers. Thus, even though reason may seem to be often submerged by tides of habitual methods, it continues, though sometimes unreasonably, to direct us--The Bridge on the River Kwai. But we can lead effective and fruitful lives only to the extent that we proceed according to reason and method. Descartes was right at least on

3

this.

Method also involves discipline. Being methodical does not just come of itself. It requires awareness of and submission to a plan of action, even though this results in considerable pain or tedium. It requires at a minimum then a high degree of individual self-discipline. But as the maintenance and progress of civilization and culture are a social affair, in which being methodical is pre-eminently necessary, most of our activity on this level involves a social discipline. Electing a president, for instance, requires long-range and detailed planning on national, state and local levels and the cooperation of thousands.

## Methods of Philosophy

Although philosophers have perennially studied the nature and types of methods, up until the rise of modern philosophy they did not claim that philosophy has its own peculiar method. Instead, taking philosophy to be the most broad sort of warranted knowledge, they tended to identify the method of philosophy with the general methodology of thought. For Plato all truth (and especially philosophy) is to be acquired through dialectics. Aristotle described the development of philosophy in terms of deductive chains of reasoning based on inductively established principles. It was only at the beginning of the modern period that the idea established itself, that just as theology and the natural sciences have their own special methods, so should philosophy.

Among modern philosophers some have proposed for philosophy a more or less purely inductive method. Thus Bacon said, "There are and can exist but two ways of investigating and discovering truth. The one hurries on rapidly from the senses and particulars to the most general axioms, and from them, as principles and their supposed indisputable truth, derives and discovers the intermediate axioms. This is the way now in use. The other constructs its axioms from the senses and particulars, by ascending continually and gradually, till it finally arrives at the most general axioms, which is the true but unattempted way".[1] This first method, the deductive, which Bacon rejected, Descartes accepted. "Having now ascertained certain principles of material things which were derived, not from the prejudices of the senses, but from the light of reason, so that we cannot doubt of their truth, it is for us to examine whether from these alone we can explain all the

4

phenomena of nature. And we shall commence with those which are the most general, and on which the others depend, such as the general structure of the visible world . . . But now, the principles which I have explained above are so broad that we can deduce from them many more things than what we see in the world . . ."[2] This deductive method needed a sound basis, a metaphysics, which is then the fundamental philosophical discipline. Metaphysics, however, was to be established by Descartes and a few elite thinkers. They would use his methodical doubt, which is thus the special method of metaphysics.

It is however especially since Kant and because of his example that modern philosophers have taken to speaking of a method that is totally peculiar to philosophy. For Kant, it was his transcendental method; for Hegel, his dialectical method; for Bergson, the method of intuition.

Our own century has produced a remarkably wide range of opinions regarding the nature and method of philosophy. Thus, the fact that some of the natural sciences, like physics and psychology, were for a long time considered a part of philosophy and became separate sciences only after they had acquired a certain mass of factual data and developed their own methods, has led some to consider philosophy only as potential natural science. In this view philosophy is merely the preparatory, inchoate stage of natural science and is due to disappear as science progressively answers all our questions. Its method is merely an artful search for problems to be solved. This was apparently what William James meant when he said that philosophy was "a collective name for questions that have not yet been answered to the satisfaction of all by whom they have been asked."[3]

Some men of an idealist cast, like R. F. A. Hoernlé and W. M. Urban, have regarded philosophy as a logically articulated faith. Men have spiritual needs they wish to satisfy and values they wish to retain. Philosophy is the development of consistent and coherent views of the universe which satisfy these needs and establish these values. Hoernlé has written, "There is a deep-seated need in the human mind . . . the need to feel at home in the universe. From this source spring all philosophies and all religions. . . It is a need which at once demands to understand the universe and to approve--nay, to live it."[4] Acknowledging that the worth of a philosophy derives from its truthfulness,

Hoernlé maintains there can be no conflict between philosophy considered as truth and as comforting belief. With such a concept of philosophy Hoernlé has little of a positive nature to say of philosophical method. The best that he can tell us is that "there is weighing of considerations, a trying out of alternatives, a mobilizing of all the resources of one's experiences and reflection, a feeling one's way from a distracted and unstable to a coherent and stable outlook."[5]

Since Husserl initiated it some seventy years ago, phenomenology has not gained many adherents in English-speaking countries, but it has had an immense influence on the continent. One of the main reasons for its success has been the promise of its method. Philosophy, said Husserl, must go to things as they are in themselves, for it can make no real progress unless grounded upon a clear and adequate grasp of the objects of the universe. This it can attain only by a manifold abstraction or "reduction". On the side of the observer this involves first the elimination of all subjectiveness: the object is what counts, not his own cognitive or emotional processes; second, the elimination of the theoretical: any hypothesis or previously gained factual knowledge should not enter, so that the mind may attend simply and wholly to the object itself; third, the elimination of all tradition, that is, all that was previously taught or told about the object. On the side of the object there is a dual reduction. The mind considers only the essence of the object, leaving aside on the one hand its existence, and on the other its accidents. One of the first and most influential phenomenologists to apply the method to ethics was Max Scheler, who sought to establish a non-formal theory of values by attending to our higher emotional encounters, in which we achieve an intuitive but neither sensory nor rational grasp of the values involved.

The logical positivists also proclaimed a new doctrine regarding the nature and method of philosophy. There are, they said, two types of propositions. Some are verifiable by experience; these make up the sciences. The others are not so verifiable; they are thus nonsense statements, exemplified by the typical sentences of traditional metaphysics, epistemology and normative ethics. What then is philosophy? It is the logical syntax of scientific language. Here, scientific language means only declarative sentences verifiable experientially and its logical syntax refers to the rules whereby these sentences may be formed and transformed, rules which are established (and are valid) without consideration of the meaning of the words which make up the sentences. The method of philosophy thus consists of those procedures used to analyze the language of science. It has two phases; the first is called formal or syntactical logic and studies the structure of the language without consideration of the words themselves; the second is semantics, which studies the relation of words and propositions to the extramental reality they refer to.[6]

C. J. Ducasse has proposed an interesting theory concerning philosophical method. Philosophy and science cannot be distinguished by their methods because "scientific" means only knowledge-yielding and both in this sense are scientific and use essentially the same methods. The distinction between them thus must come from their subject matter. This however may be either primitive or derivative. The primitive subject matter of philosophy is appraisals, or valuations, which are particular, spontaneous and stated. Particular--made by concrete persons concerning specific objects; spontaneous--made by these persons directly and instinctively, so to speak, not deductively or from habit; stated--that there may be a basis for discussing them. Such appraisals are experiential facts and form the data of philosophy. The methods to apply to these data are those of the natural sciences, generalized and modified for the purpose. Ducasse summarized his methodological position in this way: "The conceptual apparatus of which a philosophical theory consists, and the processes by which it is constructed, have already been described. They include tentative definition of the particular philosophical predicate with which the theory is concerned, tentative specification of a method for identifying cases of what has thus been defined, testing the validity of those constructs empirically by reference to particular philosophical facts already known (primitive or derivative, as the case may be), and making systematically explicit whatever is implicit in the theory so constructed, once its validity has been sufficiently tested. Some of the things implicit in it are axiological laws, i. e., norms, which are then describable as rational norms or theoretically grounded norms, in constrast to the purely and directly empirical ones mentioned above."[7] Proceeding on tnis basis, Ducasse formulates several methodological precepts which bear an obvious resemblance to those of Descartes.

Since the rise of neoscholasticism some one hundred years ago, its adherents have generally agreed that the proper method of philosophy is a judicious combination of analysis and synthesis, thus going back to what is essentially an Aristotelian and Thomistic position. The analytico-synthetic method is moreover often referred to as common to all scientific knowledge. Thus Mercier has written, "philosophy is science at its most advanced stage: its method is that of science. . . . Since philosophy is the science of being in general, of all beings, it embraces simultaneously the conceptual order and the empirical order. It studies first one then the other analytically, to afterward account for them synthetically. . . In each of the philosophical disciplines one follows the analytico-synthetic method".[8] The neoscholastics, we may note, ordinarily raise no question as to the possibility of a more specific or of a special method for philosophy, although they recognize many such methods for the natural sciences.

One of the more prominent types of philosophy in English speaking countries has, since the end of the war, been linguistic analysis. It also has its own view of the nature and method of philosophy. For analytic philosophers most philosophic difficulties result from misuse of words. And so, the function of philosophy is mainly to analyze our modes of everyday speech, resolve their confusion and thus eliminate our problems. The method linguistic philosophers use follows directly from their notion of the function of philosophy. The very name, linguistic analysis, is taken from their method. We owe to analytic philosophers a growing body of often-times subtle studies of the various shades of of meaning and of the many uses of words. Although some analysts, like Austin, would deny that linguistic analysis is all that there is to philosophy, they all retain the attitude that it is the indispensable and central approach. Thus, Strawson has urged the need for a purged kind of metaphysics which would forego causal explanations and would limit itself to describing how we actually think about the world. But he would achieve this by analyzing our language and thought to bring out the fundamental general notions underlying them.

This variety of examples suggests the following conclusions. First, the notion that one has of the nature and role of philosophy determines what one accepts as its proper method. Because Descartes wanted philosophy to provide certitude, he opted for a mathematical method, the only sort, he felt, that could provide certainty. Similarly, for Husserl the role of philosophy is to provide us with objective knowledge of the world. Consequently its method, he believes, can only be that of reduction, since it is the only one capable of eliminating all subjectivity from our knowledge. Secondly, the more broad and comprehensive one's view of the function of philosophy, the more general will be the method which one accepts. Thus, the scholastics for whom philosophy is the study of the universal order, describe its method in very broad terms, as being analytico-synthetic. On the other hand, Carnap, who sees the function of philosophy to be the clarification of scientific language, correspondingly assigns a method to it that is severely delimited. Thirdly, we cannot then adequately evaluate a method without at the same time and to some degree evaluating the philosophy of which that method is both a source and result. We judge methods also by their fruits.

## Specification of Methods

This wide range of views as to what the method of philosophy should be suggests further that it is necessary to clarify and to specify just what is meant by the question, "What is the method of philosophy?" What is one looking for when he asks this question?

We may distinguish first of all between technical and the so-called logical methods. Some methods consist of manipulations of phenomena, their precise measurement and the determination of the precise conditions under which they occur. They essentially involve physical acts and constitute what are called technical or laboratory methods. Every positive science develops its own. As they are only of secondary interest to the philosopher, we shall not consider them further here. There are however other procedures which deal with the more purely mental type of activity involved in the search for truth. These are the "logical" methods and it is they which attract most of the attention and use of philosophers.

Within the logical methods we find certain rules and procedures which are similar in all of them and which together form a general method. The other rules and procedures are thus the differentia of the special methods.

Descartes epitomized this general method in the well-known four rules of thought he proposed:

The first rule was never to accept anything

as true unless I recognized it to be certainly and evidently such; that is, carefully to avoid all precipitation and prejudgment, and to include nothing in my conclusions unless it presented itself so clearly and distinctly to my mind that there was no reason or occasion to doubt it.

The second was to divide each of the difficulties which I encountered into as many parts as possible, and as might be required for an easier solution.

The third was to think in an orderly fashion when concerned with the search for truth, beginning with the things which were simplest and easiest to understand, and gradually and by degree searching toward more complex knowledge, even treating, as though ordered, materials which were not necessarily so.

The last was, both in the process of searching and in reviewing when in difficulty, always to make enumerations so complete, and reviews so general, that I would be certain that nothing was omitted.[9]

In sum, Descartes is concluding here that the criterion of truth is evidence, that the two major procedures of thought are analysis and synthesis and that we need a check for these procedures.

Analysis and synthesis are notions which have had a long and tortuous history and consequently they have received different and even contrary meanings.[10] In mathematics the modern senses of "analysis" are quite different from those of antiquity. In philosophy, for the scholastics, analysis was an inductive process; for Descartes, a deductive one. Some have called the division of a genus into its species a synthesis, while others have seen in it an analysis. Since however analysis and synthesis are the main procedures of general methodology, it would be well to define them unequivocally.

Etymologically their meaning is clear. Analysis breaks up a whole into its parts, while synthesis combines the parts into a whole. The confusion arises from not distinguishing logical from real wholes. For, to divide a genus into its species is quite different from dividing an animal into its parts. On the grounds of historical precedence, the confusion may best be resolved by accepting as a basis real wholes. Part and whole, then, are analogous to simple and complex, to chemical elements and their compounds, to organs and their living bodies, to causes and their effects, to laws and their subsumed examples, to conditions and their results, to the comprehension of ideas and their extension, to the prior in being and the posterior.

We may then define synthesis as the combining of the simple to form the complex, of elements to form compounds, etc., while, conversely, analysis is the breaking down of the complex into the simple, etc. These are the meanings generally accepted for these terms at present.[11] They correspond moreover to their traditional acceptations.[12]

In this way the previously noted confusion may be resolved. The division of a genus into its species is not an analysis but a synthesis, because in this case division consists of adding specific differences to the genus and this is a composition, a synthesis.

We have referred to analysis and synthesis as the two main procedures of thought. It may however be objected that induction and deduction are. We may respond in this way. Induction is a regression from the instance to the law, from the effect to the cause, from the posterior in being to the prior. Induction is then a form a analysis. Deduction, on the other hand, is a progression from the law to the specific case, from the cause to the effect, from the prior in being to the posterior. It is therefore basically a synthesis.

In practice however it generally seems inadequate to refer to a method simply as "synthetic" or "analytic". For in man's quest for truth the diversity of objects and ends necessitates highly differentiated and specific methods. Thus, observation, experimentation and induction are analytic processes, while classification, deduction and the use of hypotheses and analogies are synthetic. Used separately or combined in diverse ways, these form the special logical methods.

From a different point of view method may also be divided into a) means of discovery, or of invention, that is, the processes used to uncover the truth, and b) means of instruction or of demonstration, the processes designed to convey to others what has been discovered. This distinction is of importance, since teachers and researchers generally tend to present their knowledge in a synthetic fashion, whatever may have been the procedure used in its actual discovery.

The method of invention, especially in the less abstract sciences, is usually the analytic, for generally what is given to us are facts and effects, whose causes and conditions we must determine by analysis. Similarly, the method of presentation is usually the synthetic, for the minds of the hearers are ordinarily most at ease in following through a series of causes and effects when these are presented in their natural order.

These last observations are of course relative. Thus the method of invention in mathematics is usually deductive whereas some sciences may best be taught analytically--for instance, anatomy. At any rate it seems obviously preferable to designate as the method of a science the one whereby that science was developed rather than the one whereby it is merely taught.

Methods of invention may in relation to a particular science be proper, valid or improper. The proper method is the one which produces the most knowledge the most economically. Valid methods are those which produce warranted results. Improper methods are those which are fallacious or which produce results in an unnecessarily roundabout way. The distinction is thus one of degree. A method is proper to a science if it is valid in all or most cases; it is then the principal one to be used. Thus in anatomy observation is a valid method; dissection however is the proper method; on the other hand deduction is improper.

It will help to set our problem in focus if we show in a few simple cases how the above distinctions apply to the non-philosophical sciences. In mathematics the proper method of both invention and demonstration in synthetic; for the mathematician generally starts off with his definitions, postulates and axioms and from these deduces his science. In the physical sciences the method of invention is usually analytic, for here the scientist must infer his definitions and laws from experience; once however he has gained these it is usually easier for him to pass on his information by presenting concrete cases as instances of the laws. In the biological sciences like botany, the method of invention is likewise analytic; however the method of teaching, depending on the circumstances, may just as well be analytic as synthetic. In the social sciences, because of the normative character of jurisprudence, economics and political economy, their development has both inductive and deductive phases; however on account of the peculiar complexity of their objects they are usually best taught by retaining the same methods.

We can now see more clearly what one means when he asks what the method of philosophy is. He would at least ordinarily be inquiring about the method whereby one develops or works out a philosophical theory. He would not be concerned with the method of exposition or of presentation. The problem then is whether one can adequately describe the method of developing one's philosophical viewpoint in terms that are very general, as did Bacon and Descartes,or whether it is possible or necessary to use some more specialized type of procedure.

## Conclusions

Coming back to the variety of modern views concerning the nature and method of philosophy, a comparison of them reveals a noteworthy fact. The neoscholastics seem satisfied to assign to philosophy the completely general method of analytico-synthesis, which is also held by them to be the basic method of all the other sciences. Their justification for this is that philosophy is our most general sort of knowledge of the universal order. The non-scholastics on the other hand tend to ascribe to philosophy a method of its own. They do this on the basis of the analogy of philosophy with the other sciences; if philosophy is really a science, a body of warranted generalizations, it must then like all the other sciences have its own specific method. Since this analogy seems valid we must then face the question of the possibility of a specific method for philosophy.

We can however carry this line of reasoning even further. Philosophy is not a science but a group of sciences. If then philosophy, as science, has a specific method, might not each of the sciences which make up philosophy have its own method?

There are grounds even in the neoscholastic tradition for such a position, at least in part. They are found in the commonly accepted division of sciences into theoretical and practical. For if the prevailing mode of development in the theoretical sciences is different from that of the practical, then it would seem that their methods would also be different, just as the method of the research chemist is different from

13

that of the civil engineer, since methods vary as the purpose and subject matter change. Now an examination of the difference between the speculative and practical disciplines of philosophy shows that their prevailing modes of development do differ.

We may distinguish speulative from practical thinking on several counts. First of all, on the basis of the ends they seek. The speculative sciences are followed primarily for the satisfaction they afford the intellects of their devotees; in them we seek knowledge for the sake of knowledge. In the practical sciences we seek truth in order to realize in the concrete a given ideal or end. As Aristotle phrased it, "The end of theoretical knowledge is truth, while that of practical knowledge is action."[13] Because of this difference in ends they are also distinguished by their subject matter. The proper concern of the former is the necessary relations between things, considered apart from their conditions of existence. The latter, on the contrary, is engrossed in the actual, the concrete, the individual, seeking as it does to remodel the real, to reconstruct conditions in accordance with its purposes. In other words, the practical sciences can be concerned only with what we can make or modify, whereas the speculative sciences deal with what we do not make. (Nevertheless, of course, we can consider artifacts in a relatively speculative fashion). Besides this, the speculative and the practical are also differentiated by their regulatory principles. Thus, in the ontological order the law of identity and the law of contradiction reign supreme; in the moral order the basic principle is to do good and to avoid evil. The metaphysician considers goodness as a transcendental quality of being; the moralist, as the source and cause of his choices. Finally, the speculative and the practical are also distinguished by the type of necessity dominant in each. For, the necessity discovered in natural entities is intrinsic and strict, whereas in the practical order, where we deal with the contingent, the necessity is only hypothetical. A goat has to be what it is, but whether we will milk it or kill it depends on our situation and decision.

Philosophy that is speculative either absolutely or relatively will be analytic in its prevailing mode of development. Since it has to start with the data provided by the senses, which are composite, it can know its objects only by resolving them into their universal formal principles. In other words, it proceeds by reduction of its objects into general and

14

specific differentia, by division and by demonstration of properties. Conversely, practical philosophy will be _grosso modo_ synthetic. Since it is by definition productive, it starts with the product aimed at and it shows how this is reached by certain operations and causes.

The inventive methodology of all sciences will then differ, depending on whether they are theoretical or practical. In the former case they will be predominantly analytic; in the latter case, synthetic. In building up an analytic science, the main methodological tasks are to find the facts and the viewpoint for these which will provide insight into the underlying universal principles. Thus, in regard to the distinction between animate and inanimate, the progress made by Aristotle seems due to his vast knowledge of biological facts, plus the guidance he received from his metaphysical theories; nowadays the problem is still to be able to distinguish the pertinent facts about viruses in order to tell whether or not they are life forms. On the other hand, in the construction of a practical science, once the object aimed at is established, the main problem is to determine what means will best attain that object. Now these also are facts, but being appraisals they are facts of the mental rather than of the physical order. As such they cannot be ascertained by the same methods that are used to establish facts of the physical order. Theoretical and practical sciences thus have to have different kinds of methods.

The problem which remains, and which is a large one, is whether or not we can specify further and more adequately what the methods of the various philosophical disciplines are. Perhaps the most promising way of answering this question would be to determine how progress has been achieved historically in these areas. This should provide considerable insight into what methods are proper and valid. But as we indicated earlier, it would require an overall evaluation of all the different kinds of philosophies, since the effectiveness of any methodology depends primarily on the nature of the endeavor and only secondarily on how it is applied. It will thus remain a debated issue as long as there are competing philosophies.

# CHAPTER TWO

# AN HISTORICAL SKETCH OF ETHICAL METHODOLOGY

In philosophy perhaps more than in all other intellectual disciplines, the statement and solutions of problems are most easily understood through a genetic approach. This also allows a degree of concreteness and a possibility of detail which can go far to limit an errant imagination by providing both writer and reader with a specific, factual background. For this reason we shall consider in this chapter the highlights in the development of ethical methodology up to the nineteenth century.

## Early Greek Thought

A question closely connected with ethical methodology is that of the psychological and historical conditions which permit the development of moral theory. The early history of Greek thought and in particular the remarks of Aristotle on this point are enlightening.

Ethics as a science arose as a practical application of a philosophical viewpoint and attitude. On the one hand, ethics presupposes as philosophically solved certain questions, such as that of human responsibility. On the other, men had always had moral codes, usually based on or closely connected with their religion, but they accepted them on authority, either of God or the gods, or of custom.[1] On occasion they undoubtedly solved a moral problem through purely rational procedures; this however was an exceptional, not a consistent, effort. It was only when the Greeks, dissatisfied with the patent inconsistencies and insufficiency of their traditions and alarmed at the corrosive and unconstructive criticism of the Sophists, sought to establish a theory of behavior in the same way as they had tried to explain the universe: on empirical and rational grounds, that ethics was born, the child of the many moral problems which agitated them and of their confidence in the autonomy and power of mind. Similarly, all the great ethical systems have resulted from the desire to justify rationally a course of conduct.

17

The reason however why the Greeks had so many problems and were so aware of them was that they were a commercial, colonizing and seagoing people and so had a much closer contact with several other different and conflicting cultures and were forcefully shown the relativity of human institutions. Thus, Aristotle's observation[2] that a man needs a wide background of experience to succeed in ethics seems to apply as well to societies. Ethics, indeed philosophy in general, has been the most fertile in the culturally more turbulent epochs of history, which were the richest in variety of experience: the fourth century before Christ, and the thirteenth and nineteenth after.

## The Socratic Method

It was in these circumstances that Socrates gained the distinction of being one of the few thinkers who have in the course of their lives radically changed the course of philosophy. In the centuries preceeding him, the Greeks had first limited their speculation to the exterior cosmos; the Sophists discussed psychological problems, but generally concluded to the impossibility of all science. Socrates not only stemmed this primitive agnosticism, he imbued Greek thinkers with a permanent, strong, often overriding interest in ethical questions, so much so that five centuries later Epictetus could say, "Socrates speaks like a man who is really the kinsman of the gods," and ". . . Socrates made men imitators of himself."[3]

Virtue for Socrates consisted of knowledge. Socrates, states Aristotle, "thought the virtues were rules or rational principles, for he thought they were, all of them, forms of scientific knowledge."[4] Plato had reported the same:

> Or do you think that knowledge is a noble and commanding thing, which cannot be overcome, and will not allow a man, if he only knows the difference of good and evil, to do anything which is contrary to knowledge, but that wisdom will have a strength to help him? I agree with you, Socrates, said Protagoras.[5]

If then virtue is knowledge, many men have neither. How can they attain them? Socrates thought his method was the answer. It contains four elements: induction, the maieutic process, dialectic, and irony.

18

As regards induction, Xenophon reports, "Socrates held that those who know what any given thing is can also expound it to others; on the other hand, those who do not know are misled themselves and mislead others. For this reason he never gave up considering with his companions what any given thing is."[6] Thus, the Socratic induction consisted of examining various examples and applications of an object to clarify and define what it is. Xenophon also provides us with the striking case of how it worked in defining what is a pious man.[7] And Aristotle himself summed up for us Socrates' contribution in this matter with these words, ". . . it was natural that Socrates should be seeking the essence, for he was seeking to syllogize, and 'what a thing is' is the starting-point of syllogism; for there was as yet none of the dialectical power which enables people even without knowledge of the essence to speculate about contraries and inquire whether the same science deals with contraries; for two things may be fairly ascribed to Socrates: inductive arguments and universal definition, both of which are concerned with the starting-point of science."[8]

By maieutic process Socrates meant a kind of philosophical midwifery, in which he helped men to bring forth their ideas into the world. However, its main importance lay not in the actual bringing forth, but in the consequent examination and testing to see if the supposed seed was viable or only an empty husk:

> Socrates. Such are the midwives, whose task is a very important one, but not so important as mine; for women do not bring into the world at one time real children, and at another time counterfeits which are with difficulty distin-guished from them; if they did, then the dis-cernment of the true and false birth would be the crowning achievement of the art of midwifery--you would think so?

> Theaetetus. Indeed I should.

> Socrates. Well my art of midwifery is in most respects like theirs; but differs, in that I attend men and not women, and I look after their souls when they are in labour, and not after their bodies: and the triumph of my art is in thoroughly examining whether the thought which the mind of the young man brings forth is a false idol or a noble and true birth.[9]

The maieutic process is dialectic, that is, it occurs between two or more people who discuss a problem as thoroughly as they can and who thus at least clarify it if they do not solve it. There is no formal teacher-student relationship; rather the participants are all teachers and students, each teaching and learning from each other. Thus, Xenophon and Plato never speak of Socrates' students, only of his friends and companions and of their "deliberations in common."[10] Then too, at his trial Socrates, reminding his audience that he could only "speak in my accustomed manner,"[11] proceeds to cross-examine Meletus and to thereby uncover in short order the self-contradictions of his indictment.

A major feature of the dialectic is the Socratic irony. In his conversations Socrates would willingly allow that he was actually rather ignorant and would profess willingness to learn of anybody who had any knowledge to impart. Whoever claimed to be such, however, he would question and the usual result was that the person soon involved himself in patent contradictions and made his former certainties seem to be delusions, while Socrates' supposed lack of knowledge assumed the appearance, ironically, of wisdom.

Philosophers today still make use, in its essentials, of the Socratic method. They still arrive at definitions the way he did. They agree that they should carefully scrutinize and test any creature they may produce. Except perhaps for a few eccentrics, they admit they progress only by criticizing and enlarging on their own and previous positions.

## The Platonic Dialectic

The problems of interpreting Plato have strained the ingenuity of scholars for the last hundred years. They are due first to the difficulty of determining whether Plato is presenting Socrates' or his own position. They also result from his lack of systematization, which, combined with an uncertain chronology and his long career, renders any reconstruction somewhat hypothetical. The same may be said of his methodology.

Plato always maintained the Socratic dictum that virtue was knowledge. However, to explain this last, he developed his theory of ideas, in which all real knowing is a reminiscing, which eventually leads to the Good, the highest idea of all, that illumines the mind the same way the sun lights all things. Men's memories, nevertheless, must be prodded by the concrete objects of this world and by the questions of their fellowmen: the Socratic method still holds.[12]

Plato continued to call it dialectic, but he had shifted its meaning. To it he assigned, besides its primary reference to a discussion, the sense of what occurs in and results from a dialogue, the search for and apprehension of the ideas. "And when I speak of the other division of the intelligible, you will understand me to speak of that other sort of knowledge which reason herself attains by the power of dialectic, using the hypotheses not as first principles, but only as hypotheses--that is to say, as steps and points of departure into a world which is above hypotheses, in order that she may soar beyond them to the first principle of the whole; and clinging to this and then to that which depends on this, by successive steps she descends again without the aid of any sensible object, from ideas, through ideas, and in ideas she ends."[13]

However, to arrive at the ideas Plato used two new processes. He called the first division. By it he meant dividing and subdividing a class of objects until he had finally ascertained all the species and genera included in the group. "The ancients, who were our betters and nearer the gods than we are, handed down the tradition, that whatever things are said to be are composed of one and many, and have the finite and infinite implanted in them: seeing, then, that such is the order of the world, we too ought in every enquiry to begin by laying down one idea of that which is the subject of enquiry; this unity we shall find in everything. Having found it, we may next proceed to look for two, if there be two, or, if not, then for three or some other number, subdividing each of these units, until at last the unity with which we began is seen not only to be one and many and infinite, but also a definite number; the infinite must not be suffered to approach the many until the entire number of the species intermediate between unity and infinity has been discovered,--then, and not till then, we may rest from division, and without further troubling ourselves about the endless individuals may allow them to drop into infinity."[14] By extending division to all classes of objects, the dialectician is able to attain a unified, well-articulated view of the whole realm of ideas. "Then, surely, he who can divide rightly is able to see clearly one form pervading a scattered multitude, and many different forms contained under one higher form; and again, one form knit together into a

single whole and pervading many such wholes, and many
forms, existing only in separation and isolation. This
is the knowledge of classes which determines where they
have communion with one another and where not."[15]

The second process, the use of hypotheses, Plato
borrowed from the mathematicians. He is rather obscure
as to how they are to be integrated with his theory of
ideas, but he states that "the soul is compelled to use
hypotheses."[16] They are points of departure into a
world which is above them; they are thus the base of
dialectic.[17] They should be verified in regard to what
results not only if they are true, but also if they are
false.[18] After they have been thus tested, it is the
task of the dialectician to relate them to a further
hypothesis, to verify it in the same manner, and to
continue thus until he reaches that which is sufficient
in itself, the Good.[19]

The knowledge of these eternal Forms is an essential condition of the good life. Indeed, it is by it
that a man is good. When one knows the good he cannot
but act in accord with it. For " . . . no man volun-
tarily pursues evil, or that which he thinks to be
evil. To prefer evil to good is not in human nature."[20]
Virtue then is identical with knowledge. "If then virtue is a quality of the soul, and is admitted to be
profitable, it must be wisdom or prudence, since none
of the things of the soul are either profitable or
hurtful in themselves, but they are all made profitable
or hurtful by the addition of wisdom or of folly; and
therefore if virtue is profitable, must not virtue be a
sort of wisdom or prudence?"[21] Thus the philosopher,
being the spectator of all time and of all existence,
knows and pursues what is best, whereas he who is not
wise cannot be happy.[22]

## Aristotle: Dialectics and Science

Aristotle also calls ethics dialectical. However,
he means by this something quite contrary to what Plato
did.[23] Dialectics, for the latter, was the highest and
most certain type of knowledge; it was truly science.
Aristotle defines science as universal, necessary and
certain knowledge based on definition and deductive
demonstration. He thus opposes science to dialectics,
which is knowledge based on opinion, and hence only
probable. "Now a dialectical proposition consists in
asking something that is held by all men or by most men
or by the philosopher, i. e., either by all, or by
most, or by the most notable of these, provided it be

not contrary to the general opinion. . . Dialectical propositions also include views which are like those generally accepted; also propositions which contradict the contraries of opinions that are taken to be generally accepted, and also all opinions that are in accordance with the recognized arts."[24] For Aristotle, dialectics merely prepares the way for true science; it is, we might say, <u>ancilla scientiae</u>.

More precisely, in Aristotle's sense dialectics is concerned with how an <u>aporia</u> or "problem" can be discussed or debated. On the one hand, it points out general procedures one may use to resolve a problem and how to do so consistently. On the other hand, it shows too how to uncover and bring out whatever inconsistencies one's antagonist may have fallen into. Dialectics then is not concerned with discovering what the truth of the matter is but only with plausibility and self-consistency.[25]

Dialectics is of special import for science in two ways. In the first place it is historical, descriptive and critical and thereby clears the ground for science. It is historical in a broad sense. Thus, the first book of the <u>Metaphysics</u> records various views of earlier philosophers; in preparing the <u>Politics</u> Aristotle is said to have collected the constitutions of one hundred and fifty eight cities; in the <u>Ethics</u> he carefully notes what are the accepted opinions regarding, for instance, happiness.[26] It is descriptive; the second book of the <u>Metaphysics</u> is a statement of some of the main problems of philosophy. It is critical, inasmuch as the two preceeding phases provide Aristotle with concrete points which he can scrutinize and accept or reject, in part or in whole. Hence the importance that he attaches to the <u>aporia</u>, the study of conflicting views on a problem; the <u>aporiai</u> act as the framework of the dialectic.

The second major function dialectic has in regard to science is to provide first principles. Negatively, it shows where the first principles are not to be found, by its criticisms of accepted opinion. It derives them also in a positive way, for ". . . the premisses of demonstrated knowledge must be true, primary, immediate, better known than and prior to the conclusion, which is further related to them as effect to cause."[27] "Our own doctrine is that not all knowledge is demonstrative: on the contrary, knowledge of the immediate premisses is independent of demonstration."[28] "Thus it is clear that we must get to know the primary premisses by induction; for the method by which even sense-perception implants the universal is inductive . . . From these considerations it follows that there will be no scientific knowledge of the primary premisses, and since except intuition nothing can be truer than scientific knowledge, it will be intuition that apprehends the primary premisses--a result which also follows from the fact that demonstration cannot be the originative source of demonstration nor, consequently, scientific knowledge of scientific knowledge. If, therefore, it is the only other kind of true thinking except scientific knowing, intuition will be the originative source of scientific knowledge. And the originative source of science grasps the original basic premiss, while science as a whole is similarly related as originative source to the whole body of fact."[29] There are however two types of induction: a) the intuition of an essence as "When one of a number of logically indiscriminable particulars has made a stand, the earliest universal is present in the soul; for though the act of sense-perception is of the particular, its content is universal--is man, for example, not the man Callias,"[30] and b) the eduction of a general proposition, for ". . . induction is a passage from individuals to universals, e. g., the argument that supposing the skilled pilot is the most effective, and likewise the skilled charioteer, then in general the skilled man is the best at his particular task."[31] Thus, for Aristotle induction is a function of dialectics, not of science.

## Aristotelian Ethics: Dialectical and Empirical

In the Aristotelian sense of the words ethics is therefore not scientific but dialectical. For, science deals with necessary certitudes, dialectics with the probable and possible, and in ethics we must be content "to indicate the truth roughly and in outline, and in speaking about things which are only for the most part true and with premisses of the same kind to reach conclusions that are no better."[32] For, "matters concerned with conduct and questions of what is good for us have no fixity, any more than matters of health. The general account being of this nature the account of particular cases is yet more lacking in exactness; for they do not fall under any art or precept but the agents themselves must in each case consider what is appropriate to the occasion, as happens also in the art of medicine or of navigation."[33] And finally, "To examine all the opinions that have been held were perhaps somewhat fruitless; enough to examine those that

24

are most prevalent or that seem to be arguable."[34] The Nichomachean Ethics is hence also dialectical in the original meaning of the word, referring to a discussion of all viewpoints of a problem.

Perhaps the best example of dialectical procedure in the Nichomachean Ethics is found in the first book, where Aristotle seeks to define what are happiness and the good.He starts off with the common opinion as to what constitutes the highest good. "Verbally there is very general agreement; for both the general run of men and people of superior refinement say that it is happiness."[35] However, men disagree as to what happiness consists of, so he then examines whether the various goods proposed, pleasure, honor, virtues and money, actually bring happiness.[36] To help clarify the question, he then shifts from a sociological, as it were, to a biological viewpoint. "Have the carpenter, then, and tanner certain functions or activities, and has man none? Is he born without a function? Or as eye, hand, foot, and in general each of the parts evidently has a function, may one lay it down that man similarly has a function apart from all these? What then can this be. . . . Now if the function of man is an activity of soul which follows or implies a rational principle . . . human good turns out to be activity of soul in accordance with virtue, and if there are more than one virtue, in accordance with the best and most complete."[37] From here he goes on to show that this view harmonizes well with opinions of both the philosophers and the masses.[38]

The Aristotelian ethics is also empirical. This manifests itself in several ways.

It is apparent first of all from Aristotle's statements regarding methods. "Let us not fail to notice, however, that there is a difference between arguments from and those to the first principles . . . For, while we must begin with what is known, things are objects of knowledge in two senses--some to us, some without qualification. Presumably, then, we must begin with things known to us . . . For the fact is the starting-point."[39] "We must, as in all other cases, set the observed facts before us and, after first discussing the difficulties, go on to prove, if possible, the truth of all the common opinions about these affections of the mind, or, failing this, of the greater number and the most authoritative; for if we both refute the objections and leave the common opinions undisturbed, we shall have proved the case

25

susfficiently."[40]

Again, Aristotle accepts, or starts off from, terms and definitions as found in experience. Thus he relies heavily, as has already been shown, on the aporiai.[41] This, we would emphasize, is an empirical procedure, for the generally accepted opinions are the result of generations of experience. He has frequent recourse to examples, as when he treats of continence.[42] Then too he says, "Because when we wish to show some particular good, we either show by defining that the same description applies to the good and to the thing which we wish to show to be good, or else have recourse to induction."[43]

An empirical method not only starts off from experience, but it also verifies its conclusions by facts. This, states Aristotle, is how ethics should be developed. "We must consider it, however, in the light not only of our conclusion and our premisses, but also of what is commonly said about it; for with a true view all the data harmonize, but with a false one the facts soon clash."[44] And again, "About all these matters we must try to get conviction by argument, using perceived facts as evidence and illustration . . . and it is well to criticize separately the reason that gives the cause and the conclusion both because of what has just been said, viz, that one should attend not merely to what is inferred by argument, but often attend more to per- ceived fact."[45] And finally, "The opinions of the wise seem then, to harmonize with our arguments. But while even such things carry some conviction, the truth in practical matters is discerned from the facts of life; for these are the decisive factor. We must therefore survey what we have already said, bringing it to the test of the facts of life, and if it harmonizes with the facts we must accept it, but if it clashes with them we must suppose it to be mere theory."[46]

We can also see Aristotle's empiricism in his treatment of the virtues. For, the "human good turns out to be activity of soul in accordance with vir- tue,"[47] and too, most of the Ethics is a specification of the virtues and vices. Hence, the method used here is of importance for the whole. It is consciously empirical. ". . . the accounts we demand must be in accordance with the subject-matter; matters concerned with conduct and questions of what is good for us have no fixity, any more than matters of health."[48] Therefore virtue is the mean, as determined by "a man of practical wisdom."[49] But the actions of a man of

26

practical wisdom are known only by experience. Thus, as we saw above, he later said, "We must, as in all other cases, set the observed facts before us us and, after first discussing the difficulties, go on to prove, if possible, the truth of all the common opinions about these affections of the mind, or, failing this, of the greater number and the most authoritative."[50]

## The later Greeks

Epicurus was also an empiricist in his ethics, but in a much more direct way. For, he held, the end of man is pleasure, as is proven by the fact that all men from birth naturally seek pleasure and avoid pain. "We are inquiring, then, what is the final and ultimate Good, which as all philosophers are agreed must be of such a nature as to be the End to which all other things are means, while it is not itself a means to anything else. This Epicurus finds in pleasure; pleasure he holds to be the Chief Good, pain the Chief Evil. This he sets out to prove as follows: Every animal, as soon as it is born, seeks for pleasure, and delights in it as the Chief Good, while it recoils from pain as the Chief Evil, and so far as possible avoids it. This it does as long as it remains unperverted, at the prompting of Nature's own unbiased and honest verdict. Hence Epicurus refuses to admit any necessity for argument or discussion to <u>prove</u> that pleasure is desirable and pain to be avoided."[51] Right and wrong are thus immediately given in experience. "For the end of all our actions is to be free from pain and fear, and, when once we have obtained all this, the tempest of the soul is laid; seeing that the living creature has no need to go in search of something that is lacking, nor to look for anything else by which the good of the soul and of the body will be fulfilled. When we are pained because of the absence of pleasure, then, and then only, do we feel the need of pleasure. Wherefore we call pleasure the alpha and omega of a blessed life. Pleasure is our first and kindred good. It is the starting-point of every choice and of every aversion, and to it we come back, inasmuch as we make feeling the rule by which to judge of every good thing."[52]

The Stoics combined empiricism with an aprioristic viewpoint. For them, human happiness consisted in living in conformity with one's self, with nature, and with the universal order. To know how to do this, a man had only to apply his reason to phenomena and it would spontaneously grasp its duties. "Some person asked, How then shall every man among us perceive what is suitable to his character? How, he replied, does the bull alone, when the lion has attacked, discover his own powers and put himself forward in defense of the whole herd?"[53] Epictetus later clarified this picturesque response. "But as to good and evil, and beautiful and ugly, and becoming and unbecoming, and happiness and misfortune, and proper and improper, and what we ought to do and what we ought not to do, whoever came[54] into the world without having an innate idea of them?"[54] Nevertheless, we require good teachers to show us how to apply these innate ideas properly.[55]

In modern times the Epicurean empiricism and the Stoic rationalism were to reappear in many forms.

## Scholasticism

Since we may reckon scholasticism to have started with Boethius and to have continued beyond the fifteenth century, it includes a rather heterogeneous group of thinkers. They are all similar in this, however, that they used more or less the same method. We should however distinguish the early from the later scholastics, as the latter clearly differentiated philosophy from theology. Following the lead of St. Augustine the early scholastics did not disengage their philosophical from their theological speculations. Gradually however the distinction between the natural and supernatural orders was made more precisely, so that by the thirteenth century St. Albert the Great and St. Thomas, while maintaining and explaining the mutual relations of faith and reason, nevertheless establish the autonomy of both within their own spheres.

The intent which characterized the scholastic method was to combine, harmonize and develop into a fully articulated whole, revealed and natural truths. This purpose was implied by the Anselmian formulae, "faith seeking understanding" and "I believe, that I may understand." It was explicitly stated in regard to the doctrine of the trinity by St. Bonaventure. "We treat of the most holy trinity in a threefold way since it befalls us firstly to believe in it, secondly to understand what we believe, and thirdly to say or express what we understand. Believing however comes to us through authority, understanding through reason and expression through universal and rational speech. Therefore, we shall treat of the divine trinity and unity themselves, first according to what is believed; secondly, according to how these beliefs are grasped through reason; and thirdly, according to how what we believe and understand can be rationally and universally expressed."[56] It was restated by St. Thomas in answer to the question "Whether Theological Conclusions Should be Arrived at through Authority or Reason?": "Some disputations are set up to remove doubts about whether a point is right or not and on such a theological disputation the authorities which are accepted by those with whom we dispute are to be used to the utmost. . . . But some disputations are conducted by professors in the classroom, not to remove error, but to instruct the listeners, to lead them to an understanding of the truth in point: then is it necessary that the investigating minds rest upon a firm foundation of truth and that those teaching know why what is said is true."[57]

The repeated references to authority in the above manifest a major feature of the scholastic method as it was practiced in the Middle Ages: it was a bookish (as opposed to experiential) philosophy; it initiated its discussions of problems from what had already been written about them by recognized masters, either in the distant past or more recently. However, this procedure was historically justifiable, for it took Europe centuries to reassimilate the intellectual capital of Greece. This was the reason for the large number of commentaries; hence also the constant reference to the authorities. Such a procedure was also acceptable methodologically as long as the authorities were verified by experience: the decline of scholasticism was marked by a failure to refer back to reality. Nevertheless, it must not be thought that this reliance on texts necessarily curtailed the originality and breadth of thought of the scholastics; the work of the medievalists in the last hundred years has disproved this. Nor can the Middle Ages be charged with a lack of critical acumen in their use of authorities; the popularity of Abelard's Sic et Non and St. Thomas' acknowledgedly free way of "reverently" explaining a passage are only two of the many instances which invalidate such a position.

Closely connected with this medieval approach is the use made, in establishing definitions, of etymologies and the meaning of words. For these were considered as impersonal authorities since they contain and divulge the experience of the ages. We may note the similarity here of the contemporary analytic philosophers and the scholastics.

Counterbalancing the credence they gave the ancients, the scholastics had a highly optimistic confidence in man's reason--it reminds one of Dewey's faith in intelligence to solve the problems of the modern world. However, they gave it a rather different basis. Already in the eleventh century Berengarius of Tours stated, "Clearly it takes a great heart to have recourse to dialectics in all things, because to appeal to it is to appeal to reason. And whoever does not appeal to reason relinquishes his own dignity, since it is through his reason that he is made to the image of God, nor can he be renewed from day to day in his resemblance to God."[58] This initial view was greatly strengthened by a practical consideration underlined by Abelard: since the authorities seemingly contradict themselves, every man has to use his reason to decide when and what to accept. Even in the twelfth century a few men like St. Bernard protested against the application of logic to theology, but they were lost in the tide. In the thirteenth, all the great theologians implicitly accepted Abelard's basic position, which was faith in the right use of reason.

The right use of reason, however, necessitated, in the eyes of the scholastics, a special language of the reason. Metaphors and similes, passion and rhetoric were acceptable in literature and sermons, but not in scientific works. So, they were banished. Instituted in their place was an ideal of a formalized, strictly logical procedure. M.-D. Chenu described the results in these words: "It is quite true that the style in which the Schoolmen wrote and thought sacrificed everything to technique and that the latter's austerity stripped it of any of the resources of art. Or perhaps it would be truer to say that, in his style, the Schoolman fashioned for himself a special rhetoric, in which imagery, comparison, figure of speech, symbolism, were immdiately conceptualized without any catering to sensible diversion. Any figure of speech was reduced to an example or turned into an allegory, both processes in which reason crudely exploits the imaginative faculty to the detriment of its very productiveness. Hence the abstract character of the scholastic style which is all taken up with classifications, divisions, distinctions, formal oppositions, all media that favor precision in thought and in the art of discussion."[59]

This formalization extended not only to the language, but often even to the composition of whole volumes. Thus, the <u>Summa Theologica</u> is made up of parts divided into questions, which in turn are subdivided into articles. These are all of the same form. First the opinions in favor of a position are given: <u>Videtur quod</u>. Following are those against it: <u>Sed contra</u>. The author's solution comes next: <u>Respondeo dicendum</u>. The unfavorable opinions are then refuted in the same order as they were given. This procedure obviously makes the <u>Summa</u> dry reading if one attempts to read right through; on the other hand, it fully manifests the architectonic structure of the book; then too, it simplifies the work and saves the time of the reader, who can immediately go to the core of the author's position, without wading through a mass of objections.

As the <u>Summa</u> is recognized to be the high point of medieval moral philosophy, we shall take Aquinas as our only example of that period. We find that within the methodological framework outlined above he employed deductive procedures to a large extent--which is to be expected, as the <u>Summa</u> was written as an expository text. However, in general we can say that in working out his theories he made use, as he saw fit, of a wide variety of all types of development: appeals to experience, analyses and interpretations of texts, progressive constructions of definitions, the use of analogies and the application of distinctions, all of which led Chenu to say, "Here is an observation of major import, inciting us to take note, in the present case as well as in many others, of the near indefinite diverseness of the procedures of analysing, reasoning, and dialectical research employed by Saint Thomas."[60]

There are however two characteristics of Thomas' method which deserve here special consideration.

The first is its empiricism. This point has gained greater attention recently because of the claims of some,[61] influenced perhaps by the rationalistic manner of developing ethics of some Thomists, that Thomas' moral philosophy is purely aprioristic. We would first of all note that Aquinas recognized at least in theory the empirical nature of ethics, for he was well aware of Aristotle's thorough acceptance of this point and never disagreed with it.[62] Then again, there is reason, superficially, to accuse Thomas of apriorism, for, as we have pointed out, the <u>Summa</u> is an expository treatise and as such often presents its arguments in deductive form. We should not however allow this to obscure the fact that he sought to base his premisses empirically, even though he may sometimes have given little or no indication of their source, as he could assume that his readers were familiar with Aristotelian

31

ethics and the rich ascetic literature of the Middle Ages. As a prime example of this we may take the way he defines "virtue", which, some have maintained, is completely rationalistic. His procedure, as has been pointed out by G. Klubertanz,[63] is solidly based on experience even though it did involve the use of the metaphysical notions of act and potency: starting with such facts as the different ways men act and acquire habits, he shows how "virtue" is used in different but related senses to refer to certain such habits and the acts which they bring about. As Klubertanz concluded, "Thus, under the limitations of his time and circumstances, the work of St. Thomas is as empirical as a moral philosophy can be. Of course, his ethics depends on his psychology and his metaphysics. An ethics without metaphysical bases is an ethics without a clearly known and proved ontological order to serve as standard. Such an ethics would have its norms--by way of assumptions, subject to all the distortions of prejudice, the status quo, social pressure. The presence of metaphysical and psychological principles in ethical theory does not make the latter either a priori or rationalistic but philosophical."[64]

The other noteworthy characteristic of Thomas' method is its use of intuition. By intuition he means the immediate grasp and contemplation of an essence or principle. It thus stands in contradistinction to the discursive acts of the intellect. Hence for Thomas the difference between the way men and angels know lies in that the latter know only by intuition, whereas men must, because of the weakness of their intellects, use both intuitive and discursive approaches. The comparison he makes between them indicates that such is the meaning he attaches to intuition. "So in a similar way the inferior, that is, the human form of intelligence goes to its perfection in the knowledge of truth by a kind of movement, a discursive process of understanding, advancing from one thing known to another. If the human mind were able, in seeing a given principle, to see straight away all the conclusions that follow, it would never be involved in any such process. And this, in fact, is the condition of the angels; in the truth which their nature enables them to know they apprehend immediately all that such truths can possibly imply for them. This is why they are called intellectual beings; for even in our case, the things we grasp immediately we say we see 'intellectually', and so we give the name 'intelligence' to our latent habitual capacity to intuit first principles. But the human soul in general we describe as 'rational', to indicate its way of acquiring true knowledge by a discursive process, a way imposed by the dimness of intellectual light in it. If our souls were endowed with an angelic abundance of intellectual light, then in the very act of intuiting first principles we would understand all their consequences; we would know by intuition all that reasoning can deduce from them."[65] More precisely, we can distinguish three different types of cases in which intuitions occur in human cognition: first, in simple apprehension, where the mind grasps an essence; second, when the mind perceives a set of related entities and contemplates this unity; third, when the mind understands an analytic judgment.

It would be difficult to overestimate the importance of intuition in Thomistic ethics. Consider some of the major instances. Goodness itself is intuitive, being a feature we can discern in some objects, whereby they are fit for the end for which they are used. The primary moral principles, being self-evident, are intuitive, and they form the basis of ethics. The knowledge that the ultimate end of human life is happiness is also intuitive, the last end being, in the practical order, a first principle and something we arrive at, not by discussion, but by natural approval.[66] That happiness consists in the attainment of the universal and infinite good is also intuitive.[67] We have too an intuitive grasp of the objective reality of moral obligation, which we perceive as a command of conscience binding us to be true to our nature.[68] And finally, our feelings of moral approval and guilt are objects of intuition. It is such considerations that led G. Esser to state that "St. Thomas admits the intellectual operation of intuition in moral matters. Intuition in moral matters means for him that the norm of morality, which is human nature and its ultimate end, is an objective reality, of which man has evident cognition. The intuition of human nature and of its ultimate end embraces several partial views in the comprehensive unity of the destination of man for his ultimate end. It is this concept of intuition, by which moral values are apprehended as objective realities, which is a distinctive feature of Thomistic moral philosophy and sets it apart from other systems of ethics."[69]

The problem yet before us here however is to characterize in a more essential and precise manner the scholastic and Thomistic methodology. This it would seem, reduces itself in general to three phases. In the first Thomas fixes the primary concepts, principles and various solutions; he ordinarily takes them from among the opinions of the authorities, but he may also find them in the very words and adages of every day speech. In the second, he takes these elements and compares, criticizes and refines them to arrive at their core meaning. These, in the third, he confronts and verifies with reality. J. Leclercq describes this process in this way:

It consists of taking as a point of departure for philosophical reflection the most common of notions, and even the words by which we express these notions, words of our everyday speech, whose normal meaning we scrutinize. In this way we seek the ideas to which these words correspond, and beyond these ideas the grasp of reality which they express. By starting off in this way, with words which everyone uses and with notions which appear elementary, we arrive after some work of purification and elimination at notions that are properly philosophical and at findings which sometimes at first sight seem quite contrary to common views, even though the latter entail them.

These everyday terms are besides taken in quite diverse senses, sometimes quite equivocally. Analysis permits us to uncover such equivocal terms, to discern the primary and essential meanings, to denounce the improper ones and to avoid the contradictory ones.[76]

This, it is plain, is a consolidation of the dialectical methods of Plato and Aristotle. It is Platonic inasmuch as it can give scientific knowledge and relies heavily on the comparison and criticism by one another of theories and facts. It is Aristotelian in its reliance on the Organon. To quote Leclercq again, "This goes back to a method which we find as early as Socrates, which is taken up too by Plato and Aristotle, and which we also meet with in medieval writers; St. Thomas applies it constantly. . . . In Plato's Dialogues Socrates harasses in this way his interlocutors with questions which force them to discover what is implicit in their thinking and to coordinate their ideas; his conversations often meander along for tedious lengths. St. Thomas, who comes at the culmination of this tradition, follows a more direct route. He likes to start off with a verbal definition but pushes immediately to the philosophical notions it implicitly contains. The procedure is nevertheless

fundamentally the same . . ."[71] There is a noteworthy
similarity here between the approach of Thomas and that
of the contemporary linguistic analysts, despite the
vast divergence of their metaphysical positions.

## Modern Trends

With the rise of modern philosophy came a break in
the unity of methodology. Two opposing tendencies, with
their characteristic manners of thinking, assumed an
ever more dominant role: the rationalist and the
empiricist.

## Rationalism

The major event in the inception of rationalism
was Descartes' Discourse on Method. Its importance lay
in this, that it sought to lay the ground-rules, so to
speak, of method in general. However, since the only
scientific procedure with which Descartes was satisfied
was that of mathematics, his methodology was essentially deductive.

Although Descartes never wrote a definitive
ethics, he would have liked to, as he considered it to
be the ultimate extension and completion of his
philosophy. From the sure foundation of his physics and
metaphysics he thought it possible to deduce with
mathematical certainty the principles and most of the
applications of the right.[72]

This Cartesian dream Spinoza, at least in his own
sight, made real. Observe, said Spinoza, the mathematicians. They start with a group of definitions and
axioms, and from these deduce a vast body of certain
and true propositions. These, he says, we call true
because they are all consistent with one another and
with the definitions and axioms. In the same way, they
are certain because they are true and because the
definitions and axioms are self-evident certainties.
Now, the mathematicians arrive at these propositions by
deducing them, that is, by seeing that there is a
necessary relation between them and the definitions and
axioms. However, Spinoza had no illusions about the
deductive method. Had he not himself written, in
deductive form, The Principles of Cartesian Philosophy,
although he knew that Descartes' theories were wrong?
What counts then is that the axioms and definitions,
our intuitions, be correct. Spinoza believed that he
had achieved intuitions of the primary elements of the
cosmic process. Since one of these is its absolute

determinism, the same necessity reigns in the real as in the geometrical world, and hence the same method is valid. Since he, Spinoza, is acquainted with this method and has these intuitions, he can show men what their function as humans is and how they should fulfill it.[73]

The phase of continental rationalism initiated by Descartes may be termed metaphysical; with Kant started the critical. In the former the main interest was the ontological structure of the world. In the latter it was the very possibility and conditions of knowledge as determined by an immanent evaluation.

We see Kant's ethical method mainly in the Foundations of the Metaphysics of Morals and the Critique of Practical Reason. In the first two sections of the Foundations, Kant uses a regressive analysis. In the third section, he lays the way for the use of a progressive synthesis, which is the method of the Critique. By analysis he means deriving from a given proposition the principles logically implied by it; by synthesis, determining for these principles the necessary and ultimate conditions of their existence.[74]

The analysis of the two first sections of the Foundations proceeds from acknowledged moral facts to their underlying principles, the same way that the Critique of Pure Reason derived from the data of experience their rational a priori conditions. This process is best seen in how Kant himself carried it out. Our consciences hold as absolutely good only a good will (in this context a good will refers to the source of those acts in which we recognize a moral rightness). Now, a good will is one which performs its duties simply because they are duties. Thus, its basic attitude is one of respect for the moral law. However, men concur in placing a sharp distinction between what is and what ought to be. Since the law states what ought to be and since it is not given in experience, it is then an a priori form of morality. It is formulated by Kant in what he calls the categorical imperative: "Act only on a maxim through which you can at the same time will that it should become a universal law." Another formulation which he gives is, "so act as to treat humanity, whether in your own person or in that of any other, never as a means only but in every case as an end also." These, it may be noted, do not state the law so much as give the characteristic which every maxim, or concrete law, must have. Thus, with them Kant expects to deduce whatever maxims he needs for the guidance of conduct.

Just as in <u>Transcendental Dialectic</u> Kant had found the ultimate conditions of knowledge in the ideas of the soul, the world and God, so in the third section of the <u>Foundations</u> and in the <u>Critique of Practical Reason</u> he sought by a similar synthesis to reach the ultimate conditions of morality. These he found in the transcendental postulates of liberty, immortality and God. With them morality can exist; without them it cannot.[75]

Despite what Kant said about his method, however, it seems essentially to be the deductive verification of hypotheses. Thus, he starts off with a fact to explain: a good will. Duty done for its own sake can explain it; therefore duty done for its own sake is the cause of the good will. Respect for law can explain duty done for its own sake; therefore respect for law is the principle of duty. The moral law exists, inscribed in our hearts; liberty can explain it, as only free beings can be subject to moral laws; therefore men are free and liberty is the foundation of the moral law. Duty done for its own sake demands as a natural consequence happiness; men cannot be happy in this world; immortality can explain how they will gain their just meed; therefore men are immortal. A retributory God can explain how men will receive their due; therefore God exists. The very word Kant uses to designate liberty, immortality and God: postulates, is suggestive of his method.

Other thinkers whose ethical theories were basically deductive were Rousseau and the Eclectic School.

Rousseau not only influenced Kant, he was also the guiding spirit of those French statesmen(?) who, as Comte remarked, proclaimed in thirty years ten "eternal and irrevocable" constitutions. Whatever the applications made of it, Rousseau's ethics was largely a system of natural rights deduced, strictly and exclusively, from what he imagined the natural state of man to be. Thus he states in his <u>Discourse on Inequality</u>, "Let us start by laying aside all facts." On the other hand, he believed men equal by nature and did not fear to proclaim what he deduced from this: Down with property, which makes men unequal; Away with the law which guarantees property; Down with governments, which make the law; Away with society, which creates governments.

The Eclectics, being good solid bourgeois, rejected such views as nonsense. Led by Cousin, Jouffroy and Damiron, they dominated the French universities in the nineteenth century. Although they found Rousseau's conclusions unacceptable, they retained his method, applying it with a bit more sobriety if no less exclusively. Jouffroy summarized their position well. We must, he says, start off by determining what are the constitutive principles of human nature, which can be done simply by observation and introspection. This point established, we can deduce from it man's natural purpose and destiny in life. From here, we can infer whatever else we need to know about how we should act. From man's end we can deduce what rights and duties he has as an individual; from this we can establish the rights and duties of societies, how governments should be set up, and even international law. Thus the whole of ethics is just one long series of deductions from an initial insight into what it is to be a man.[76]

## Empiricism

Running a simultaneous course with continental rationalism was an empirical tradition whose major figures were English: Bacon, Hobbes, Locke, Hume and the utilitarians. It will serve our purposes to examine more closely Hobbes and Hume.

Hobbes was the first modern materialist of importance. His ethics is of especial interest because it shows clearly the implications of such a viewpoint. Thus he says, "But whatsoever is the object of any man's appetite or desire, that is it which he calleth for his part good; and the object of hate and aversion, evil; and of his contempt, vile and inconsiderable. For these words of good, evil, and contemptible, are ever used with relation to the person that useth them: there being nothing simply and absolutely so; nor any common rule of good and evil to be taken from the nature of the objects themselves . . ."[77] On this basis, his personal ethics is a cataloging of what men in general like and dislike, as determined by observation and introspection. His method is thus inductive.

In his social ethics however, he proceeds in a different manner. Since self-interest is identical with morality in his view, he deduces from self-interest a series of general rules regarding what it is in man's interest to do in regard to his fellowman: to seek peace, to live up to one's agreements, and the like. These general rules that he deduces form a fairly comprehensive social code.

Hume did not develop in a detailed way his moral theories. However, he did come out strongly for an empirical method in ethics. In the following remarkably lucid and to the point passage he outlines the phases and characteristics of such a method. "In order to attain this purpose, we shall endeavour to follow a very simple method: we shall analyze that complication of mental qualities, which form what, in common life, we call Personal Merit: we shall consider every attribute of the mind, which renders a man an object either of esteem and affection, or of hatred and contempt; every habit or sentiment or faculty, which, if ascribed to any person, implies either praise or blame, and may enter into any panegyric or satire of his character and manners. The quick sensibility, which, on this head, is so universal among mankind, gives a philosopher sufficient assurance, that he can never be considerably mistaken in framing the cata- logue, or incur any danger of misplacing the objects of his contemplation: he needs only enter into his own breast for a moment, and consider whether or not he should desire to have this or that quality ascribed to him, and whether such or such an imputation would proceed from a friend or an enemy. This very nature of language guides us almost infallibly in forming a judgement of this nature; and as every tongue possesses one set of words which are taken in a good sense, and another in the opposite, the least acquaintance with the idiom suffices, without any reasoning, to direct us in collecting and arranging the estimable or blameable qualities of men. The only object of reasoning is to discover the circumstances on both sides, which are common to these qualities; to observe that particular in which the estimable qualities agree on the one hand, and the blameable on the other; and thence to reach the foundation of ethics, and find those universal princi- ples, from which all censure or approbation is ulti- mately derived. As this is a question of fact, not of abstract science, we can only expect success, by fol- lowing the experimental method, and deducing general maxims from a comparison of particular instances. The other scientific method, where a general abstract principle is first established, and is afterwards branched out into a variety of inferences and conclu- sions, may be more perfect in itself, but suits less the imperfection of human nature, and is a common source of illusion and mistake in this as well as in other subjects. Men are not cured of their passion for hypotheses and systems in natural philosophy, and will hearken to no arguments but those which are derived from experience. It is full time they should attempt a like reformation in all moral disquisitions; and reject every system of ethics, however subtle or ingenious, which is not founded on fact and observation."[78] It is worth noting that Hume, who is usually considered inimical to the Aristotelian and scholastic tradition, here reminds us very much of Aristotle in his insistence on the facts, and of the scholastics in his references to language. Nevertheless, Hume has greatly influenced the empiricists who came after him, and especially the linguistic analysts of the present century.

## Conclusion

In regards to moral methodology, three major theories have been proposed. The empiricists, without denying the necessity of deduction, claim that ethics is in the main developed by ascertaining moral facts and laws on the same basis and with the same approach that the positive sciences use to explore the physical world. Most rationalists and idealists, while allowing that inductive and historical procedures are useful in establishing certain preliminary facts, nevertheless insist that moral theory is primarily a priori and deductive. Finally, the tradition established by Socrates, Plato, Aristotle and Aquinas has proceeded, in developing ethics, in a more or less explicitly acknowledged manner which we have denominated dialectical, and which is characterized by the use of as many other specific methods: inductive, deductive, historical, linguistic or other, as may seem applicable in any particular case, and by the comparison, criticism and control of the results of each by that of the others, to thus elaborate a multifaceted view of every problem studied.

# CHAPTER THREE

## THE EVOLUTIONARY APPROACH TO ETHICS

In the last hundred years evolutionary ethics has been upheld by several well-known thinkers, besides gaining a wide popular audience. We shall study it here from the methodological point of view. By analyzing the way evolutionary moralists proceed, we shall try to show to what extent their manner of theorizing is acceptable in the light of such usual methodological criteria as consistency and applicability. We shall therefore first review how evolutionary ethics has developed. In a second section we shall discuss various points about the procedure of its contemporary adherents. In conclusion we shall briefly indicate some general conclusions which seem required.

### Historical Development

Evolutionary ethics is one form of the biological approach to moral philosophy. It thus has its roots in the hedonistic and materialistic currents of Greece and, in modern times, the English empiricists. It had other important sources in the eighteenth century: the encyclopedists did much to spread empiricist and hedonist views; Condorcet popularized the idea of indefinite progess in all fields, including the moral; the rise of romanticism further prepared the psychological climate by its insistence on the irrational and disorderly aspects of the universe.

The immediate sources of evolutionary ethics are found however in the utilitarianism and positivism of the early nineteenth century. These provided its basic positions and attitudes, while biology gave it a "scientific" basis. Evolutionary theories had been current since the last quarter of the eighteenth century. Thus, Buffon explained the biological development of species as the effects of the environment, perpetuated by heredity; Lamarck claimed these changes were due to the inheritance of acquired characteristics. It took several decades however for such ideas to develop into what we now refer to as evolutionary naturalism.

41

In 1851 Spencer published his <u>Social Statics</u>, in which he attempted to shape these trends into a cohesive unity. A real science of ethics is necessary, he held, and it shows that evil arises because we are ill-adapted to natural conditions. The development of life entails a progressive physical and mental adaptation which will result in the eventual disappearance of evil. The evolution of human society is in the direction of complete concord and cooperation. A scientific ethics can thus guide men to happiness by pointing out to them the conditions under which they can attain it.

In such a moral theory the method consists essentially of trying to infer from the data and hypotheses of biologists the direction in which the human species is developing, accepting this as the purpose of life, and deducing from it a moral obligation to act always in such a way as to be in step with evolution.

Eight years after the appearance of Spencer's <u>Social Statics</u>, Darwin published the <u>Origin of Species</u> in which he amassed in a persuasive lineup the scientific evidence for biological evolution. Then in 1871, in <u>The Descent of Man</u>, he attempted to show that men's intellectual and moral faculties were also the result of the evolutionary process. Thus, he said, the purpose of life is "the rearing of the greatest number of individuals in full vigour and health, with all their faculties perfect, under the conditions to which they are subjected."[1] Darwin however was primarily a scientist and he preferred to leave to others the task of developing the philosophical implications of his theory. Hence his importance in the history of ethics is due mostly to the use which others made of his biological discoveries.

Thus, Spencer's later work, <u>The Principles of Ethics</u>, is largely a re-presentation of his early ideas buttressed by the facts which Darwin and other biologists had established. He believed that the evolutionism he had previously championed was now substantiated scientifically. His aim and method, however, remained the same. Ethics was to be developed in the light of both the evolutionary direction of life and the utilitarian criterion of the happiness of individuals and groups.

In the nineteenth century evolutionary ethics had a number of zealous adherents and they popularized the doctrine in numerous books and articles throughout the world. In Anglo-Saxon lands Spencer did this with the aid of Leslie Stephen and W. K. Clifford. In Germany the oracles of scientific evolutionary ethics were Haeckel, Büchner and Moleschott. The French had two varieties to choose from: the strictly materialistic type of Metchnikoff and an idealist form proposed by Guyau, to whom it had been suggested by Fouillée. John Fiske and Henry Drummond developed theistic versions which appealed to religiously-minded people. Nietzsche, on the other hand, basing himself on the notion of the survival of the fittest, proclaimed the ethics of the Superman.

Spencer and his allies considered evolution as something of a new gospel, which promised heaven on earth for those who evolved rightly. Thomas Henry Huxley believed such optimism unwarranted. In his Romanes Lecture, Evolution and Ethics (1893), he attempted to show that civilization is the result not of evolution but of counter-evolution; for, the person most fit to survive is not necessarily the best morally. "I have termed this evolution of the feelings out of which the primitive bonds of human society are so largely forged, into the organized and personified sympathy we call conscience, the ethical process. So far as it tends to make any human society more efficient in the struggle for existence with the state of nature, or with other societies, it works in harmonious contrast with the cosmic process. But it is none the less true that, since law and morals are restraints upon the struggle for existence between men in society, the ethical process is in opposition to the principle of the cosmic process, and tends to the suppression of the qualities best fitted for success in that struggle."[2] And again, "Let us understand, once for all, that the ethical progress of society depends, not in imitating the cosmic process, still less in running away from it, but in combating it."[3]

Such views had a far-reaching effect on Huxley's conception of ethics and its method. For, under such circumstances ethics is aimed "to the end of facilitating the free expansion of the innate faculties of the citizen, so far as it is consistent with the general good."[4] Its method is "the same method of observation, experiment, and ratiocination, as is practised in other kinds of scientific work,"[5] to determine the course of conduct which will best conduce to that end. But Spencer's evolutionary criterion is to be rejected.

For several decades the ethics of evolutionism seemed to have been dealt a death-blow by the criticisms of Thomas Huxley. It was however revived. A summary formulation of the renewed theory was given by Julian Huxley in the forties. His grandfather, he pointed out, had concluded that the ethical process combated the cosmic. At present however this contradiction of the cosmic by the ethical could be resolved "on the one hand by extending the concept of evolution both backwards into the inorganic and forward into the human domain, and on the other by considering ethics not as a body of fixed principles, but as a product of evolution, and itself evolving."[6]

The solution of this contradiction and the renewal of evolutionary ethics, wrote Huxley, was made possible by two developments at the turn of the century, Freudian psychology and Mendelian genetics.

Freudian psychology showed that the seeming absoluteness of moral obligation is merely due to a compulsive all-or-nothing mechanism of the primitive superego. "This quality of absoluteness is later reinforced by the natural human desire for certitude, as well as by certain peculiarities of our language mechanism. . . Thus the absoluteness of moral obligation turns out on analysis to be no true absolute, but a result of the nature of our infantile mental machinery combined with later rationalization and wish-fulfilment."[7] Since one of the stumbling-blocks of evolutionary ethics was the existence of absolutes, Freud rendered an immense service to morality by making clear the real nature of moral qualities. Besides this, modern psychology has greatly changed ethics by bringing out many new facts and a new approach.[8]

Modern genetics aided in this renewal of evolutionary ethics by stressing the fact of man's immense genetic variability, which has important results, both biologically and ethically. Among these are those personal differences which allow us to speak of moral temperaments. Modern genetics has also provided the basis for a comprehensive selectionist theory of evolution. For, it has shown that although mutation provides the raw material of evolution, it has little or no effect on its direction. All other suggested agencies of evolution, Lamarckism, orthogenesis, vitalistic immanent tendencies and divine guidance have been proven unnecessary, since natural selection is logically necessary and is in itself a satisfactory explanation of the facts. A further development has been the closer analysis of the results of evolution.[9]

We now know, Huxley avers, that in all evidence it is better to have a realistic rather than an unrealistic ethics. Furthermore, it should be realistic both internally and externally. The first occurs when an individual adjusts himself objectively to the moral standards of his society; the second, when the standards of society are realistically adjusted to science.[10]

All this however is merely knowledge of our psychological situation. It does not tell us whether our standards are ethically better.

> However, ethics do not merely vary at random: they also evolve. That fact provides our clue. Our ethics evolve because they are themselves part of the evolutionary process. And any standards of rightness or wrongness must in some way be related to the movement of that process through time.

> Now that the moment has arrived when we are able to perceive evolution as an all-comprehensive process of which human existence forms a part, it is impossible any longer to rely on any static guarantees for ethics. Our fuller knowledge discloses not a set of absolute or fixed standards, but a direction of change.[11]

At the beginning of life evolution was biological, proceeding through mechanical interaction and natural selection. With the advent of men it has become conscious and has acquired quicker methods of gaining and transmitting experience. Since such is the case, "ethics can be injected into the evolutionary process. Before man that process was merely amoral. After his emergence onto life's stage it became possible to introduce faith, courage, love of truth, goodness--in a word moral purpose--into evolution."[12]

But how are we to know what are morally right purposes?

> When we look at evolution as a whole, we find, among the many directions which it has taken, one which is characterized by introducing the evolving world-stuff to progres-

sively higher levels of organization and so to new possibilities of being, action, and experience. This direction has culminated in the attainment of a state where the world-stuff (now moulded into human shape) finds that it experiences some of the new possibilities as having value in or for themselves; and further that among these it assigns higher and lower degrees of value, the higher values being those which are more intrinsically or more permanently satisfying, or involve a greater degree of perfection. The teleologically-minded would say that this trend embodies evolution's purpose. I do not feel that we should use the word purpose save where we know that a conscious aim is involved; but we can say that this is the most desirable direction of evolution, and accordingly that our ethical standards must fit into its dynamic framework. In other words, it is ethically right to aim at whatever will promote the increasingly full realization of increasingly higher values.[13]

Standards of right and wrong are to be worked out as an expansion of this aim, but always with an eye out to reconcile the claims of the present and future. Evolutionary ethics thus presents the world with dynamic general standards to replace the older ones which are crumbling.

As we analyze this renewal of evolutionary moral theory, we find that in essence its method is the same as the earlier. Huxley first marshals all the evolutionary data science can provide; this task is a good deal more complicated for him than it was for Spencer because scientists have discovered so much in the last half century and furthermore he has enlarged the concept of evolution to start it off with the first appearance of matter, to include all the processes which it has gone and will go through, to that ultimate step in which it is consciously guided by man. From this over-all view of evolution he infers its direction of change. As man is a part of nature and all nature is subject to evolution, only that is morally right which is in accordance with this evolutionary direction of change. At this point, however, Huxley slips in hedonistic considerations, just as did the earlier evolutionists. As man evolves, he says, he becomes conscious of objective values, that is, of the qualities of things whereby they are "more intrinsically or permanently satisfying." He has therefore a moral right to seek them on two counts: first, the evolutionary standard, since these values were perceived as part of the evolutionary process; secondly, their intrinsic satisfactoriness. With these standards Huxley feels he is in a position to draw up scientific rules of morality. These in effect will be merely generalized statements of what has been empirically found to be in accordance with the evolutionary direction of change or to be intrinsically satisfying.

Pierre Teilhard de Chardin, Huxley's friend and a renowned paleontologist, has defended a view that is similar in its basics but is developed within the framework of catholic theology. His ethical position is to be found chiefly in The Phenomenon of Man (1955) and The Divine Milieu (1957). In his view, a central and crucial fact about man is that he is an evolving creature of God. Evolution, Teilhard optimistically holds, necessarily and overall brings about progress. We can determine the direction of this progress and should conform ourselves to it. The ultimate end of the evolutionary process is convergence with the divine. But at the present stage of evolution it is up to man himself to organize and direct his social life in such a way as to further the evolutionary tendency to an ever closer communion with God. In man evolution has become conscious of itself, so, in order to be true to himself and to the universe man has to bring about, individually and socially, the spiritual progress of nature. Thus, the approaches of Huxley and Teilhard are similar in this way that they both base themselves on what they determine the direction of evolution to be, but they differ inasmuch as Huxley interprets and completes his analysis of evolution with utilitarian considerations whereas Teilhard does so from the point of view of a theistic and theological humanism.

Another recent and prominent advocate of evolutionary ethics has been the eminent geneticist, C. H. Waddington. In the early forties he started off considerable discussion with his article, "The Relations Between Science and Ethics." More recently, he has attempted to give a fuller and more developed expression to his position in The Ethical Animal.[14]

Waddington holds that Spencer and Huxley were on the right track when they defended the necessity of an evolutionary approach to moral philosophy. But, he argues, both had certain methodological shortcomings which weakened their presentation and also therefore the support they received. Both, he says, fell into a vicious circle. For they claim that evolutionary progress is good and that therefore the moral goodness of our acts can be defined in terms of evolutionary processes. Then too, according to Spencer, evolutionary progress consists in and is demonstrated by the increasing complexity of what evolves. But this is to take too simple a view of the matter because the development of complexity often leads in evolution to a dead end. Huxley, Waddington says, also leaves himself open to the charge of having committed the "naturalistic fallacy" by the loose way that he identifies moral goodness and evolutionary progress.

Waddington's aim is work out more explicitly and fully his earlier defense of evolutionary ethics and to thereby provide a theory which, he feels, will be superior to Huxley's. He also wishes to argue against the positivists and the analytic philosophers that ethics is a valid normative discipline and that it is besides an objective one.

Waddington frames the issue in this way. We all wish to have some rational guidance in regard to how we ought to act. As adults we find that we have acquired a set of feelings about what is right and what is wrong, and about what we ought or ought not to do. We refer to these feelings as "ethical" because of a common quality we perceive in them and we use them as guides for our behavior. The issue then is how do we determine whether or not any such feelings are correct, that is, are adequate guides for our conduct. It is only, Waddington holds, through a consideration of animal and human evolution that we are able to decide in such matters and also to make a rational evaluation of different systems of ethics. It must be stressed however that besides animal evolution, man has also gone through an evolution that is peculiarly human, which for purposes of moral evaluation is of far greater importance. Human evolution has been primarily a cultural evolution. And it is only by understanding how culture has evolved that we can see how man has achieved those characteristics that we now consider the most valuable.

It is crucial to any form of evolutionary ethics that it can show how evolutionary processes are demonstrably progressive. There are various mechanisms whereby evolution comes. Two that most biologists today recognize are mutation and natural selection. These, says Waddington, cannot however by themselves adequately explain why evolution would be anything but directionless change. But we can now see that two further factors are involved. First, natural selection affects not the hereditary factors themselves but the total organisms throughout their lives. Thus, what is passed on from one generation to the next is not just a genetic system but a whole "epigenetic system" whereby the information contained in the genetic system is provided a functional structure through which that information expresses itself. In other terms, throughout evolution each organism responds to environmental stresses as well as it can, but in any given population there will be a certain range of variation in the density and character of the responses; those organisms that are able to respond in the most adaptive manner are the ones which in time will dominate, that is, remain in existence. In this way acquired characteristics can be said to be transmitted. But, then, the "survival of the fittest" should be interpreted to mean, not the survival of the strongest but the success of certain kinds of individuals in transmitting hereditary qualities. A second aspect of the evolutionary mechanism is that organisms are not just shaped by the environment but to a certain extent choose and modify it also. Waddington summarizes his view here in these terms:

> Biological evolution, then, is carried out by an 'evolutionary system' which involves four major factors (Fig. 2): a genetic system, which engenders new variation by the process of mutation and transmits it by chromosomal genes; an epigenetic system, which translates the information in the fertilized egg and that which impinges on it from the environment into the characters of the reproducing adult; an exploitive system, by which an animal chooses and modifies the environment to which it will submit itself; and a system of natural selective pressures, originating from the environment and operating on the combined result of the other three systems.[15]

As a result of the interaction of these four systems evolutionary changes always tend in the direction of increasing efficiency.

Animal evolution continues in man but the more important and rapid changes in men are due to cultural evolution. This has been made possible by an extremely important change in the mode of evolution. In animals information (in the cybernetic sense) is transmitted from generation to generation through the genes. Consequently, any improvement in this information took a long time. Man however has reached an evolutionary stage in which he transmits information by teaching, thus making possible radical and rapid changes in what we know and how we live. Teaching methods themselves have evolved in a very rapid way in the last few thousand years. Among the main steps of this evolution were the formalization of rote learning and then the invention of writing and, more recently, of printing. As a result of this, new information can be acquired and disseminated in a matter of days.

The socio-genetic transmission of information by man requires a certain mechanism whereby he can, not only transmit, but also receive the information. This mechanism consists of developing infants into acceptors of authority. It is a logical and empirical necessity that children submit to learning from others, that they in this sense accept the authority of others. It is in this way too that we get our moral feelings and the internalized authority system that we call conscience. Modern psychology helps us to understand this process. Piaget has shown that the development of the moral sense in the child results from a spontaneous feeling in the presence of his parents that they are greater than and superior to himself. Freud and other psychoanalysts have shown how, in the formation of personality, authority systems like the ego and superego are formed in the mind and why they are so often stronger and more demanding than seems really necessary. The development of such "authority-bearing systems" is necessary so that children become information-acceptors. But simultaneously it also makes them acceptors of moral standards, values and notions. Having moral feelings is then also a necessary effect and factor of the evolutionary process.

Although not every line of evolutionary change is progressive, it is clear that evolution tends in the direction of increasing efficiency and has over the long range produced newer and higher forms of life. Evolutionary progress can then be characterized as the development, to higher and higher levels, of various capacities: "to remain relatively independent of the environment, to incorporate into the life-system more complex functions of environmental variables, and ultimately to control the environment."[16] In more crude terms, the progressive character of evolution is exhibited by the increasing possibility of richness of experience.

As result evolutionary theory can provide us with a criterion to evaluate moral feelings and moral philosophies, while also providing a more useful point of view to examine such problems. In the course of our evolutionary development we have come to consider our feelings, about certain actions, as being "ethical." Such feelings have an important function in the evolutionary scheme: to make us do certain acts and avoid others. We can determine which of these acts now are or are not in accord with evolutionary progress and thus also determine which of these feelings are warrantedly ethical. We can in the same manner establish which moral theories provide us with a correct moral code. Thus, Waddington avers, resolving moral problems is similar to resolving dieting problems. We determine what a good diet is by finding out through which foods we adequately fulfill the function of eating. We determine what acts should be considered ethical in the light of how well by them we fulfill our functions in the evolutionary scheme. The criterion of what should be done and avoided is thus a cosmic, evolutionary wisdom. "If, as I maintain, our ethical beliefs are part of the human evolutionary system, they also must be subject to evolutionary processes. Since we can discern their function, we can decide what is anagenesis with respect to them, just as we can decide what is anagenesis with respect to the biological genetic system. We can attach a real and objective meaning to the idea of an improvement in the mechanism of formation and development of the super-ego as a part of the functional machinery of human evolution. This direction of improvement undoubtedly forms one of the criteria which we must apply in judging the merits of particular ethical systems."[17] In this way too we avoid the fallacies of reasoning in a circle and of identifying moral goodness with some non-moral quality.

Despite differences in the conclusions and emphases, evolutionary moralists, it seems clear, all follow the same general approach in developing their ethics. The problem we are mainly concerning ourselves with here is how appropriate and adequate is this approach, looking at it from the methodological point of view.

Critical Analysis

It is axiomatic that a structure can be no more solid than its foundation. We may then first ask ourselves how solid a foundation for an ethical system is the evolutionary theory. We must keep in mind the difference between a fact and a theory. No one nowadays doubts the fact of evolution, that is, that living things of a higher sort have come from others of a lower sort. But the theory of evolution is another matter. To explain the facts of evolution scientists have worked out various evolutionary theories and they recognize that all of these theories have their deficiencies and inadequacies. Thus, the well-known biologist G. G. Simpson has written, "The general outline of that history and some of its characteristic details are now so well determined as to provide a factual background open to little serious question. It is, however, still true that the unknown exceeds the known and gives room for some (yet for limited) differences of interpretation. And even were all factually known, which can never become true, interpretation would still be necessary before meaning could arise from the factual record. Differences of interpretation will no doubt always arise, and this or any other readings of meaning into the history of life can never carry compulsive authority. It can only be an opinion submitted for judgment . . ."[18] E. C. Olson, in the paper he read at the Darwin Centennial, described the present situation in these terms, "We are then in the position of believing, without definitive proof, that factors beyond those recognized at present are of major importance in some areas of evolution, but of not knowing just what they are or how they may be discovered. This is an unfortunate negative situation."[19] Thus, since there is at present so much disagreement among scientists as to how and why evolution did take place, it follows that in trying to establish an ethical system on such a theory one would have to be most careful to base one's self as much as possible on those parts of the theory that are generally admitted, such as the view that the genes function in an interdependent fashion or that natural selection occurs to some extent through adaptation. But a moral theory based on such a consensus would indeed have a rather narrow foundation. If however a moralist develops his views on the basis of the total evolutionary theory presented by some scientist, although he would then have a much broader base from which to work, it would be a much more unreliable one. Even a cursory reading, however, makes it clear that evolutionary moralists like Huxley, Teilhard and Waddington base their moral systems on a whole-hearted acceptance of the particular version of the evolutionary theory that they favor.

Because of the various gaps and obscurities in the facts of evolution, there is a wide range of different, indeed, contrary interpretations and conclusions possible. On the purely scientific level the result has been a number of different schools, not only in the past but also in the present: Darwinism, Neo-Lamarckianism, Neo-Darwinism, vitalism, etc. In the present day, according to E. C. Olson, "There are, of course, degrees of difference in evaluation of successes, from healthy scepticism to confidence that the final word has been said, and there are still some among the biologists who feel that much of the fabric of theory accepted by the majority today is actually false . . . There exists, as well, a generally silent group of students engaged in biological pursuits who tend to disagree with much of the current thought but say and write little . . . many who are not satisfied with current theory are to be found in the ranks of the paleontologists and morphologists."[20] This diversity of scientific interpretation leads quite naturally to a corresponding variety of conclusions drawn by the philosophers. Thus Dewey had his instrumentalist naturalism; Harris, a personalistic idealism and Whitehead, a realistic process view. Clearly, then, the scientific theory of evolution is open to a variety of philosophic interpretations. It follows also that depending on these variations different kinds of moral theories could be developed from the same facts. It is then most necessary to clearly distinguish what is based on the scientific fact and what comes from the point of view of the interpreting philosopher.

When we consider the different versions of evolutionary ethics which have been produced, this conclusion is borne out, that they are not just inferred from scientific theory but result mainly from the philosophical presuppositions of their authors. Both Huxley and Waddington interpret the scientific data from a naturalistic point of view and their ethics is naturalistic. Teilhard starts off with the same scientific data but also with a theistic humanism and his ethics is a theocentric one. To put it in another way, science, as has been so often pointed out, is ethically neutral. Science has is its functions describing, measuring and correlating phenomena and developing on this basis theories which enable us to some degree to explain and control nature. But when any person engages in scientific pursuits he is working within a comprehensive world-picture which of itself is not scientific but philosophical and which provides him with his fundamental attitudes, presuppositions and values. From the point of view of this Weltanschauung, he will then interpret his scientific data. But such interpretations are hence a function more of his philosophy than his science. It is important to keep this in mind because evolutionary moralists generally think of and present their views as being simply and purely scientific inferences from established facts.

We should note further that an evolutionary ethics involves not just a general world-picture but as its different versions have been historically worked out, they also presuppose a set of non-scientific, ethical principles. In The Phenomenon of Man Teilhard claims he is doing and presenting work which is purely and simply scientific. But many of his conclusions as to how man should act are the result, it seems clear enough, not of a strict scientific deduction from evolutionary theory, but of his prescientific commitment to the Christian God. For, Huxley would draw no such conclusions from the scientific data. We can see the same point rather clearly in Waddington's case. One of his cardinal moral principles is the necessity to keep an open mind and to avoid looking at the world in terms of stark opposites, as just black or white. "The practical conclusion to be drawn from this line of thought is that it is dangerous to allow questions of belief to become concentrated into a single channel. We have to recognize not merely that it is impossible to eliminate beliefs from the human mind, but that a stable and equable personality must be founded, not only on one, but on several ideals."[2] The issue here is whether this is a conclusion he has derived from the evolutionary theory or a presupposition derived from his Weltanschauung and in the light of which he interprets the scientific data and theory. It has really to be the latter. Let us note first an ambiguity in the statement "a stable and equable personality must be founded . . . on several ideals." Does the "must" indicate an evolutionary or a non-evolutionary necessity? If he means the latter, then our point is granted. If he means the former, then he is inconsistent. For, it is his view that "it is necessary before socio-genetic transmissions can operate, that some sort of 'authority-bearing system' is formed in the mental apparatus of those who will transmit and those who will receive" and that "the

54

actual authoritative system set up in human minds seems commonly to carry much more weight than would be necessary to fulfil this function adequately enough."[22] If such is the mechanism through which evolution works in man, then the acceptance of several counterbalancing ideals, as suggested by Waddington,would not be in line with this mechanism; it would involve a transcending of and an imposition upon the mechanism. It could then only be justified on the basis of a non-evolutionary moral principle. Besides this, we may note, the claim that a stable and equable personality must be based on more than one ideal seems counterfactual. Fanatics often have very stable and equable personalities; on the other hand, neuroses often result from following several ideals that are not unified in a hierarchical system.

From the point of view of method, it is important to know what a moralist is using as a dual, scientific and philosophical foundation. We would want to know the justification for both and how they are related. For, if a moral system was actually founded on a dual basis of this sort and this was not recognized, the result would be that philosophical principles would be covertly introduced and, despite the claim that the result is a "scientific ethics", what one would have would be simply an uncritical presentation of a set of philosophical prejudices. Unfortunately, since the more recent evolutionary moralists have not been professional philosophers they have not been very explicit in distinguishing the philosophical from the scientific in their theories. Since the former is so crucial, this is a serious methodological deficiency.

A central tenet of every evolutionary ethics is that evolution, at least in the long run, is achieving what is identifiably and certainly progress. If this were not the case, there would then be no way of developing an ethics from an evolutionary basis. Methodologically, however, such a tenet is objectionable if biologists do not in general support it. Concerning this we may note first of all that there is general agreement that evolution has not produced a uniform progress. But some scientists insist further that there is not, in the total evolutionary process, any single, overall progressive trend. Thus, G. G. Simpson has written, "In summary, evolution is not invariably accompanied by progress, nor does it really seem to be characterized by progress as an essential feature. Progress has occurred within it but is not of its es-

sence. Aside from the broad tendency for the expansion
of life, which is also inconstant, there is no sense in
which it can be said that evolution is progress. Within
the framework of the evolutionary history of life there
have been not one but many different sorts of progress.
Each sort appears not with a single line or even with
one central but branching line throughout the course of
evolution, but separately in many different lines."[23]
From such considerations he concluded to the
impossibility of establishing any sort of evolutionary
ethics based on the notion of evolutionary progress.[24]
This line of argument, however, be it found in Simpson
or elsewhere, is clearly fallacious, because not to the
point. The proponent of an evolutionary ethics does not
base his view on the claim that progress invariably
accompanies evolution, for he would agree that it does
not. Nor, likewise, does he identify evolution with
progress. His point rather is that through the whole
course of evolution there have been successively
produced increasingly superior forms of life and that
biologists are in general agreement on the point.

Another example of such a straw man may be found
in S. C. Pepper's Ethics. In the context of this issue,
he says: "Progress . . . can only relevantly mean that
the forms that have emerged later in the evolution of
life are better adapted than those that emerged earlier."[25] Hence, he argues, an ethics based on evolutionary progress is untenable since all life forms
adapt equally well, in their own ways. But, evolutionary moralists readily acknowledge this comparability of
adaptations and so when they speak of progress, this is
simply not what they are referring to. Thus Pepper's
objection too is without foundation.

There still however remain difficulties. The long-
range sorts of progress we can point to in biological
evolution are all of a vague, general kind: extension
of life, increase in complexity, increase in efficiency
and increase in the richness of experience. The use of
these as moral criteria allows one to infer certain
moral rules. But these are also and necessarily phrased
in very broad terms. Consequently they would require
other moral rules providing for limiting cases, but
from where except a non-evolutionary source could one
derive them? If one takes evolutionary progress to consist in the extension of life, this leaves no way of
resolving problems of overpopulation and of the superiority of quality over quantity. If one takes progress
to involve several or all of those biological trends,

56

one would have to determine which in which cases has priority over the others. For instance, should we encourage growth in complexity over growth in the richness of experience or vice versa? The evolutionary moralist is faced with the dilemma of either sticking solely with his evolutionary principles and having a system too general to be effective or of giving up his purely evolutionary system to make it more effective.

If we try to resolve this dilemma by a closer consideration of human evolution, we still have problems. The development of man manifests a number of different trends. How can we tell which really constitute progress? To do this in a scientific way we would have to derive our criteria from what we know of the present and the past. But it is a characteristic of the evolutionary process to produce novelties. Since the latter are in the nature of the case unpredictable, it is at least on the biological level risky to either affirm or deny that a given trend shall continue to be progressive, even though we could establish that from a given point of view it has been so. It might be argued that on the human or cultural level of evolution it is up to man to continue consciously the progressive direction of the past. But even if this were granted, it would not give us any sufficiently specific indication of how we should act unless one brought in further non-evolutionary principles on the basis of which a proper direction could be maintained. Thus, the dilemma remains.

There is another difficulty. Evolutionary moralists generally consider ethics to be a normative discipline. In line with this they talk like other normative moralists of the obligations which men have. But there would seem to be an ambiguity in the use of the term. Waddington, for instance, speaks of obligation in terms of the super-ego and seems to reduce moral obligation to a feeling of having to act in a certain way, a feeling whose nature and origin is to be explained in Freudian terms. When however moralists speak of obligation in the more usual and traditional sense, they mean a certain moral, as opposed to physical or psychological, necessity to act in a given way. But, to be obliged in the sense that the super-ego makes us do an act is quite different from being obliged in the sense that we have to do an act because we recognize that there is a moral order that is objective and superior to us and which requires that we do it. It is this latter sense of obligation that the layman ordinarily is using when he asks about his moral obligations. Realizing this, Waddington answers queries about why we should be moral or why we should seek to further evolutionary progress with an analogy of morality to eating. You should be moral because you will be fulfilling your natural function and will be happier, just as you should follow a proper diet because you will be healthier and feel better. The point to be noted here is this. A purely evolutionary morality does not by itself provide an ultimate justification for moral obligations but can do so only by bringing in non-evolutionary considerations: utilitarian ones in the case of Huxley and Waddington, theistic ones in the case of Teilhard.

As a normative discipline ethics has as one of its main functions providing us with a rational code of conduct. Evolutionary moralists have all tried to indicate what it should be but the results show three common characteristics: their proposed rules are all very general, they deal only with a limited number of selected problems and they usually repeat some of the same points most other moralists arrive at. To illustrate, we find Waddington suggesting that we ought to encourage the progress of the mechanism of the socio-genetic evolutionary system, that we ought to encourage the development of varieties of communities, and that we should avoid nuclear war. One conclusion that suggests itself here is that the evolutionary approach is then one of rather limited scope and value, since other approaches provide behavior codes that are much more extensive and detailed. One could further argue that from a methodological view it is therefore an evolutionary dead-end.

An important and interesting facet of evolutionary ethics is its extension of the meaning of evolution. Evolution is now taken to mean not just biological evolution but it is used to refer to the cultural history of man also. There seem to be two reasons especially for so extending the meaning of the term. On the one hand it is a way of acknowledging how different, indeed, how unique, man is in the animal kingdom. This difference is not simply biological but we have in man a new dimension, that of mind, which involves quite different sorts of conditions and processes. What is perhaps most noteworthy is that with man evolution has come to a point where it is self-conscious and self-determined. On the other hand, we also make clear the nature, functions and necessity of ethics. Men have developed ethical theories because they live together in groups and have a certain culture. All sorts of problems arise as a result of their interaction and ethics is one kind of attempt to resolve these problems. By relating cultural evolution to biological evolution it is hoped to arrive at a more adequate and scientific resolution of moral problems.

There is however a rather paradoxical result of the extension of the notion. It was done in order to complete and strengthen the evolutionary ethical theory but it would seem to require its development along lines that go beyond its original premisses. It accepts as established that in biological evolution progress is guaranteed by the nature of the process but that in human cultural evolution it is up to men themselves to ensure continued progress. In this case however past evolution might be able to indicate certain general directions men should take but could not give any reasonably specific goals, motives and criteria for activities that are progressive in the present context. For instance, Soviet, Maoist and Western ideologists would all argue that the cultural trends in their countries represent the main thrust of human evolution. The only adequate way to resolve this and similar issues seems to be through a metaevolutionary analysis of the nature and conditions of human activity.

Then too, when it is used in these ways, evolution is an analogical term, that is, it is being used to refer to two processes which are quite different in nature but which have certain similarities and relations, and it is because of these that we call them by the same name. Clearly, they are fundamentally different. Evolution in the biological sense consists of changes that take place in organisms, over eons, as a result of conditions arising randomly, with no control over them by those affected. Evolution in the cultural sense refers to changes in how men live and act; these changes occur relatively quickly and at an increasing tempo; they are produced to some extent as a result of our choices and we can too to a degree control them. On the other hand, though they are different, cultural evolution is the continuation, on a higher level, of what started in biological evolution. They also both involve continual change and, hopefully, progress. It is such similarities and relationships which justify the imposition of a common term.

As a consequence of this, however, what is true of biological evolution is not necessarily so of cultural evolution. Thus, even if we grant that biological evolution necessarily produces progress, it would not follow that cultural evolution does. What is important from a methodological point of view is that any conclusion of evolutionary ethics that is based on a comparison of or a passage between biological and cultural evolution could strictly be only a probable one, no matter how plausible it might seem. Even though such conclusions were in fact true statements and could be established otherwise to be such, taken as conclusions from such premisses, they can only be probable. Thus, for example, when an evolutionary moralist says that men have an obligation to make cultural evolution progressive because it is a continuation of biological evolution which is progressive, it may perhaps be true. But to show that it is true one would also have to somehow establish that we have a general noral obligation to live in accord with nature. Otherwise one would be committing the "is-to-ought" fallacy. Huxley and Waddington would base their view that we should live in accord with nature at least in part on hedonistic grounds: doing so is in general a more satisfying way of living. But the hedonistic principle is not itself established by the evolutionary data and so from within the purely evolutionary perspective has only a hypothetical value.

This leads us to another methodological deficiency of evolutionary ethics. Both Huxley and Waddington would argue that a valid ethics can be derived only through the application of the scientific method to the evolutionary data. First of all, we should note that the term "scientific" is also an analogous one. For, it could be used in its recent sense of consisting of the cumulation of measurements and correlations of facts or in its older meaning of productive of knowledge that is certain and of real causes. Huxley and Waddington however use it in the former sense. Now, we could agree with them that biological evolution is studied properly only in this way. Such an approach though does not work too well for the study of cultural evolution, for here the qualitative factors are the more relevant. It is however not valid at all when the task is to develop an ethics. Fundamentally, a scale of values and a code of conduct require a quite different method of derivation than does man's genetic structure. What is required for an ethics is an analysis of the essential characteristics and functions of men and of their activities. This cannot be done through a laboratory approach. As we have seen, evolutionary ethics is possible only through the acceptance of a <u>Weltanschauung</u> on the basis of which biological and anthropological data are interpreted. A valid ethics can be scientific only in the older and broader meaning of the word, although it certainly should make use of data that is scientific in the narrower sense. Thus, evolutionary moralists err by conceiving of method and of science in a univocal instead of an analogical fashion, and concluding that the method for ethics has to be the same as that for biology.

Another deficiency that has often been noted in evolutionary ethics is that its proponents commit the "naturalistic fallacy" by identifying moral goodness with being in accord with the main evolutionary thrust. Waddington argues that this charge is not valid against his ethical position because he does not identify moral goodness with evolutionary progress but only uses the latter as the criterion by which he can judge between ethical systems. It is clear however that this is merely a verbal evasion of the charge. Its plausibility, such as it has, comes from the peculiar way that he defines moral goodness, as a feeling certain activities arouse in us. He then goes on to argue that "ethicizing," or having and living according to such feelings, is a natural function directed to furthering the progress of evolution. From this he concludes that ethical systems can be evaluated on the basis of how well they guide men toward fulfilling their evolutionary goal. What Waddington is doing here, however, is to identify what are or are not desirable ways of acting with what is or is not in accord with the direction of evolution. And the former is what we usually mean by moral goodness or badness. If now someone would counter that nevertheless this identification is a valid one, we would be back to a point previously discussed: Waddington would have to establish that it is so, and he can do this only in terms of his pre-scientific, naturalistic assumptions.

Conclusions

We may summarize our conclusions in this way. The evolutionary approach to ethics has the advantage of taking a strongly empirical point of view which leads to important insights into the nature of man and his situation. Nevertheless, evolutionary ethics, at least in its common forms, is from a methodological point of view inadequate for various reasons. Its proponents tend to accept a given version of the evolutionary theory as thoroughly established and beyond doubt, but this is contrary to fact. Besides, there is no such thing as a purely evolutionary ethics. Every form of it is based not only on a scientific theory but also on a pre-scientific world picture of one sort or another. And what is worse, often-times this world picture is accepted without much critical analysis and thus the ethics based on it is to that extent methodologically tainted. But certainly any adequate moral theory will have to be based on a <u>Weltanschauung</u> which gives an objective account and explanation of the world and man and to do this it will have to give full consideration to evolutionary data. Then too, the criteria and the conduct rules evolutionary ethics can plausibly support are also only of a rather general sort. But these can usually also be established on the basis of non-evolutionary considerations, although, we may note, evolutionary ethics can provide strong arguments for certain negative rules such as those against pollution.

# CHAPTER FOUR

# THE PSYCHOLOGICAL APPROACH TO ETHICS

In the traditional approach to the development of ethics, it is built up on the basis of data obtained from experience, from empirical sciences like biology, empirical psychology and sociology, and from philosophical disciplines such as ontology and philosophical psychology. In the psychological approach, on the other hand, ethics is based primarily and mainly on the data and theories of empirical and clinical psychology. Its proponents may accept supporting theories from other positive sciences or from a "scientific" philosophy, but they refuse to base their views on any philosophically or religiously theistic conception of the world, although they may admit its psychological importance in the lives of many people. In general, this method consists of adopting the findings and theories of scientific psychology as the essential and adequate matrix within which we should work out our ethical theory and code of conduct. Consequently, it accepts as norms of morality such goals as maturity, mental health or the satisfaction of needs and wants.

We shall first sketch out the historical development of this approach. We shall then analyze its use by one of its main proponents, B. F. Skinner. After that, we shall discuss critically the validity and use of such a method in working out a moral philosophy.

## Historical Development

Given the nature of the psychological approach, it could not have been developed until the twentieth century, but its roots go back far. Already in antiquity the Epicureans developed their ethics largely on the basis of their analysis of human drives and behavior. At the beginning of the modern period Hobbes worked out his ethics along similar lines.

One of the main hopes and projects of the Enlightenment thinkers was to establish an empirical science of man, on the basis of which a solid, natural morality could be based. In France the tendency was toward the reductive analysis of the higher mental activities to sensation and from there to move on to some form of hedonism. Thus, Condillac, following but simplifying Locke, reduces all knowledge to experience and all experience to sensation. Man can thus be considered higher than other animals because of the superiority of his sense of touch. His desires and drives are the result of previous pleasures. Hence the good is merely what gives pleasure. La Mettrie and Cabanis worked out analogous views.

In England in this same time period David Hartley worked out a utilitarian ethics on the basis of his associationist psychology. All sensations, he said, result from cerebro-neural vibrations and give either pain or pleasure. When different sensations are experienced together repeatedly, later on the experience of one of these sensations will give rise by association to the vibrations of the other sensation, and these are the ideas of the imagination. The pains and pleasures of the imagination arise in the same way. With time the simple ideas and pleasures are converted, again by association, into ever more complex ideas and pleasures. The final result is a moral sense which leads men to prefer benevolence and piety to the lower pleasures. As the mature is more perfect than the primitive, man progresses morally by following his moral sense, by doing which he may achieve infinite happiness.

Leaving aside to a large extent the associationist groundwork Hartley had built on, Jeremy Bentham, influenced by Condillac, La Mettrie and Helvetius, developed a utilitarianism based on quantitative comparisons of pains and pleasures: his well-known hedonic calculus. As men always seek to have pleasures and to avoid pain, their happiness consists in achieving the maximum of the former and the minimum of the latter. As moreover pains and pleasures may be measured quantitatively according to their intensity, duration, certainty, nearness, fecundity and purity, we may by simple calculation determine their relative values and through this the best course of action. We need not bother with the quality of pleasures because "quantity of pleasure being equal, pushpin is as good as poetry." Nevertheless, sympathy and friendship are desirable; they are sources of pleasure and useful in maintaining or extending our happiness.

The mechanistic current of thought exemplified earlier by Hobbes and La Mettrie waxed strong in the nineteenth century, when it produced a "psychology without a soul." This explained all human behavior as only the result of the physical and chemical responses of the human organism. It differed from the more primitive materialism in that it had at its disposal large masses of details regarding the interrelations of physiological and mental processes and in that it could fit into the new Darwinian universe which had a pattern but no purpose, laws but no lawgiver. Such a system received its most mature and complete formulation at the end of the century by Jacques Loeb, for whom tropism was the key to understanding all life phenomena.

The late 1800's also witnessed three new scientific developments of importance for the psychological approach. First of all, psychology started to be developed as an empirical discipline. It had existed as a philosophical science since Aristotle, but with the setting up of the first laboratory of psychology by Wilhelm Wundt it started to develop as a positive science. Secondly, Freud started to lay the basis for psychoanalysis. Thirdly, I. D. Pavlov and V. M. Bekhterev did their work on conditioning. Pavlov demonstrated and accurately measured the induction of a conditioned reflex. This was of course a specialized application of the law of association earlier mentioned by Aristotle. Pavlov however wanted to avoid the psychological implications of the word "association" and in time presented a generalized theory of behavior as resulting from purely physiological complexes of conditioned reflexes. Bekhterev emphasized chiefly the motor reflexes. He too made conditioning a purely physiological process. He went further however to suggest that complex habits were compounded conditioned reflexes and that thought itself was the responses of the muscles of the speech organs.

The twentieth century saw a rapid development of empirical and clinical psychology and the early use of the psychological approach to ethics. Thus, in the United States John Watson had been advocating what he called a behaviorist psychology which sought to do without such concepts as mind and consciousness. In 1916 he came across translations of Bekhterev, whose ideas he immediately infused into his theory. All behavior could be explained in terms of conditioned reflexes. He paid special attention to language as thought was primarily the conditioned response to words. In 1925 Albert Weiss produced a brief and clear summary of behaviorist views of psychology and ethics. "As a larger percentage of the population begins to see that human achievement need not be regarded as the product of unanalyzable components based upon magical or mythical principles, there is gradually developing a biosocial analysis of human behavior. . . The biosocial as opposed to the supernatural concept of man's destiny assumes electrons and protons as the ultimate elements from which the more complex inorganic atoms, molecules, crystals, are formed. Greater complexity is found in the organic molecules which reach one limit in the protoplasmic cell and a second limit in the larger multicellular herbivora. Social organization represents the greatest degree of complexity and begins in the animal series as those relationships which are designated as parasitism and symbiosis, and in man these processes take the form of what is known as exploitation and cooperation. Social evolution as a cosmical process is producing larger and more complex electron-proton aggregates and as an individual process is developing a social organization that yields to each individual a maximum of variety in behavior. The ultimate realization of these conditions will produce a social organization and a type of individual that have as upper limits those properties best described as omniscient, and omnipotent, and from the biological side those properties which produce a maximum degree of interchangeability of the receptor-effector functions between individuals."[1] The keynote of the ethics of such a system thus lies "in developing among all individuals on earth a greater degree of cooperation, to the end that there may be greater sensori-motor interchangeability and maximum opportunity for self-expression and variety in behavior."[2] "The development of behavioristic ethics is in the direction of making available for every individual a healthful and decent physical environment during childhood and youth."[3] "The economic organization will be in the direction of giving every individual an opportunity to train himself in a vocation which either allows a maximum of self-expression or in which the conditions of work leave sufficient energy and leisure for an avocation."[4] "The limit toward which the variety of human behavior is approaching may be one in which the individual, through a substitutional language mechanism is able to respond differentially to a constantly increasing number of spatially and temporally unlimited electron-proton configurations."[5]

In the 1930's and later the behaviorists modified their claims considerably. They did this partly in a natural reaction against the one-sidedness of Watson and partly under the influence of other theories, especially gestalt psychology and psychoanalysis.

Freud was initiating psychoanalysis at about the

same time that Pavlov and Bekhterev had started their work, but at first he ran into much more trouble getting his ideas accepted. However, the gradual but widespread acceptance of psychoanalytic concepts in many different forms has made it, from the philosophical point of view, one of the most important types of psychological theory. Freud himself seemed to consider psychoanalytic theory as capable of providing a complete philosophy of life. He could do this however partly because he did not distinguish the materialist and determininist framework whence he started from his later clinical constructs. Alfred Adler, one of Freud's rebellious disciples, made similar claims for his own Individual Psychology. It provides, he said, a scientific basis for the universal teachings of all religions and philosophies, and moreover proposes a scientific technique whereby men can live happy and meaningful lives.[6] The example of Adler also brings out a characteristic of ethical works produced by the psychological method: they tend to be written by men who are not professional philosophers, and they are of a popular, non-dialectical and non-technical cast.

Of such works one of the earliest, and still widely read, is <u>A Preface to Morals</u> by Walter Lippmann, who based his moral position on an analysis of psychological development from infancy to maturity. For him, psychological maturity is synonymous with moral maturity.[7] At the end of the Second World War, in a long technical work, the English psychoanalyst J. C. Flügel devoted two chapters to the development of a psychological ethics.[8] More recently, the psychological approach has been used by E. Neumann,[9] L. S. Feuer,[10] D. Skakow,[11] and J. Wilder.[12]

We should also note that although prominent psychologists such as H. B. Overstreet, C. Bühler and A. H. Maslow have frequently discussed moral issues and naturally used psychological theory a good deal, they are not proponents of the psychological method in ethics, for they explicitly acknowledge the need to ground moral philosophy on more than just psychology.

## Skinner's Method

A striking feature of Skinner's method of resolving issues of morality is its relative simplicity. This, he would undoubtedly argue, is also one of its main advantages. The fundamental thrust of his approach is to reject traditional ways of explaining men and their behavior in favor of a scientific one. As we do this, we gradually establish what the factors are which make us be what we are and make us function as we do. This allows us to formulate the basic meaning of moral terms such as good and bad. Then, to specify more precisely what are good or bad for a given individual or culture is a matter of further empirical study of those particular cases. However, in order to appreciate and evaluate such an approach we have to consider it in more detail.

As Skinner sees it, before this century men had to rely on prescientific views of human nature in order to explain behavior. Consequently there developed the traditional view, which is still widely held, that men are autonomous, endowed with freedom and hence responsible for what they do and deserving of punishments and rewards for their acts. Based on this was a wide range of moral theories and practices. However, what we need and have recently been developing are a science and a technology of behavior. As we come to understand more and more how the human organism interacts with the environment, effects which were previously attributed to a free will, states of mind or personality traits are seen to result from environmental conditions and able therefore to be controlled by changing those conditions. The progress of science thus requires that we give up the traditional notion and ethics of autonomous man. Moreover, contrary to a very widespread view, science can also show us how we ought to act. For, science deals with facts. But values, or how people feel about facts, are also facts. We can thus scientifically determine what values exist, what results they produce and whether these results are good or bad. Such a science of behavior will be radically different from traditional views in its explanations of behavior and morality.[13]

The science of behavior will have to be based on a scientific concept of man, which we get mainly from biology and anthropology. Humans are one of the end-products of eons of evolution, as a result of which the species has a certain genetic endowment which enables and makes it perform a given range of activities. Thus endowed, each human individual is subject to the various factors of his physical and social environment, which condition him and determine how he will react at any given moment. Thus, as we increase our knowledge of them, we are able to control their results more and more completely.[14]

With such a view of man and of his place in nature, Skinner finds it easy to define what we mean by "good" and "bad". We call a thing good if it is a positive reinforcer of an expectation, inclination or conditioning. When we look at a steak on our plate and expect that it will produce certain effects when we eat it, and it does, we may then pronounce it good. Conversely, bad things are negative reinforcers. When we discover that by pulling away from an open flame we avoid the pain of a burnt hand, the reoccurence of such events reinforces our attempts to escape and so we call the flame bad. Thus, a value judgment is just a special type of factual judgment: it describes how in fact people feel about an object. Furthermore then, value judgments, contrary to the usual positivist view, are both descriptive and normative. They not only state what kind of effect an object has, they also indicate whether or not one should seek such an object. Given the fact that people want to achieve certain goals, value judgments tell them what to do or to avoid. Consequently, Skinner also rejects the hedonistic approach to morality. "Pleasure" is simply the general term we use to refer to the feelings caused in us by good things, and similarly "pain" denominates feelings produced by bad things. So, pleasure is not the ultimate good, nor is it the main goal that men seek. What men primarily want to get are the things that feel good, not the feelings themselves.[15]

Since moral good and evil are simply a matter of positive and negative reinforcement, we can establish what the factors are that determine whether a thing is good or bad through an analysis of the relevant scientific data. First of all, there is our genetic endowment, which is basically the same in all of us and which determines how we act and react, but which also provides for each individual various idiosyncratic features. A second factor is the physical environment, which provides varying types and levels of stimuli. Even more important however is the social environment. In reaction to the natural and social environments, a people will develop a set of customary behaviors which we call its culture. The values of a culture consist of whatever things are discovered to be reinforcements of those customs. Consequently, good and evil are relative. They change as a culture changes and they are different from one culture to another.[16]

As Skinner sees it then, morality has its source in evolution, both biological and cultural. The first has produced our bodies, with a relatively stable set of inclinations, capabilities and limitations. Thus, meat is generally considered good because it reinforces well our desire to satisfy our hunger. Cultural evolution superimposes on that biological inheritance a wide range of customary behaviors, which can be maintained for centuries but which are susceptible of rapid change. Thus, that several years ago Americans started buying large numbers of the Beatle records was a result of a complex interplay of economic and social factors. We may then distinguish three kinds of goods: goods of the individual which reinforce his genetic inheritance, things which are required and reinforced by others for their own good, and things which are called for and reinforced by the culture.[17]

Skinner also holds that it is possible to improve morality, but he rejects as ineffective the traditional methods of doing so by education and the appeal to ideals. Rather, what we need to do is to develop a science of behavior and use it to redesign our culture. By determining which contingencies produce which effects in behavior, we can vary those contingencies to produce the kind of culture, i. e., the kind of customary behaviors, that are more effective and desirable. Such a behavioral technology is ethically neutral, but if we accept the task of designing a better culture, a study of cultures can establish the values we should follow. The prime value here would be the ability of the culture to survive. And we already know enough to say that secondary values would include order, security, a productive economy, educational institutions and so forth.[18]

In sum, then, Skinner's approach to moral problems is positivistic. Since we think and act the way we do simply because of the various biological and environmental factors which affect us, the proper method for ethics is an empirical and scientific analysis of them along the lines of behaviorist psychology, which establishes what are in fact the goals and practices that are followed and whether or not these practices are effective in achieving the desired ends.

Critique

As we look at Skinner's method of working out a moral theory, the most obvious problem, at least for those who do not share his positivist metaphysics, arises from his ontological assumptions, namely, that humans do not have a free will but like everything else in this world are determined in their every act; that consequently humans have no obligations or responsibil-

70

ities, understood in the traditional way to be a special sort of non-empirical relations; and that furthermore moral values necessarily change with time and circumstances. These assumptions will not bother anyone who happens to share them, but to those who do not, Skinner's conclusions will seem as unfounded as his assumptions. For if you hold men to be totally determined beings, then Skinner's approach to morality makes a lot of sense: as the scientific analysis of phenomena has been obviously successful, so a scientific study of men's behavior will establish all the factors that determine it and thus allow us to understand and control it too. However, if you consider men to be capable of that contingent self-determination commonly referred to as freedom of choice or freedom of the will, Skinner's views will appear to be simply an elaboration of assumptions that he accepts in the face of contrary evidence and without critical justification. But a good method requires assumptions that are clearly understood and reasonably based.

Skinner defends his assumptions and approach mainly on the grounds that they are simply those of science and hence are justified by its past successes and the likelihood of its future ones. Now, it is of course true that one of the postulates of natural sciences like physics and chemistry is that a universal determinism obtains in the realm of their objects. The fundamental issue here is whether or not it is reasonable to extend this postulate not only to man's biological activity but also to his conscious and deliberate acts. Skinner argues that it is, because in the last four hundred years scientists have been able to gradually though successfully extend their postulates and explanations to every natural phenomenon up to man, so that we can expect that they will be able in time to also explain all human acts in terms of the same principles. Such an argument however is specious, because it is circular. The success of a given method or postulate justifies us in expecting further successes, but only if we are applying them in the same or a similar area. However, Skinner is assuming here that deliberate human acts are basically of the same sort as any non-human activity, which is precisely the point at issue.

Then too, it is methodologically unsound to accept any assumption or principle that goes directly contrary to an established fact. But this is what Skinner is doing. For, man's freedom is a fact attested to by its acceptance over the centuries by most men and by various philosophical traditions. Unless then Skinner can show that this acceptance is unwarranted because it results from some misconception or misinterpretation, we would have to say that his assumption is counterfactual. To this however Skinner retorts that the traditional view of autonomous man explains freedom in terms of non-empirical notions such as human nature and will; the natural sciences at first followed similar practices but they have been able to progress only to the extent that they have laid aside such mentalistic types of explanation; similarly, then, we can and should develop a technology of behavior that will explain all our actions as necessary results of environmental causes. Here, then, the issue comes down to three points. The first is whether it is sound and valid to explain human nature (or anything else) in terms of any non-empirical factors. But this is clearly a matter of metaphysics, of how one interprets reality in general. Skinner's assumption follows his metaphysics, but if the latter is counterfactual too, the former is not thereby made acceptable. The second point has to do with whether or not Skinner is correct in saying that science has progressed only to the extent that it has abondoned non-empirical notions. While it is obvious that a part of the progress of science came about through the elimination of various superstitious and anthropomorphic explanations of phenomena, it is equally clear that science has advanced largely by interpreting nature in terms of mathematics, which is totally non-empirical. The third point deals with the mechanistic and deterministic assumptions of the physical and biological sciences. These have worked very well in regard to sub-human phenomena. But it does not at all follow that by eliminating "mentalistic" views in regard to human behavior science will thereby be enabled to explain it more satisfactorily. It would then of course produce a mechanistic explanation of man. This is fine, if man is only a machine, but if he is not one, then such a view is itself just a superstition. However, to determine whether or not we are simply machines we must rely ultimately on our experience of ourselves and of our activity. We should not rely on a theory which starts by denying that experience, instead of trying to explain it.

One of the main claims of the psychological approach to ethics is that the development of a scientific psychology has made possible and now necessitates the sort of moral views Skinner is proposing. Such a view however is highly overblown, as is clear from the fact that one of the most vigorous developments[19] of the last few decades is humanistic psychology, which includes many leading psychologists like Allport, Horney and Rogers and which rejects the deterministic interpretations of behaviorism. Thus, A. H. Maslow has written, "Psychology should study the human being not just as passive clay, helplessly determined by outside forces. Man is, or should be, an active, autonomous, self-governing mover, chooser and center of his own life."[20] Furthermore, Skinner's ethics are the results not so much of his psychology as his metaphysics. Deterministic and relativistic forms of ethics are as old as antiquity. Skinnerians are just elaborating them with the help of certain contemporary scientific notions.

One result of Skinner's assumptions and method is that ethics should become a radically different kind of enterprise. The traditional view has been that one of the main functions of moralists is to establish some kind of natural and necessary hierarchy of values in terms of which people can put a rightful order in all that they do. Skinner, however, in line with his positivism, rejects such a conception. Denying any teleology in nature, he concludes that moral values have to be invented, not discovered. As he put it, "Man has not evolved as an ethical or moral animal. He has evolved to the point at which he has constructed an ethical or moral culture." And again, "The intentional design of a culture and the control of human behavior it implies are essential if the human species is to continue to develop. Neither biological nor cultural evolution is any guarantee that we are inevitably moving toward a better world."[21] Thus, since we choose our values, how we rank them also has to be a matter of individual preference, determined of course by our particular cultural and social environment. We see two main problems with his approach here. First, there is the question of the objectivity of his interpretation. This is again a metaphysical issue, which we cannot discuss here but we should note that such views reflect not so much the findings of biology or psychology as his parascientific Weltansicht. If one does not accept the latter, there is no need to accept the former. Secondly, there is the matter of consistency. On the one hand, Skinner is clearly concerned with showing us how to live a good life, which is a traditional view of the functions of ethics. But on the other hand, since he judges this to be merely a matter of upbringing, there being no intrinsically correct standard of right and wrong, it is quite contradictory for him to argue that any action or way of life is in general preferable to any other. He cannot consistently hold that "if it <our culture> continues to take freedom or dignity, rather than its own survival, as its principal value, then it is possible that some other culture will make a greater contribution to the future."[22] To determine what is or is not "a greater contribution" requires some sort of transcultural standard, for if a greater contribution is simply achieving what we happen to prefer, it makes no sense to say that we should not choose to develop a culture that values freedom and dignity.

This kind of inconsistency, which from the point of view of methodology is very perturbing, pervades Skinner's discussion of valuation. Thus, in the course of arguing against the objection that we ought not to try to plan and control our culture because this may cut off some lines of evolutionary development, he states, "The only hope is planned diversification, in which the importance of variety is recognized."[23] But if, in line with his definition of goodness and his rejection of any absolutes, the good life consists in being surrounded by things which positively reinforce us, then there is no point in trying to design a culture to produce a greater variety (it is clear that he means here a variety in the ways of responding and not just a variety of reinforcing objects), since this would involve changing our responses and what is presently good. If we have no necessary, absolute standards to go by, then the good life would involve, not changing our modes of being conditioned, but simply the increasing of opportunities for positive reinforcement. But there is a further inconsistency here, for by claiming variety as such is important and indeed the only hope, he is thereby accepting variety as a necessary, absolute value. A similar inconsistency also shows up when Skinner argues that although our culture has some remarkable advantages, it may turn out to have a "fatal flaw" and consequently some "other culture may then make a greater contribution to the future."[24] It is clear however that logically one can speak of flaws and greater contributions of cultures only if one accepts some sort of transcultural set of values. Thus also, when he argues that it is necessary to redesign our culture "if the human species is to continue to develop,"[25] this entails some kind of absolute standard whereby species can be determined to be better or worse.

It should be noted that although Skinner rejects the notion of any sort of absolute, he does hold that "there is a kind of natural morality in both biological and cultural evolution."[26] At any given time, evolution has produced certain types of beings, conditions and conditionings, as a consequence of which various things are at that time good or bad. These results were necessary under the circumstances but are fundamentally contingent: slightly different conditions eons ago would have produced a quite different world now. Thus, the ultimate sources of goodness and evil are biological and cultural evolution. The former has determined what kind of bodies and basic needs we have and thus also certain common values; the latter builds up from that basis along different lines, producing new sets of superimposed values. In regard to every culture, however, survival will necessarily be its primary good. Whether or not a culture survives depends on the number of people it can induce to work for its survival.[27] With modern science they can design the development of a culture so that it will survive, by increasing the ways in which the remote consequences of acts are foreseen and given a role. Now, few will deny that it is possible at least to some extent to redesign a culture in this manner. A serious problem arises here however, for in terms of Skinner's approach there are no grounds for claiming one way of doing it is intrinsically any better or worse than any other. Thus, if this redesigning was under Skinner's direction, hopefully it would proceed in the direction of liberal, democratic values, but in other hands it might quite possibly move in the direction of a totalitarian value system of a Marxist sort as in the Soviet Union or of a Nazi type as under Hitler. Since Skinner denies that there is any hierarchy of intrinsic moral values, he falls back to survival and efficiency as the basic criteria of moral evaluation. Logically then, 1984 may well represent the acme of moral development for people of our culture--if Skinner's approach is correct. As he said, we can redesign our culture to make a better world and "it will be liked by those who live in it because it has been designed with an eye to what is or can be most reinforcing."[28]

From the point of view of most other moralists, Skinner's method also entails serious difficulties as to its scope. Rejecting the traditional normative notion of ethics for a technology of behavior, Skinner quite logically sees no point in concerning himself with such matters as justice, obligations, dilemmas of conscience, natural rights or the moral rightness of civil disobedience and revolution. However, for those numerous and not inconsequential ethicians who see men as possessed of freedom of choice, and morality as based on a natural order, his position eliminates the core of morality and is thus grossly inadequate.

Another problem with Skinner's method is the manner in which he claims to lay the foundation for behavioral evaluations. He argues that we should distinguish scientific views of man from non-scientific ones, i. e., those that are merely traditional, literary, philosophical or religious. Although all such views are interesting phenomena, the scientific ones have proven themselves to be the more reliable. So, by using the findings of scientific psychology, supplemented with some relevant data from certain other sciences like anthropology, we shall be able to develop a rational technology of behavior that will enable men to live with less trouble and more fruitfully. This may initially sound plausible, but it does not stand up under analysis. When we study how scientists develop their disciplines, we find that there is no such thing as a "pure" science. This is especially obvious in the biological and social sciences. When scientists study, as scientists, human beings, they are guided in the formation of hypotheses and the search for data by the scientific concepts, theories and data that are already established. More importantly however, how they interpret and which of the latter they emphasize is determined, not just by scientific considerations, but by their philosophical interpretations of man's nature. Thus, because Skinner starts off with a determinist philosophical psychology, he prefers a behaviorist to a humanistic type of scientific psychology. But then, the determinism of his scientific psychology cannot be said to be scientifically established. Rather, it is a philosophical and prescientific interpretation, whose validity can only be decided by philosophical analysis and evaluation.

We should further note then that, since every scientific psychology has some type of philosophical view of human nature which grounds and shapes its development, it is methodologically of the utmost importance that that philosophical position itself be empirically sound and theoretically adequate. It is clear that any theory of moral behavior will necessarily be based in large part on a theory of human nature, since how we ought to act is obviously a function of what we are. However, what we are and how we act are established by various scientific disciplines like experimental, clinical and developmental ppsychology, sociology and anthropology on the one hand, and by metaphysics and philosophical psychology on the other. As we develop a moral theory, we necessarily base it primarily on the latter, since the former are themselves based on them also. Thus, the kind of metaphysics you start off with determines the kind of philosophy of man and of moral theory you will have; because of his positivist metaphysics, Skinner also holds to determinist theories of man and morality, which he supports and develops further with the help of those scientific theories that are in line with his philosophy. Thus, the adequacy of his and of any moral theory depends on the adequacy of its underlying philosophical psychology and ultimately, of its metaphysics.

A clear and noteworthy instance of this is Skinner's denial of moral evil in the traditional sense: the free and deliberate choosing to do what one holds to be wrong. In line with his metaphysical vision of the world as totally determined but whose order is a result of a thorough-going, evolutionary contingency, he rejects moral evil both because it involves freedom of choice and because, in its traditional sense, it implies that some sort of necessary and natural values are being violated. Thus, if his positivistic metaphysics is correct, then his moral theory is a quite plausible one. We would note however that they clearly run counter to the common experience of moral failure: who has not at some time in his life said to himself, "This is wrong, but I'm going to do it anyhow"?

Another basic fault of this approach is that it ignores much data that is relevant to ethics. In the past, to develop ethics moralists used insights and principles derived form common experience, history, biographies, anthropology, political economy, ontology, philosophical psychology and whatever other sources that offerred any promise. Psychology and psychoanalysis can of course also provide the moralist with a variety of facts and theories that can be useful, but they are clearly inadequate as the sole basis for working out moral philosophy. For instance, Skinnerians would condemn the use of literary and religious works to establish and clarify the range and nature of moral problems men have. The reason for this is clear enough: rejecting the notions of freedom and responsibility, they quite consistently view Dostoevski and Job as mentalistic mystifiers. But because our culture is thoroughly permeated by such notions, Skinner is much more concerned with remolding it into a quite different sort, thereby eliminating the array of traditional moral issues, which in his analysis result only from groundless misinterpretations and are thus fundamentally pointless. Perhaps worst of all however, he shrugs off the work previously done in ethics, pretty much without discussion or refutation: a major breach of the canons of dialectical development. We may in passing note that one reason for these various deficiencies is that psychology and psychoanalysis are among the most recently developed disciplines. Being less than a hundred years old, they are still having growing pains. Up until recently they were both rent by bitter feuds among their different schools. Such rivalry may be healthy, but it does not inspire confidence in the sweeping claims made by psychologistic moralists.

An effective way of checking out any method is to see how it works out. One result of accepting Skinner's approach is that it becomes very difficult to understand and to explain the phenomenon of problems of conscience like remorse. We usually distinguish between regret and remorse. If a person accidentally breaks an expensive dish, it is not surprising if he regrets it, but he would be considered unreasonable and neurotic if he claimed to have remorse over it. On the other hand, if a person would deliberately damage another's property, it would usually be considered in his favor, should he later feel remorse about it. With the psychological approach, the distinction between regret and remorse is recognized, but the latter would be considered an unnecessary distortion produced by a traditional upbringing; we feel remorse in certain circumstances only if we have been brought up to do so. However, with a more scientific view of behavior, since disorderly acts are seen to be the result either of ignorance or of some more or less clear necessitation, we may regret what we have done but we also realize that to feel remorse over it would be unreasonable and neurotic. For, feelings or remorse could be justified only in terms of freedom and responsibility, which are unscientific notions. To evaluate such an approach then, we have to determine to what extent it helps us to understand more adequately the moral phenomena we experience. We may note here two points. First, the Skinnerian interpretation does not square with the universality of the phenomenon of remorse. Secondly, it is clear that the difference between Skinnerians and libertarians is not so much over matters of fact as over the interpretation of those facts. That is, the main source of their differences lies finally in their metaphysics.

Various other results of Skinner's approach also merit consideration. For example, as every culture has advanced, it has developed legal, judicial and penal systems. These are clearly based on the principle that men are free and responsible, as has been acknowledged for centuries. In the Skinnerian view, however, all that has just been universal error, like the belief that the sun orbits the earth. The behaviorist argues that society's laws and sanctions are simply its means of maintaining order and of achieving certain goals and that humans are no more free than the animals in a circus show. We would hold that whether or not such a position ought to be accepted has to be determined ultimately by our own experiences of ourselves acting. That men have been totally in error about this over the centuries, as is claimed, is a point that should be and has been investigated but which seems quite unlikely in the light of all the evidence.

Then again, if Skinner is right, this would have momentous consequences in regard to our treatment of misbehavior. For obviously in that case what is necessary is that we turn all our prisons and reformatories into psychological and psychiatric clinics. Further, a large proportion of our policemen and teachers should be trained psychologists with a solid grasp of the principles and application of the technology of behavior. Finally, we should seek to replace traditionally-minded legislators and officials with others that are more scientific: a country will never improve if people from the president on down keep on thinking and talking in such mentalistic terms as human rights, responsibility, sin and repentance. One point that behaviorists presently tend to emphasize is that in all this they seek to act always in accord with the laws and customs of the land and not to just impose their views on others. In the light of such consequences as just noted, the Skinnerian approach again seems unpromising. Allthough it is clear that a knowledge of the sciences of man should be helpful to legislators, lawmen and teachers, in the last fifty years vigorous attempts to apply such an approach have been widely implemented, and they have not noticeably improved our morality or law-abidingness. Besides this, the end result of the consistent application of this approach would be that psychologists would be in charge of producing happiness in the whole populace by conditioning and reconditioning it as they judge proper and necessary. And it is obviously impossible, from the very terms of the theory, that anybody have a right to object to the way he is being conditioned.

In regard to conditioning, the psychological method manifests here another weakness. Skinner holds conditioning and genetic structure to be the determinants of morality, since the good is whatever reinforces them. The weakness results firstly from the fact that they may be inconsonant. It makes sense to base morality on man's genetic structure, for this is just another way of referring to his essence or nature, the persisting set of qualities, capabilities and inclinations that all men have in common. However, the conditioning we incur as a result of our cultural, physical or social environment could be reinforced by things which go counter to our genetic inclinations, e. g., dietary practices which eliminate necessary nutrients. To correct this deficiency Skinner would have to make what might at first seem a simple change but which in fact would have radical implications: he would have to define the good as that which reinforces genetic inclinations and those acquired inclinations that are compatible with them. Such a change is methodologically necessary to maintain consistency but is radical, because it would in effect reduce to a considerable extent the relativism to which behaviorists generally hold. For, moral practices change mostly because of environmental changes, not evolutionary modifications. A second reason for this weakness is that although conditioning may well explain why certain acts are done, this is not the same as to explain why these acts are moral.

There is a related inadequacy with Skinner's methods of dealing with the notion of goodness. To be adequate, a moral theory has to justify some sort of hierarchy of values, so that it can serve as a rational guide to conduct under varying circumstances. In the Skinnerian approach, the only distinction suggested is that the primary value in the redesigning of a culture is survival, which presumably would also have primacy for individuals. There is also implied the criterion of reinforcement: since the good is whatever reinforces our inclinations, then the stronger the reinforcement, the greater the good. For practical purposes of value taxonomy, however, this is not of much use in the relativistic context in which Skinner set up the problem. What may be a strong reinforcer for one person may very well be a very weak one for another. Thus, many young men quit school and work long, hard hours in order to have a car, while others remain students as long as they can in order to avoid having to work. That is, once our biological needs have been satisfied, our individual reinforcers vary considerably in kind and degree. This weakness of the method, then, is endemic to the relativistic assumptions used.

Despite these various difficulties and weaknesses that we have noted, the psychological method of developing an ethics has helped to clarify certain points. Thus, Skinner has as one of his main theses that the way to change moral practices is to change the environment, i. e., the contingencies of reinforcement. Skinner naturally emphasized them because of his naturalistic asssumptions. Even if these are not accepted however, it remains clear that we are all more or less strongly influenced by environmental conditions and pressures, which thus play an important role in shaping our attitudes, habits, characters and behaviors. On the other hand, because the libertarian recognizes the importance and the potential role of free choice, he tends usually to emphasize that and to correspondingly neglect the contingencies of reinforcement and the technology of behavior. But that too is a mistake. For instance, an ethical scandal of our times is the way millions of people needlessly and irreparably damage their health by smoking. The problem and the serious danger have been public knowledge for twenty years now. Appeals to self-contol and enlightened self-interest, the libertarian preference, have been moderately successful: in the older, male population there has been a heavy decrease in the number of smokers. Otherwise it has not worked very well. Changing the reinforcement contingencies could produce a drastic improvement within five years. The elimination of all tobacco advertising would not have an immediate effect, but in time smoking would lose much of its aura of glamor and many fewer youngsters would be inclined to take it up. Cutting out all government subsidies and support would produce at least two desirable effects: less tobacco would be grown and the cost to the consumer would go up. As the supply decreases and costs go up, fewer would start the habit and more would drop it. Increasing the tax on tobacco products would also help along the process. Raising insurance premiums for smokers to match the considerably higher risks and costs should be a particularly effective measure. Also helpful would be a government program to make it financially rewarding for tobacco farmers to switch to other crops. While various such steps would not eliminate the problem, it is highly probable that they would cut it down effectively. In such a manner, with a little imagination there is a wide range of moral problems whose solution by individuals or society could be aided by the systematic application of a Skinnerian technology of behavior.

The proponents of the psychological method claim
that the only adequate way of developing ethics is by
basing it completely and primarily on the concepts and
theories of a scientific psychology. Even if we reject
this claim, it is clear that the findings of the various branches of psychology can often be helpful in
working out one's moral philosophy. For instance, scientific inquiries into the exact ranges of innate and
learned tendencies could be helpful to moralists, since
natural tendencies are major factors in determining an
objective teleology as a basis for morality. Then
again, psychological investigations into the various
causes and results of affective behavior have direct
relevance to the moralist's treatment of responsibility
and of the moral act. Similarly, clinical studies of
the unconscious, manias, phobias, addictions and per-
versions can be very helpful to the moralists in working out a more fully nuanced and correct treatment of
subjective morality. For instance, it is much more
clear now than it was a hundred years ago that inces-
sant stealing and lying may be more of a psychological
than a moral defect. Also of some use for a fuller
understanding of conduct is research into the various
aspects of conditioning and habituation. For, we now
have clearer ideas of the relations of moral acts to
their occasions, of how moral responsibility may be a
function more of the response to the occasions than of
the acts themselves, and of how we should proceed in
the making of good, and the breaking of bad, habits.
Thus, in a variety of such ways the moralist can use
the findings of psychology to develop a more precise
theory. As the history of ethics has shown, a quite
adequate ethics can be worked out without the help of
modern scientific psychology, by using a well-grounded
rational psychology, but it would obviously be unreasonable for ethicians today not to nuance their views
further by making whatever use they can of the past
century's advances in scientific psychology. We should
also note, however, that these advances have not involved anything revolutionary, but have been largely[29]
taxonomic and in the accumulation of refined data.
Indeed, as more aggressive critics like Koestler and
Bertalanffy have noted,[30] modern psychology has not
uncovered any really important insights into man's
nature but has for the most part just provided a new
terminology for old ideas: another plausible reason why
the psychological method of developing ethics has not
worked out well.

In the light of all this, then, we have to conclude that the psychological method of developing a moral philosophy is quite inadequate. As practiced by Skinner, it is hobbled by his deterministic and positivistic assumptions which ineluctably produce a moral theory which is essentially conservative and static: it identifies goodness with the satisfaction of the inclinations resulting from biological and social evolution. As a further consequence, it ignores or misinterprets many crucial aspects of the moral life. However, even if the psychological approach would be used with some other form of empirical or clinical psychology, it would still not work. For, although in developing moral theory we obviously should make use of psychological data and theories when they can be helpful, nevertheless, moral philosophy, as even Skinner's work illustrates, is primarily based on and results from the metaphysics and philosophical theory of human nature which one accepts.

# CHAPTER FIVE

## THE SOCIOLOGICAL APPROACH TO ETHICS

By the sociological method of developing moral philosophy we mean any way of working out a theory and a code of human conduct which bases itself mainly, if not exclusively, on the data and theories of the social sciences. Just as in the psychological approach to ethics the fundamental assumption is that empirical and clinical psychology are capable of the fully adequate guidance of man in his conduct, so in the sociological approach the basic assumption is that although society is to a certain extent a function of its component individuals, their characters and acts reflect to a high degree sociological laws and hence are determined and predictable. Thus, in discovering the laws of communal life sociology concomitantly states for men how they ought to act.

Here, we shall not be concerned with any particular theories the sociological moralists have worked out. We shall look rather at their method, at how they attempt to develop a moral philosophy. Our interest thus remains primarily methodological. First of all, we shall take a look at how actually the sociological approach has been used. We shall then point out what we consider to be the main difficulties with such a methodology. In conclusion we shall indicate various ways in which the social sciences can be of use in developing a moral theory.

## Historical Development

The sociological approach was first adumbrated among the Sophists, who based their moral relativism in part on their observations of the differences of mores from one country to another. Its foremost precursors however appear only toward the end of the eighteenth century, as a reaction against the extreme individualism that was then common. Among the moral philosophers of that era were Shaftesbury, who maintained the primacy of the individual's conscience and sentiments, and Rousseau, who held that men were naturally good but were always corrupted by society. The crest of this

individualism was reached in the revolutionary procla-
mation of the Rights of Man and in the Kantian theory
of the autonomy of the will and the dignity of the person. According to the revolutionists the individual is
the social unit and society is merely the means which
individuals use to arrive at their own ends without
harming or being harmed by the others. It was against
this primacy of the individual that the early practitioners of the sociological method opposed that of society. They held that what is of primary importance is
not the individual but society, which is anterior to
each individual, which makes him all that he is and
which continues on when he disappears. The function of
the individual is thus to do his share in maintaining
the institutions which are the core of society; he must
not, in the name of some supposed personal right, perform any act which tends to destroy them; he must reject any end, such as the primacy of personal development, which negates their spirit.

We find early traces of this approach in the arguments against revolution of Edmund Burke, for whom
the individual must submit to the general demands of
the body politic. In France certain catholics like de
Bonald and de Maistre found in the church the perfect
society, in submission to which both state and individuals would find right guidance.[1]

To the left of these men were Saint-Simon and his
disciples, such as Fourier, who aimed at a complete
reformation of society by persuading the masses to accept and live up to ideals and laws of universal love.
Traditional morality was likewise to be recast as shown
necessary by science and the new social ideals.

It was however Auguste Comte, the founder of both
positivism and sociology, who made the first full-blown
use of the sociological method in ethics. To explain
the evolution of man's knowledge of nature he formulated his well-known law of three stages: man first
explained phenomena theologically, by gods and demons;
he then rose to the metaphysical stage, in which he
explained them by general a priori concepts; finally he
arrived at the positive stage, in which he realized
that they occur according to strict law which he can
discover by observation and experiment. However, said
Comte, the positive spirit still has one major task
ahead of it, to establish the science of sociology,
that is, to establish the laws of those human activities which are not explained by either the biological

or physical sciences--Comte, we must remember here, refused to admit psychology as a distinct science. Sociology is thus the crowning achievement of science replacing both theology and philosophy. For, it is the function of the sociologist, since only he knows the scientific laws of society, to establish the social order which will be the salvation of all. Political economy, law and ethics are thus all mere applications of sociology.

Comte made the application of sociology to ethics in his <u>Cours de Politique Positive</u>.[2] He acknowledged that ethics is not created by scientists but rather is progressively elaborated by Humanity in common, in its perpetual struggle against nature. The sociologist merely studies what Humanity has created; he outlines its structure; he formulates its laws; he states the ends it has set up and he points out the means best suited to attain them. Sociology, said Comte, has shown that moral progress consists of living for others. Putting Humanity in the place which God had previously held in society, he paraphrased the evangelical precepts of love of God and neighbor in his basic principle of positivistic ethics: <u>Vivre pour autrui</u>, by which he meant, Live for Humanity. Thus, ethics became essentially a search of means to subordinate all pleasure-seeking and egoistic tendencies to an overriding altruism. Comte evaluated everything, the choice of a vocation, the economic system, the political setup, according to how they advanced the social good. In his later years he instituted, to fill the gap left by the traditional religions, the cult of Humanity, a secularized version of catholicism, and the code thereof constituted his applied ethics.

This positivistic tradition of sociology was carried on in France during and after the second half of the nineteenth century by the school of Emile Durkheim, who however dropped Comte's more fantastic projects, such as the cult of Humanity. Indeed, about all he retained from Comte was the name and the ideal of sociology as the integral science of human group activity, developed on an empirical basis.

Major theses which Durkheim developed, and which are of basic importance for a sociological ethics, related to the object and method of sociology. To a large extent he borrowed them, although he seemed loath to admit it, from the Germans, who in turn reflected in this the influence of the early romantics. For, the latter at the end of the eighteenth century were responsible in great part for the renewal of interest in history, in the interpretation of which they often made heavy use of such factors as the "soul" of a people and the national "spirit" or "genius."[3] This idea of society as a real, individual thing was propagated by German sociologists such as Wagner, Schmoller and Schäffle. By adopting a similar stand, that is, that society is not merely a collection of individuals but an entity different from them, with its own specific properties and laws, Durkheim felt he could provide sociology with a well-defined object susceptible to empirical study. For him the task of sociology was to discover these objective and permanent properties and laws of societies, and it could do so because social phenomena also were subject to the principle of causality. "All that it asks is that the principle of causality be applied to social phenomena. Again, this principle is enunciated for sociology not as a rational necessity but only as an empirical postulate, produced by legitimate induction. Since the law of causality has been verified in the other realms of nature, and since it has progressively extended its authority from the physico-chemical world to the biological, and from the latter to the psychological, we are justified in claiming that it is equally true of the social world."[4] Although he admitted the possibility of contingency, his application of causality to social phenomena led him to sociological determinism. Speaking of their coercive power he said, "To be sure, we do make constraint the characteristic of all social facts. But this constraint does not result from more or less learned machinations, destined to conceal from men the traps in which they have caught themselves. It is due simply to the fact that the individual finds himself in the presence of a force which is superior to him and before which he bows; but this force is an entirely natural one. It is not derived from a conventional arrangement which human will has added bodily to natural reality; it issues from innermost reality; it is the necessary product of given causes."[5]

Such was the view of sociology accepted by Durkheim and his colleagues, among whom was Lucien Lévy-Bruhl. It had very definite effects on their ethical conceptions.

It led them first of all to reject all previous ethical systems. For, they said, these claim to be scientific and normative, which is a contradiction in terms. They are largely deductive, whereas ethics should proceed inductively. They are moreover all founded on unjustified assumptions.

There is, said Durkheim, a certain type of facts which we call moral. These facts are characterized by being obligatory, by being connected with sanctions. Sanctions however can come only from society. For, an individual does not apply sanctions against himself and God is an unscientific hypothesis. Thus, moral facts are essentially social facts and the study of morality is a branch of sociology.

The object of moral sociology then is moral facts. Its purpose is to treat them like any other phenomena to learn their causes and laws. Its method will be the usual one of sociology, that of indirect experimentation, or comparison, especially in the form of the method of concomitant variations. In seeking to establish the genesis and function of moral rules, it will have to consider every moral rule by itself, in the concrete circumstances in which it arose.

Moral sociology, Durkheim continued, has only recently been born, but it has already produced important results. It has shown that moral rules are essentially formulations of the fundamental conditions of social solidarity. Their purpose is to make the masses of individuals unified and coherent wholes. Morality is thus social discipline. Hence, society is also the source of obligation, which is the pressure it applies on individuals through tradition, laws and sanctions to obtain conformity with the rules it has developed for its own self-preservation and growth.

Moral sociology, however, being a science, merely tells us what the moral facts are; it is not normative; it does not tell us how we ought to act. Nevertheless, its ultimate purpose is to lay the basis of a rational moral art. This moral art will be the application of whatever knowledge and guidance that moral science can offer. For although the latter is not normative, it does provide some guidance. For it indicates the direction which as social beings we should take; it clarifies the ideal towards which society is moving. It shows what rules and institutions have become superannuated, impediments to social life. It determines the state of health of society.[6]

For, societies can be either healthy or diseased.

A major function of moral science is thus to determine what is normal and pathological for a given society. With different conditions, what is normal in one society will not be so in another. Hence, the normal state of each group must be determined for it individually. Moral science can do this because of the uniformity of causality in societies. The concern of the scientist then is to determine the relation existing between the constitutive attributes of each type of society and the circumstances surrounding it. Along this line, Lévy-Bruhl went even further; for him, a society was neither good nor bad, but simply what it could be, given the conditions wherein it found itself.

Such was Durkheim's sociological approach to ethics. However, his theory has been criticized and modified by his own successors in the positivist movement. The work of Eugene Dupréel perhaps best represents at present the use of the sociological method in ethics. Although relatively unknown in English-speaking countries, Dupréel is widely respected on the continent, as is evidenced by the fact that the Revue Internationale de Philosophie devoted a whole issue in 1968 to a consideration of his thought and influence.

Dupréel first of all criticized and rejected Durkheim's central concept of society as a collective conscience, an entity different and separate from its members. This, he said, was to explain the clear by the obscure. Furthermore, most individuals belong to several different societies. Durkheim's explanation would entail the mulplication ad infinitum of collective consciences, without explaining anything. Hence, "A society is not the sum of its members but the unity which they constitute through all the social relations of which they are the terms. "[7]

Moreover, claimed Dupréel, by acknowledging that moral sociology gives man some moral guidance, and by admitting that it lays the basis for a moral art, Durkheim in reality was committing the old error of making ethics normative; the only difference here between Durkheim and the traditional moralists was that he claimed to deduce moral obligations, not for the whole human race, but only for a given group. But the notion of a normative science is equivocal and unacceptable. We may act on the basis of facts provided by science; we may have an applied science; we can never have a normative science, for science can tell us only what is, not what ought to be. Thus, the sole function of moral sociology is to investigate and ascertain what moral rules a given society has adopted and the reason for which it adopted them. The moralist has no business telling others what they ought to do. For it is only society itself which can set up moral rules and ends.

It is up to society as such, that is, to a consensus of its members, to decide what shall be not only the rules but also the ends that it shall propose for itself. This society is not a Being endowed with a fixed nature which determines its ineluctable ends: it modifies its nature to the extent that it changes its ends and its rules. In no way could any scientific truth lead it to submit to legislation that it would not spontaneously adopt. Although the scientist can certainly seek inspiration in what he knows in order to determine what would be desirable goals and good rules, he will never be able to do anything except to propose them, along with all his arguments, to the conscience of all, starting with his own, for free acceptance.

. . .

No matter how we stretch the idea of science, we shall never draw from it a means of legitimately making one moral system rather than another benefit from the prestige of scientific truth. The sole science of human actions, which is confined to the search for the strict truth, seeks to know the moral values that are accepted or proposed, to understand why consciences receive them the way they do, but it does not itself propose any in any case.[8]

For although society is made up of, and hence results from, individuals, nevertheless the character and actions of these individuals are for the most part effects of their communal life. Their morality is thus a social fact, that is, it results from the interaction of these individuals. Ethics, whose object is their morality, is thus a branch of sociology. It must, to remain a science, stay completely factual, that is, be non-normative.[9]

The social character of morality is more precisely shown by a consideration of the subject matter of ethics. For, the moralist seeks to describe and explain judgments of approval and disapproval. These however

91

imply a person who judges, one who is judged, and one for whose benefit the judgment is rendered.[10] Moral acts are thus essentially social.

An analysis of some of the specific acts which society calls moral shows that they have two characteristic notes: their agent accepts an immediate or eventual disadvantage and he conforms to a rule. Thus, the Good Samaritan had to spend some time and money to help his wounded neighbor, and in doing so conformed to the precept of charity. "Sacrifice and regularity: with these two words we surely seem to express the twofold characteristic of every act on which common sense or every-day living are inclined to confer moral value. Should these two conditions together be lacking, an act will not be of a moral sort; we shall hold it to be indifferent, not bringing to its author either moral merit or demerit, or it will be immoral, that is, the cause of demerit."[11]

Moral rules are a specific type of social rules. Thus, they are established the same way as the latter. It is a sociological law that ephemeral social relations between the same people tend to establish between them a lasting social relation. For example, a person who repeatedly patronizes the same meat shop will eventually have with the butcher mutual feelings of familiarity and confidence, and both will establish certain habits of dealing with each other. For the same psychological reasons, this butcher will tend to treat all his other customers in the same way. In general then we may say that the multiplicity, diversity and interpenetration of social relations have the natural effect of creating in men's consciences and behavior permanent tendencies. When these are widespread, they become conventions--of politeness, of law, of weights and measures, of morality. More precisely, moral rules are those conventions which society recognizes as duties; they are the mutual concessions which the group recognizes as binding on its members at all times.[12]

Morality is thus essentially social. The characteristic notes of both are the same: sacrifice, or mutual concessions, and conformity to agreed rules. "We can perceive that morality, in its quintessence, is nothing but the social itself; it is what constitutes the conscious or implicit assent of individuals to combine the activity. . . . Morality is not like a quality which superimposes itself on an already existing social life; it is rather concomitant and consubstantial with

92

it."[13]

The more fundamental rules will then be the cornerstone of the social order. Thus, every group maintains certain minimum standards of neighborliness (<u>bienfaisance</u>), which includes good-will, sympathy and kindness, and of justice.[14]

The observance of the moral rules constitutes the objective moral order. Underlying and maintaining this however is the subjective moral order, the memories, the foresights, the habits, the intentions, the volitions, in a word, the consciences of individuals. These may pass through three stages: a first, in which one conforms to a rule simply from instinct or habit; a second, in which the moral rules become explicitly known and obeyed as such; this results from the conflicts of individuals, who, to resolve them, appeal to their neighbors whose discussion clarifies and makes explicit the law: in an advanced society of course this stage is reached largely through education in which the individual absorbs in a limited time the cumulated progress;[15] a third, in which the moral rules are viewed as ends in themselves, being either statements of the ideal or deductive reflections of the ideal. This third phase is characterized by a tendency to unify moral rules under the highest ideal possible. Thus, men like Socrates and Jesus find themselves in opposition to the moral laws of their group because they seek to substitute for the existing rules others which they consider as flowing from a more desirable ideal. However, just as the passage from the first to the second phase is a result of conflicts between individuals, so the passage from the second to the third is the effect of conflicts between groups; it is a social process. It is only because different groups present different ideals that an individual can choose between them and thus realize his moral autonomy.[16]

However, society does not merely perfect moral liberty, it also confers it. For, that man is morally free is only a social convention. "This convention means nothing more than this: the individual is capable of acquiring merit and demerit. As soon as there are individuals whose reciprocal relations have become such that they react to blame and praise in the way intended by the one who judges them, it proves to be excellent from a practical point of view to assign merit and demerit, or in other words to treat these individuals as free and responsible beings."[17] This is the exact contrary of the traditional view that a man can merit because he is free. What happens, says Dupréel, is that society exerts sanctions for its rules by attaching merit or demerit to different acts; then it logically accepts the convention of calling free the ones on whom it confers merit or demerit for these acts.

Society gives man not only his liberty, but also his personality, that is, his soul. It does this by attributing to men not just the qualities they exhibit, but also certain conventional prerogatives such as liberty. "Our soul is not a substance existing by itself, a completely consummated being which maintains itself no matter what happens and which would make of itself a good or bad use. It is the happy harmony of our spiritual efforts that are sustained by the approbation of the minds that live at the same time as we and of those, more numerous, that lived before us. It corresponds to a physical individual who transcends himself thanks to the help of his fellowmen. Persons exist only to the extent that others recognize them as such, to the extent that they travail at justifying the reasons for affirming them to be persons, by making fertile the convention which affirms them. In other words, to be a person one must practice the virtues proper to a person. There are persons only in societies in which the members mutually consider themselves to be such because they show themselves worthy of being so considered."[18]

Without using any of the religious or metaphysical assumptions of the past, the sociological method in ethics can thus explain the whole of moral reality, its basis and its rules, as a result of convention.[19]

Although sociological ethics has not received in America the full and technical development it did in Europe, it has had its more or less explicit proponents here. Among the better known we might mention W. G. Sumner and Kinsey.

Critique

The question we now wish to raise is a methodological one: whether the kind of approach the sociological moralists use is a valid, proper or useful one in developing a moral theory. Since Dupréel has most fully exemplified and worked out the method, we shall concentrate our consideration on him.

First of all, let us consider his rejection of

ethics as a normative science. He rejects it, as we have seen, in the name of science. For, whatever cannot be established scientifically should not be accepted. Since we cannot go from an "is" to an "ought", a normative science is impossible. Such a line of argument, we may point out, is however, despite Dupréel's claim that he is proceeding in a purely scientific way, not at all scientific but patently metaphysical. His conclusion is clearly not a matter for empirical justification but a result of his interpretation of the nature of reality. On the other hand, it is a fact that for over two thousand years it has been a common, indeed, the predominant view, that it is possible to have a normative science. But those who make such as claim have generally held that such an ethics would be scientific only in the broad sense, that warranted knowledge in this area is possible but without being established by statistical or laboratory methods. We can then say that Dupréel is right, at least in the sense that ethics as a normative science is not possible if we take science in the narrow contemporary sense in which it is restricted to the positive and mathematical sciences. But for him to deny the possibility of ethics as a normative science in the broader sense is to reflect an old, increasingly discredited positivistic prejudice. If a non-positivist is justified in holding that warranted knowledge other than that found through laboratory work or mathematical analysis is justified, then Dupréel's rejection of all normative sciences is not.

We may note too that Dupréel's denial of the possibility of a normative moral science logically leads to difficulties which he seems simply to ignore. For he also admits that the moralist must pay attention to the reasons adduced for moral rules and must indeed institute a philosophical criticism of them. However, the purposes of this criticism as Dupréel sees them are negative and unconstructive: to avoid any lacunae in the analysis and to be able to sidestep any non-ethical problems which may come up.[20] In view of his initial position a positive criticism would seem well nigh impossible, for it could proceed only on the basis that there are some moral principles which are fundamental, which may be used to evaluate all moral rules. But such principles would be objective moral norms and Dupréel is sure that they cannot exist.

There is another difficulty resulting from Dupréel's rejection of any normative ethics. All adults to some extent have problems about whether or not they shall follow a given socially accepted rule. How can they solve these problems without a normative ethics? Admittedly, Dupréel, as he states in his preface, is not writing a book of practical morality. But what kind of treatise on practical morality could he write to help people solve such problems when he believes that "it is up to society as such, that is, to a consensus of its members, to decide what shall be not only the rules but also the ends that it shall propose for itself"?[21] In response to the anguish of those who are racked by moral scruples, Dupréel announces their trouble arises from a pseudo-problem: because obligation is a social convention. If this is the case, it would certainly be well for them to be aware of it. Nevertheless, it still would not resolve their problem, for if obligations are merely social conventions, one has only to be clever enough to circumvent them with a minimum of trouble. The problem however still remains: on what rational grounds and in what way is one to decide what he will do? Are there, for instance, as some sociologists, anthropologists and psychologists say, certain needs and relations common to all men as such, as a result of which only certain decisions would be proper? If this is the case (and the evidence supporting it in a number of instances is overwhelming), it is on such grounds that we should try to derive whatever general, objective rules of conduct that we can. These would not eliminate moral issues and the need for decisions of conscience, but would make it posssible to handle them in a rational manner. An approach like Dupréel's which opts for an arbitrary, voluntaristic solution to moral difficulties is methodologically suspect.

Dupréel's treatment of duty and obligation is open to the same sort of objection. He rejects the usual acceptation of these terms because they are incompatible with his positivistic presuppositions. His explanation of them is very simple: they are words society surrounds with a certain aura to ensure obedience to the rules it sets up. He is presenting, in short, an early, continental version of the emotive theory. "The authorities of society not only teach the rules and the distinction of good and evil, they also take strong measures to make people's wills inclined to conform to them. One says that the rules _oblige_; to obey them is a _duty_."[22] It might be objected against such a view that it runs counter to the experience of the generations that have seen in moral rules factual statements about a non-physical sort of necessity which society discovers and defines but does not create, any more than it creates the laws of electricity. Not so, answers Dupréel, because to hold this involves one in the impossible task of defining the good _per se_. For, "To define the moral act in terms of the good rule is always, as we have seen, to want to choose a certain good through an arbitrary preference. At the same time it is to engage moral science in the vicious circle in which classical thought revolves: the good rule is the one that is conformed to the right; the right is that which is in accord with the good rule. In reality, to decide that a rule is good, one must place himself in the point of view of the social group in which this rule is accepted, or in the point of view of the consciences which are convinced of its excellence."[23] Hardly anyone could withhold agreement with this last sentence, but we may note that its implication is contrary to Dupréel's thesis, for society and the consciences of men generally agree that duty and obligation have an objective and not merely a conventional basis. The issue here then involves two points: (1) Does defining morality in terms of a set of good rules always involve arbitrary choices? (2) Does classical moral philosophy fall into a vicious circle because it does this? Aristotle's ethics is about as classical as one may hope to find, so we can use it as a case in point. But in determining what is good and what are proper moral rules, Aristotle is clearly and explicitly concerned with avoiding any arbitrary or a priori imposition of views and with establishing what is good by an objective correlation of what we know of our characteristic capacities and functions, our ends and the means at our disposal.[24] Thus, the circular reasoning Dupréel speaks of is not to be found in Aristotle, for whom the individual act is judged in terms of a moral rule while the rule itself is a result of reflection on the empirical data concerning human nature, our ends and our activities taken as means to those ends. Nevertheless, Dupréel's view on the meaning of duty and obligations are not themselves without some empirical validity. It is certain that society is continually conditioning its members to act in what it considers to be morally obligatory and dutiful ways and that individual persons have a widely different understanding of the nature of moral obligations. But to think that moral duties and obligations consist only of such conditioning is to take a grossly limited view of the matter.

Dupréel makes it sufficiently clear that his intention is only to describe moral realities. At the same time too he forswears any attempt to explain away any facts on the basis of a priori definition or theory. Such methodological principles are unexceptionable, but unfortunately he does not remain true to them. His point of view in assessing the facts is frankly positivistic and the results reflect this. To non-positivists, such results will necessarily seem misinterpretations. One crucial instance of this is Dupréel's denial of the existence of objective ends and functions in nature. Now, it is a fact that we know of no tribal or larger societies that do not have legal and moral codes. It is also a fact that despite many striking differences the moral codes especially are fundamentally similar: the last six precepts of the Jewish Decalog have their counterparts everywhere. The common explanation for these similarities is that despite subconscious and external pressures man is a rational animal and tends to act according to grounded motives. The codes are similar because they are all motivated by the desire to reach the same ends; these ends, and the means thereto affirmed by the laws, are basically similar in all codes because they are based on universal human needs and inclinations. Thus, a leading English sociologist has written:

> The conclusions that emerge from this survey of the main types of variations in moral opinion and sentiment may now be briefly summarized. Firstly, morality is universal in the sense that everywhere we find a recognition, implicit or explicit, that conduct has to be controlled or guided by reference to principle. Secondly, in content moral systems vary greatly but the variations are far from arbitrary. . . But, thirdly, there is evidence of development in the sense of growth of insight into the nature and conditions of well-being made possible by a wider experience of human needs and capacities and of the conditions of social co-operation. . . . It follows from these considerations that in comparing different moral systems we should have, firstly, to elicit the primary experiences of value on which they are based. Since these relate to basic human needs, bodily and mental, they would probably be found much the same everywhere.[25]

If men all have the same basic needs and capacities and if they tend naturally to satisfy these needs and to develop these capacities, as Ginsberg and many other sociologists find, it is crucial from the point of view of ethical methodology to acknowledge it. It is on the basis of such facts that one should develop one's <u>Weltanschauung</u>; we should not deny such facts just because they are incompatible with the anti-teleological metaphysics of positivism.

The fact that society has conflicting moral rules and ideals presents Dupréel with a dilemma. If society is to resolve these conflicts, it will have to do so either on objective grounds or by arbitrary choice. Admitting the first would require Dupréel to give up one of his central assumptions, that there is no universal and objective morality. If he holds for the second, on what grounds can he say that an individual ought to prefer the arbitrary choice of society to his own?

We have seen how for Dupréel the moral and the social are ultimately identical. Along this line he has also said, "The cause and the rationale of the rules of morality are then the establishing and the maintenance of positive social relations of every sort."[26] One odd result of such a position is that a hermit or a person shipwrecked on a deserted island could not have, at least for the most part, a moral life. Far more importantly than this however, the consequences of such a view are morally and socially pernicious. From the principle that the moral is the social, it is only a short step, which many social scientists have taken, to state that the individual is for the social, that the person is for the state. This is the basic principle which has justified in the eyes of totalitarian leaders the most monstrous excesses. If we can judge a method to any degree by its results, then the sociological approach is one which at the very least would require some basic qualifications or modifications.

In close relation with this is Dupréel's view that the moral is also conventional. On this point he has said, "It is from a starting point that is conventional that all reality and all explanations will radiate. Our free decisions which are arrived at through our reciprocal sacrifices and which we institute through common consent are the central point whence everything is ordered and receives consistency and direction."[27] We have here a rather strange phenomenon. Dupréel's expressed motive is to find the scientific, that is, the deterministic law according to which moral codes have evolved. We can say he has followed this program well, for the moral science which he presents us has just about eliminated freedom as most people understand it. Suddenly however on this precise point, the moral rules themselves, which are subject to determination by objective factors, within the limitations of our logic and of our knowledge of the relevant facts, Dupréel champions the arbitrary. Moral rules become "free decisions" which we "establish through common consent." Suffice it to say that the basic similarities of the precepts of the codes of all known societies are proof enough that they are not undetermined but reflect basic conditions of human life. It is moreover equivocal to state that moral rules are established through common consent, as though it were an affair like the election of president. Their establishment seems analogical rather to that of chemical laws.

Like other positivists, Dupréel also maintains a unmivocal view of method. Now as long as one is only in sociology, there is usually a certain methodological advantage to considering the acts of men as though they were completely determined, for there are to be discovered in this way some objective and important factors of behavior. But even in sociology such a univocal view of method, such a consideration of social acts as to be understood by the same means whereby we deal with physical phenomena, is unfactual and hence unscientific. For, the freedom of men is a fact and cannot be denied without warping the whole of sociology. The problem of distinguishing free from non-free is of course difficult. But when we are in moral sociology, that is, when we study the sociological data concerning the acts men call moral and immoral, we cannot even methodologically bind ourselves to a physical and univocal view of phenomena, for in the moral sphere every act is free, at least to some extent, and hence must be seen as such to be understood. It would then be an even grosser error to attempt to solve moral problems simply by transferring to ethics the methodological limitations accepted in sociology. Method is an analogous concept, and the method of every science must be suited to its object and the type of necessity this object involves. It is thus impossible to have a physics of social or moral life; for in physics we are in the realm of the determined, whereas human behavior belongs to the sphere of the self-determined, the free.

We must also take exception to Dupréel's derivation and treatment of the characteristics of the moral. He argues in this way. "We find that judgments of approbation and disapprobation in the study of which it has seemed possible to circumscribe the study of moral philosophy are an operation which presupposes definite relationships between three individuals: the one who judges, the one who is judged and the one because of whom one judges."[28] Because of this, he concludes, moral acts are essentially social. He then analyses some specific moral acts to show their two main characteristics, namely, involving a sacrifice and conformity to a rule.

First of all, we may note that although it is a function of the moralist to study judgments of approbation and of disapprobation, this is not his primary concern. He is more interested in the reason why such judgments may be valid or invalid. That is, his primary concern is with the goodness or rightness of acts. To make the moral opinions of men the central object of ethics is simply to confuse the secondary with the primary. Besides this, Dupréel also overlooks a crucial fact: making judgments about moral matters does not necessarily presuppose three distinct individuals being involved. Indeed, a good deal of the time we all make moral judgments without any such interpersonal involvement, that is, I may judge my own act and I may do so simply because I wish to guide myself rightly. Hence, Dupréel's conclusion that moral acts are essentially social is false. Furthermore, to establish what the specific characteristics of the moral are, it does not suffice to take only a few possible cases. They may not cover the whole gamut of moral acts. And indeed, we find that the characteristics which Dupréel arrives at are hardly common to all moral acts. For instance, when a driver obeys the signals of the traffic policeman, there is no sacrifice on his part. Then again, all moral conduct involves conforming to certain very general principles, such as to do good and to avoid evil, so that if we take "rule" in a broad sense moral acts will necessarily involve conformity to a rule. The fundamental reason for this is that as rational animals it would be contrary to our nature to act irrationally, that is, without a grounded motive, so that we are always subject to this rule, at least, that we should always act rationally. Thus, it makes much more sense to identify the moral with the rational than with the social. But should we, as Dupréel seems to, take "rule" in a more restricted sense to mean one concerned with specific types of action, besides being promoted and sanctioned by society, it seems that we frequently enough commit morally good acts which are not in conformity with any such rule. For we often argue that we should under certain conditions violate a rule, when following it would defeat its purpose. To make morality simply a matter of following rules is to make it impossibly inflexible. Morality is rather a matter of achieving our ends in a proper manner; the rules are just to help us guide ourselves and to simplify our task. Then again, an act may conform to a rule but the intention of the agent may make it wrong. When, for instance, A informs the police about B's wrongdoing, in order to revenge himself on B, who would deny that A's act is wrong, even though it conforms to the rule that citizens should report all illegal activities? Yet again, most of us would have qualms about declaring immoral an act which is contrary to a rule but which is done conscientiously and out of noble motives. We must then conclude that Dupréel based his analysis here on an inadequate induction.

Concerning Dupréel's position in regard to human freedom, it is clear it is not derived empirically. As we have seen, he holds that society exerts sanctions for its rules and then accepts the convention of calling free those acts which it considers meritorious or the contrary. There is no evidence whatsoever that this ever occurred anywhere. What has taken place is clear enough. Dupréel is starting off with the common positivist thesis that man is determined in everything he does. But he is faced with the fact, which he has to explain, that the majority of men consider themselves to be free. His reduction of freedom to a convention is clearly an attempt to explain away the fact in order to retain his initial assumption. Sociologists know of no society that does not have rules and sanctions and does not at least implicitly accept that men are responsible and free. Even in Moslem lands where Allah is held to predestine all, men are held responsible for what they do.

In relation to this issue, we may also note that Dupréel's use of "soul" could be misleading. What he calls the soul seems to be what scientific psychologists refer to as the psychological personality, as opposed to personality in the metaphysical sense. That the soul taken as the psychological personality exists and is to a large extent the product of society, we would not deny. But the issue of whether or not a substantial soul such as metaphysicians conceive of it exists is a problem which concerns metaphysics and philosophical psychology, but not sociology. The two senses are quite different and the existence of the psychological personality does not prove the non-existence of the personality in the metaphysical sense.Moreover, the latter can without contradiction be conceived of as the necessary basis of the former, so that it could be argued that if Dupréel admits the former he should accept the latter.

We have seen several instances of how the positivist viewpoint from which Dupréel works serves a a matrix within which he develops his sociological ethics. In working out a moral philosophy it is unavoidable that one work from within some philosophical point of view. The trouble with Dupréel's metaphysics however is that it has limited and warped his interpretation of the facts. A particularly vitiating consequence of his point of view is his belief that sociology by itself gives[29]an adequate description of our moral experience. For, this belief leads directly to an excessive exaltation of the role of society in our lives. Since he holds that man is not innately free and that there is no kind of objective teleological order whatsoever in nature, he concludes that human conduct can be reduced to the laws of social interaction. If this conclusion is right, then a physics of morality is possible; but if his premises are not factual then his whole project is simply an academic tour de force. We do not find those premises supported by the evidence, so although we would readily agree that sociology can provide many insights into human behavior, we would not hold that it can provide an integral explanation of it.

## The Use of the Sociological Method and of the Social Sciences

We may turn now to the question of the positive value which the sociological method and the use of the social sciences may possess for developing an adequate moral philosophy.

As we see it, Durkheim and Dupréel have made an important contribution to our understanding of human behavior by their emphasis on certain facts: that ethics is not only a theory and a body of rules but also a sociological phenomenon worthy of study, that the same moral code exists simultaneously in the minds of many men, that different societies have different codes, that these codes developed in part as a result of social pressures and in part as a result of conscious reformulations, and that these codes have too effects which under similar condition are similar. These are all facts suitable for empirical study and of great interest for the moralist. By encouraging the systematic study of such phenomena in what they have called moral sociology, Durkheim and Dupréel have established a non-normative and non-ethical discipline, which, while it may never make any great change in ethics possible or necessary, nevertheless does make available in many matters more precise information which can be useful to the moralist.

Sociologists have already illustrated what can be done in this area in a variety of ways. Durkheim himself did his well-known pioneering investigations of suicide, having as one of his main goals the discovery of how to restrain the growth of this social evil. In The Protestant Ethic and the Rise of Capitalism Max Weber studied modern western man's switch from a religiously oriented system of values to one that is secularistic. Also of importance from the point of view of moral philosophy is Weber's analysis of the transformation of moral ideas into social institutions. In his investigations of sexual behavior Kinsey insisted that he wanted to make no moral judgments about his subjects' behavior, but nevertheless his findings were often interpreted as justifying a greater permissiveness in sexual conduct. A work which has attracted relatively little attention from moralists, though it seems worthy of their close study, is Geoffrey Gorer's description of Lepcha society which is overwhelmingly monogamous but also accepts premarital and extramarital intercourse as naturally and morally proper.[30] The empirical conditions and effects of such a view clearly have interesting implications for our western society, in which similar standards are being suggested with increasing frequency. A final and more recent example is the Moynihan report on The Negro Family. Whatever its technical deficiencies may have been, its purpose was to provide a factual basis for a social policy that would be morally sound.

There yet nevertheless remain many areas of sociological investigation that are untouched but which could be most helpful to the moralist. Among the more obvious that come to mind would be communal life as led by the "hippies" and on the Kibbutzim, to determine the effects it has on people and the practices that tend to become common under such conditions. Studies of this sort should provide valuable insights for both the psychologist and the moralist. Another promising subject area would be the effects over a period of years of the free dissemination of pornography, as now obtains in Denmark. Even there, we may note however, pornographic materials remain relatively expensive and their sale is legally limited to adults. Since the crux of the moral problems revolving around pornography and its control lies in the issue of its long-term, cumulative effects on children and adolescents who are more or less regularly exposed to it, studies of the present developments in Denmark would not be nearly as valuable as would be those made later, should all legal and economic restrictions be lifted. Also of considerable interest would be investigations of the psychological effects on the attitudes of a whole people, when they have made abortion legal and easy to obtain, as in Japan, Hawaii and elsewhere. While it may not be likely that such data would resolve the moral issue, they could at least illuminate it somewhat.

One may ask precisely what kind of facts a moral sociology may uncover. The large majority of ethical rules deal with social problems. However, the moralist cannot either justify or apply these rules simply by working with his principles in the abstract. He must take into consideration the actual social conditions in which men live, to ensure that following the rules will help men achieve the proper goals and not lead them away from them. Thus, the rules dealing with respect for parents may change considerably from a primitive agricultural community to a modern welfare state--and this will be due to a number of variables: the economic conditions, personal attitudes, conventional views and social pressures. Examples would be the desire older people may have not to be continually subject to the noise of their grandchildren or the economic necessity to live in a small apartment. How a person would manifest his appreciation of his parents and try to help them under present conditions would have to be different than how it was done in colonial times. By the study of the social environment the scientist can oftentimes ascertain conditions and factors that are pertinent to the reflections of the moralist, who may very well have overlooked them if he depended simply on common sensical observations as was done in the past.

Sociology not only provides factual data of use to the moralist, it also presents theories which may help to illuminate the history of ethics or to clarify certain moral issues. A good illustration of this is

Sorokin's theory of cultural change. Integrated cultures, he says, are either sensate, ideational or idealistic. Sooner or later every such cultural form undergoes a breakdown and is replaced by another--usually the sensate by the ideational and the ideational by the idealist. Thus, western culture for the last four centuries has been predominately sensate and, since it now manifests clear signs of disintegration, we can expect within a century or so to have a radical cultural transmission.[31] In the light of such a theory the issue of the relativity of morals, for instance, requires a rather different approach than the one now commonly used and based on the presuppositon that our western culture has discovered in science the secret of perpetual progress. What emerges is the possibility of a moral theory that transcends both cultures and cultural forms. Should a moralist accept Sorokin's theory as valid, he will then too vary the emphasis of his work, depending on which cultural form he considers of greater intrinsic worth and on which phase his culture is situated in. In general we may say then that to the extent that sociologists genuinely illuminate the nature of social relationships and pressures, their work can be of use to the moralists. On the other hand, we must admit that what the sociologists have uncovered so far has helped to clarify somewhat and to establish in a more firm way points that men have long been aware of, but they have not yet come up with any factual data or theory involving a radical modification or development of ethical theory. From the cooperation of moralists and sociologists we can expect, it would seem, progress but not revolution.

A very promising area in which moralists and sociologists could cooperate would be to determine empirically what might be the most effective ways of promoting and achieving moral ideals. If moralists and sociologists would get together to plan such projects and to evaluate their results, we could expect to see a new and important series of investigations whose value would not be only practical but could also in the long run have unexpected repercussions on moral and sociological theory. To illustrate the possibilities here let us consider this example. Moralists generally agree that respect for law and order is not merely a desirable characteristic among citizens but a virtue necessary for any healthy society. It is clear however that while some segments of American society have possessed it to a high degree, others have rather noticeably lacked it. There arises then a cluster of questions whose answers are subject to empirical verification: What are the factors which are important in building it up and in breaking it down? To what extent is it a result of education and of social pressures and of careful, personal choice? By what means can it be nurtured? Which of these means would be consonant with the human dignity of those affected? The point to be noted is that although sociologists have investigated such questions, they usually have not done so in cooperation with moral philosophers. They should however start. A number of universities have recently established centers or institutes for the study of the urban environment and its problems. Prominently involved in them are faculty from busines, sociology, education and law. But if the philosophers have been asked to participate, they do not seem to have responded in any great numbers. But they would surely have much to offer, and much to gain. For if anyone should be able to help keep matters in proper perspective, it is the philosopher. And a philosopher who is out of touch with the present day realities will inevitably be sterile.

Sociology may also be useful to ethics by establishing scientific facts and theories which may serve to limit the excessively speculative tendencies of some philosophers. For there are in every discipline some who, in their eagerness to push theoretical conclusions as far as they can, do not investigate adequately the facts which may invalidate their position. However, just one established fact suffices to overthrow the most finely argued theory. We have seen a good illustration of this. Shall we accept Dupréel's theory of human freedom being a convention or is it incompatible with sociological facts? Or, again, any evaluation of the "welfare state" in any country from a moral point of view would have, to be valid, to be based on solid sociological data. Any approval or condemnation of it based only on ideological considerations would necessarily be suspect.

In conclusion we may note that moral sociology, as Durkheim conceived of it, remains an ancillary of some value to ethics. It is nevertheless a discipline distinct form ethics, since its purpose is to tell us what is and not what ought to be. It cannot then on the grounds of its data establish that any act is morally right, though it may help ethics to establish what is right by determining the social circumstances which affect our conduct. But the sociological method of developing ethics is itself too arbitrary and unempirical to be a useful or adequate approach.

# CHAPTER SIX

## ANALYTIC APPROACHES TO ETHICS

Since time immemorial men have looked for moral guidance to their prophets and priests; many still do. But since the Sophists it has been a part of our western tradition to expect our philosophers to provide at least a large measure of our ideas and theories about right and wrong conduct. This continues to be the case, even though in English-speaking lands there have lately been a number of philosophers who at least give the impression of disclaiming that it is a function of philosophers to give moral guidance or to provide a moral code. Nevertheless that expectation seems to be justified, if for no other reason than that if philosophers do not satisfy it, in all likelihood it will not ever be adequately fulfilled.

If then we accept this common and traditional view of normative ethics, that it is indeed one of the major functions of philosophers to develop it, one question that immediately arises is methodological: how ought we to do it? But since so many English and American thinkers have espoused analytic philosophy in the last few decades, a related issue also presents itself: how and to what degree could analytic philosophy help the moralist in determining the best approach to use in developing a moral theory and code? Since analytic moralists have frequently shown a keen interest in methodology, this whets our desire to know what they have to offer.

Some, perhaps, might believe that such a question betrays an ignorance of what analytic philosophy is all about. It is concerned, they would say, with the analysis of language and the clarification of our thought processes but not at all with such first order problems as how we ought to behave. Such an answer, I would suggest, does reflect the thinking of many of the earlier analytic philosophers but neglects a very interesting evolution of this tradition. Various analysts, and not the least influential, show increasing concern with the traditional ethical problems and their general tendency, I would suggest further, is more and more to resolve them along lines which cannot be said to be very new, since they are to a certain degree similar to

Aristotle's.

My intent here is to sketch some of these developments in order to show how this evolution in ethical methodology took place and make some evaluation of it at its different stages. More importantly though, I would want to show what kind of contribution analytic philosophy could make towards the elaboration of a more effective method of working out a theory and code of moral behavior.

For our purposes it will suffice to take up in turn and briefly the four main analytic approaches of intuitionism, emotivism, prescriptivism and good reasons.

## Intuitionism

Since G. E. Moore is generally considered to be one the main pioneers of analytic philosophy and ethics, we can start off with him. His influence has been rather multifaceted because different aspects of his work, and not necessarily those that he thought the most highly of, led to quite different sorts of results. Although he was read widely in English philosophical circles, it seems that he had an even greater impact through his personal contacts in the classroom and elsewhere. There is also the matter of historical context. He lived his early life when English philosophy was dominated by idealists like Bradley and Bosanquet who tended to present their views in such broad and abstract terms that Moore found their thinking fuzzy and confusing. His protests and method, which took the form of an insistence on the need to achieve clarity by analyzing each problem as it comes up to establish precisely what it involves, were among the main causes of the decline of idealism and of the rise of analytic philosophy.

Moore made clear his great concern over methodological issues right from the beginning of his _Principia Ethica_. He starts off his preface by observing that very numerous difficulties of philosophers result mainly from a quite simple cause: "the attempt to answer questions, without first discovering precisely what question it is which you desire to answer." He notes further that if philosophers would only resolutely try to do this, that "many of the most glaring difficulties and disagreements in philosophy would disappear." Most philosophers, he believes, have not even tried to do so. I would simply note here in passing that such a generalization is historically inaccurate, and is not true even in regard to the idealist writers who dominated English philosophy at the time, even though he may have had them mainly in mind. At any rate, this was the genesis of the general methodological principle that was to become one of the main sources of analytic philosophy.

Applying this principle to ethics, Moore then distinguishes two kinds of questions moral philosophers deal with. The first deals with the nature of things that ought to exist for their own sakes, that is, the meaning of "good". The second concerns the kinds of action we ought to perform or, in other words, what kinds of acts produce good things. By understanding the nature of these two questions, Moore holds, we are able to grasp what is of the utmost importance: "the nature of the evidence, by which alone any ethical proposition can be proved or disproved, confirmed or rendered doubtful." But, we can also see that with this approach he is laying the framework for a comprehensive treatment of morality, for both a theory and a code of conduct.

This methodological principle, that when one wants to resolve a problem, the first thing to do is to ascertain clearly and precisely just what the issue is, is one that is old and unexceptionable. Since ethics is concerned with determining what good conduct is, Moore's first application of it has to do with the nature of "good". As he applies it however, he arrives at a conclusion that is original and surprising: that goodness is a simple, non-natural property. For, since we commonly judge some acts to be good and others not, it follows that goodness is a property of some acts. When however we try to specify what goodness is, we find, Moore holds, that "good", like "yellow", is such an elemental quality that though we can experience it we cannot define it, except in the sense of pointing out examples. We simply intuit what it is. On the other hand, it is not perceivable in the same way that yellowness is: it is a non-natural property.

Resolving the second basic ethical question, of how we ought to act, requires a quite different method. For once we are aware of what goodness is, we can establish which acts will cause that which is good in itself, but this can be done only by empirical investigation. That is, under the same conditions a given kind of act always produces the same effect, but we know what these causes and effects are only through empir-

111

ical study. But once we know what these effects are we can see whether they are good or not and we can then infer that acts which cause effects that are good are the kind of acts which we ought to do.

In regards to his dual approach to solving ethical issues, the validity of the second clearly depends on that of the first, if we combine them the way Moore does. For, to hold that we can establish empirically the morality of an act by determining what its effects are and observing whether or not they are good, patently assumes the intuitiveness of goodness. By itself, of course, the view that we can in one way or another empirically establish the morality of acts is one that goes back to the Greek moralists and that usually has not been conjoined with an assumption like Moore's. Minus that assumption, it has been taken up and developed in the good reasons approach of later analytic philosophy. On the other hand, Moore's way of resolving the question of what goodness is, by holding it to be a non-natural property known by intuition, has gotten very few adherents. It did however help prepare the way for the development of a quite different view, that of emotivism. For if one holds intuitionism to be untenable, one reason that could be offered is that goodness is not an intuitable property, since it is not a property at all.

Emotivism

Emotivism, since it first appeared in the nineteen twenties, represents basically a positivistic view of morality and ethics. Because they tried to be as radically empirical as they could, the positivists rejected the possibility of scientifically verifying any ethical values. So, in their view ethics was literally nonsense--but important nonsense: moral judgments and theories play such a crucial role in the lives of men that they cannot be ignored. But, it was argued, even though there can no normative science of moral values, there can be a science of moral behavior. And what it seeks to establish is that moral judgments and values do not describe or correspond to real entities but are simply the expression of our feelings. Hence the term emotivism. Thus, in Carnap's view value statements, having no theoretical sense, belong to the realm of metaphysics and like all metaphysical statements are extremely dangerous in their deceptiveness. Ayer was equally blunt but more explicit. The method of a strictly philosophical ethics consists of the analysis of ethical terms in order to properly categorize the statements made with them. Ethical concepts, he maintained, cannot be validated because they are merely pseudo-concepts, referring to nothing. Furthermore, then, moral statements can be neither true nor false and they cannot really be contradicted. "For in saying that a certain type of action is right or wrong, I am not making any factual statement, not even a statement about my own state of mind. I am merely expressing certain sentiments."[1] Ayer also remarks that besides expressing feelings with them, we frequently use ethical terms to arouse similar feelings in others and thus get them to act in ways which we approve of.

Emotivism however received its most full and influential statement at the hands of Charles L. Stevenson. He also was especially concerned with clarifying the meaning of ethical terms and in establishing a proper method for ethics. But, unlike Ayer, he maintained that ethical statements can at least in part be true or false and that real disagreement is possible concerning them. To explain why this is so, Stevenson analysed what is involved when people agree or disagree. Agreement and disagreement are of two basic types, depending on their object. First, they may concern beliefs, that is, statements which can be empirically established or revised in the light of empirical data. Secondly, they may concern attitudes, that is, "purposes, aspirations, wants, preferences, desires, and so on." We may disagree or agree concerning either beliefs or attitudes, or both. Problems about beliefs have to do with the truth of an explanation or description; problems about attitudes, "with how they are to be favored or disfavored, and hence with how they are to be shaped by human efforts."[2]

Ethical disagreements, Stevenson points out, usually involve differences both in beliefs and in attitudes. As a result, he maintains, the main problem of ethical analysis is to establish how beliefs and attitudes are related. It is clear that generally attitudes are based on beliefs, so that a change in beliefs can bring about a change in attitude. But, on the other hand, beliefs do not determine our attitudes; on the contrary, it is our attitudes that determine what beliefs we shall consider relevant to a particular moral issue and ethical disputes end when we come to agreement in our attitudes, even though we may still have disagreements in beliefs.[3] Thus, scientific controversy is distinguished from ethical in this, that the former is concerned mainly about the validity of beliefs, whereas the latter is over differences in attitudes. It also follows then that the methods of resolving the one will not suffice for resolving the other.

An adequate analysis of the meaning of moral statements will have to be based on a correct general theory of meaning . Among its fundamental points would be the following. Meaning itself is a power or dispositional property, developing within an elaborate process of conditioning, of a sign to affect a hearer. A work may have both descriptive and emotive meanings. The emotive meaning of a sign is its capacity to stir up some feeling or attitude, whereas its descriptive meaning is its power to produce cognitive processes of various sorts.

The analysis of various working models of moral statements shows that they have two components, one descriptive, the other imperative. The first component describes the speaker's attitudes, whereas the imperative component has the function of changing or intensifying the hearer's attitudes. Thus, a moral statement may be either true or false in its descriptive aspect but not in its imperative one. The imperative component has the emotive meaning of a moral statement and it is precisely its emotive meaning that constitutes it as an ethical statement.

We can then disagree about ethical matters. When we try to resolve a moral disagreement or to justify a moral statement, we cannot give a proof of our position in a narrow, strict sense but we can give reasons for it, which may in a broad though acceptable sense establish it. Sometimes the reasons given are about matters of fact. They can then be discussed and rebutted or accepted, like any other factual matter. Even if they are accepted though, this does not necessarily result in a consensus of moral views, for the relation between a moral statement and the reasons for it is not logical but psychological. That is, they usually "do not strictly imply the judgment in the way that axioms imply theorems; nor are they related to the judgment inductively, as statements describing observations are related to scientific laws. Rather, they support the judgment in the way that reasons support imperatives. They serve to intensify and render more permanent the influence upon attitudes which emotive meaning can often do no more than begin."[4] However, many moral disagreements are resolved, not by giving reasons but by persuasion, by the use of emotive speech.

Stevenson holds therefore that when ethical dis-

putes are rooted in disagreement in beliefs, it is possible to resolve them by rational argument. But if an
ethical dispute involves, not a disagreement of beliefs, but simply of attitudes, then logic and reason
will be to no avail.[5] We must then resort to persuasion, Such a methodology, he holds, will work out more
satisfactorily than those used in the past, even though
it cannot promise to resolve all disputes, and much
less to establish any universally accepted code.[6]

An examination of Stevenson's approach shows some
serious weaknesses. His distinction between disagreements of beliefs and of attitudes is of central importance for him, since he holds that the method of resolving the one will not usually work for the other.
Put in those terms, the distinction initially seems
plausible enough, as does his further observation that
although beliefs may frequently shape our attitudes, in
the long run it is our attitudes that determine which
beliefs we accept. However, when we examine the matter
more closely we find first that this terminology is
misleading. For, by belief he means, not something that
is believed, but something factual, a truthful description or explanation.[7] There is also a problem with "attitude". An attitude, he tells us, may be of approval
or of disapproval and disagreements in attitudes are
what mainly distinguish moral issues from scientific
ones. But now, if moral attitudes cannot be established
in the same way we do a fact or a truthful description,
two questions arise. How then do we establish them? And
what are the implications of this in regards to the
nature of ethics? To the first, Stevenson answers that
"if any ethical dispute is not rooted in disagreement
in belief, then no reasoned solution of any sort is
possible."[8] But since he also holds that our attitudes
determine ultimately what beliefs we shall accept, it
turns out that for him in general our moral views are
not rationally established, objective truths, though we
can explain them in the sense that we can establish
what causes us to have such views, and we can resolve
moral difficulties by using on an opponent what will
cause him to change his mind. Thus, Stevenson's use of
this distinction results in making ethics simply a
branch of psychology: an empirical investigation of how
and why we come to approve or disapprove of various
acts.

Stevenson quite correctly insists that an adequate development and understanding of ethics has to be
based on a comprehensive theory of meaning and signs.
For it he accepts however a causal theory, which has

been rigorously criticized and rejected even by many analytic philosophers. The basic objection to it is that it confuses the causal and the logical features of terms. That is, when an act is described in moral terms, the statement may produce various sorts of effects on its hearers. This cause-effect relation can certainly be profitably studied by psychologists and sociologists, but the meaning of the statement and of its terms is not simply the power they have to produce a constant effect, given a set of social beings who have been properly conditioned over a long period. For, the meaning of terms is one of the things that makes it possible for them to produce their constant, conditioned effects. It is only after we have understood what a statement means and after we have judged it to be correct or incorrect that it will cause us to approve or disapprove of it. But this brings us to another aspect and objection to Stevenson's approach. He holds to his causal theory of meaning because he accepts a determinist view of man. However, should one hold, as many philosophers have, that men, though conditioned in many of their responses, are capable of persuading and of being persuaded rationally, then one would have no compelling reason for accepting Stevenson's theory of meaning.

Another difficulty with Stevenson's methodology results from its general direction and scope. He is especially concerned with showing how disagreements between people, be it over beliefs or attitudes, may be resolved. This certainly is worthwhile, but it would hardly seem to be the proper main goal of a rational normative discipline. If ethics is to be scientific, it must be more concerned with establishing universal truths and validity rather than a mere consensus. Stevenson, however, while admitting the possibility sometimes of the latter, rejects that of the former, arguing that unless a dispute is rooted in disagreement in belief, it is not possible to establish any solution through rational inquiry. By doing this, however, Stevenson is stripping ethics of precisely that which, in the eyes of most men, made it of value.

To sum up and to conclude, the basic objection to Stevenson's method is that it results in a rejection of the possibility of ethics having the function traditionally assigned to it: to provide a reasoned and reasonable basis for conduct.

Prescriptivism

Among the analytic critics of emotivism was Richard M. Hare. He too objected that Stevenson made a logical mistake by trying to assimilate the use of moral judgments to processes quite unlike them. To express a moral judgement is not the same thing as to make someone act in the manner one wishes. But what especially bothered Hare in emotivism was the denial that ethics is based ultimately on reasoned arguments. Moral questions are raised by rational agents and discussions of their answer are subject to the appropriate logical criteria. While he agreed with Moore and Stevenson that we could not make any factual or objective claims for our moral values and judgments, nevertheless, he argued, it does not follow that we cannot establish ethics on a reasoned and rational basis.

What Hare wanted to do then was to develop a theory that could account for our use of moral terms, of moral generalizations and of moral reasoning. He wanted to show that even though moral judgments are not factual statements, ethics is a rational discipline. For, many moral problems are the result simply of linguistic confusions, so we can solve such problems simply by resolving the ambiguities which gave rise to them. He therefore defined ethics as the study of the language of morals, that is, of how we talk about moral matters. Thus, for him we should make decisions about conduct in the light of ethical theory, but the method of ethics is linguistic analysis. We determine the right way of thinking morally by becoming familiar with the logical characteristics of moral terms, moral judgments and moral reasoning.

In The Language of Morals Hare worked out his approach along the following lines. Since moral language is one species of prescriptive language, he analyzed the latter to determine its various types and their similarities and dissimilarities. In regard to particular moral imperatives, these, Hare insisted, result from a process of deductive reasoning. Like all reasoning, moral reasoning is based on principles, in this case, principles of behavior, which in moral reasoning we apply to a particular situation. Some of these moral principles are deduced from others, but the ultimate or most fundamental of one's moral principles are established by one's decision or choice. To achieve correct conclusions in our moral reasoning, we must on the one hand always strive for logical propriety and, on the other, we must accept as our moral principles only such generalizations as bear universalization. Since logicality and universalizability are rational sorts of criteria, ethics then is a rational discipline.

Methodologically there are several criticisms that immediately suggest themselves in ragard to Hare's approach. First of all, there is his notion of ethics. To redefine ethics as the study of the language of morals quite obviously does nothing to resolve or eliminate the problems of ethics as it has been traditionally defined. Besides that, it only confuses matters to try to change the meaning of a term of such long-standing and continuous use. If he wished to treat of the language of morals, no one would object to that, but he should have referred to it as meta-ethics or by some other, different term. Secondly, though his analysis of prescriptive language is ingenious and somewhat complicated, we need simply note that he himself afterwards considered it seriously defective in certain ways. Besides this however, his use of "prescriptive" is loose and thus troublesome. He takes it to mean the same as evaluative and commendatory (p. 146) and advisory, instructional and guiding (p. 155). But these terms clearly do not mean all the same thing. It is thus invalid to argue that because a term is "prescriptive" in one of these senses, that it is also in any of the others. Then too, Hare from the beginning takes it for granted that moral language is primarily prescriptive. This however is not at all obvious or necessarily the case. And when he does get around to discussing the prescriptive nature of moral terms (chaps. 9 and 10), all he does is to give examples of how they are used prescriptively, which of itself does not prove that that is their primary use. Besides, even if one moral term (say, "ought"), is primarily prescriptive in its use, this does not mean that all other moral terms have to be used primarily in that way too. Thirdly, it is clear even from Hare's own treatment that working out a theory of moral conduct rerquires more than just linguistic analysis. The universalizability of a specific rule, for instance, cannot be established merely by analysis. In Hare's favor, it is also clear that by acknowledging the need to follow the relevant logical rules and to be consistent in the use of terms, Hare has taken important steps in making ethics a more rational type of discipline than it was for Stevenson, no matter whether we take ethics in his or the more traditional sense. Nevertheless, and this is the most damaging point, Hare's approach also makes ethics fundamentally irrational. Since he holds ultimate principles of behavior can be established only by one's decision and since he recognizes no objective, factual or logical limit to what one may accept as a principle, his approach, whether he likes it or not, thus makes it impossible to rationally establish that it is objectively the case that one should ever do or not do anything.

## Good Reasons Approach

As Hare was working out his prescriptivist views, other analytic philosophers were developing what has become known as the "good reasons" approach. It has proved to be a popular one but since its main proponent is generally considered to be Stephen Toulmin, we shall consider his exposition of it especially. Like Hare, he too wants to show how a rational ethics is possible. And like all analysts he hopes to resolve his problems through an analysis of moral thinking. The analysts we have considered up to now have been concerned mainly with the logical analysis of moral terms. Toulmin however believes that the problem can be resolved more adequately by approaching the opposite end, by analyzing instead what is involved in moral reasoning.

In An Examination of the Place of Reason in Ethics Toulmin first takes up and rejects what he calls the three main traditional approaches to doing ethics. The first is the objectivist view represented by, among others, Moore, for whom goodness is an objective, albeit non-natural, property. The second is the subjectivist view, according to which morality is simply a function of our feelings. The third is emotivism. These theories, Toulmin argues, are not only unhelpful, they are also false.[10] Apart from the specific difficulties which he points out in regard to each, they all share the same general inadequacy of not being able to explain the difference between good and bad reasons in ethics. As a consequence, he holds, "all they can do is to elaborate their terminology, in the double hope of hiding their initial mistakes, and of getting their theories to fit our ideas of goodness and rightness in spite of these mistakes. And, in so doing, they make their arguments vague beyond redemption."[11]

For Toulmin when we are working out the right approach to morality the basic issue is this: In making a moral decision what kind of reasoning ought we to accept? To answer this question Toulmin first considers at some length what is meant by reasoning and explanation. He then turns to moral reasoning itself. This can be understood and evaluated only in terms of the function of ethics. That is, we can establish what are or are not good reasons for accepting a given conclusion only if we know why people engage in moral or ethical inquiry. Its function, as Toulmin sees it, is "to correlate our feelings and behavior in such a way as to make the fulfillment of everyone's aims and desires as far as possible compatible."[12] In other words the purpose of ethics and of moral deliberation is to make possible an harmonious and satisfactory community life. This provides us with the criterion for what will constitute a good reason in moral matters. Looking at how this has been worked out in practice, we find that in everyday deliberation we have a good reason for approving an action if it is in accord with a common moral maxim, such as "Do not steal." For, these maxims are the result of the experience of community life over centuries. Sometimes however situations arise in which we are led to question one of the accepted moral rules. Going back to the basic criterion, we will have a good reason to either accept or modify such a rule if doing so will help the members of the community to lead fuller and happier lives. Now, such judgements are obviously based on the assumption that the general direction and traditions of one's community are to be maintained. But what if we want to question the very way of life of our community? Toulmin responds that the only practical use of such a question is to help us make a personal decision as to whether we shall remain in our present community or go and live in a radically different one. We can reason about this but our conclusion will be simply a matter of our personal choice, not of moral right or wrong.[13]

For Toulmin, ethics is then a rational discipline, since it establishes its conclusions by reasonings whose grounds we know to be true. In sum, its method is the following. We establish by an analysis of linguistic usage the meaning and function of ethics. This provides us with our basic criterion for what constitutes a good reason for accepting a moral conclusion: whatever helps to eliminate conflicts and makes for an harmonious social life. Thus, for most day-to-day moral decisions the commonly accepted moral rules are reliable principles of conduct. In other cases, however, when the question is about a moral rule itself being too lax or too restrictive, we have to return to our basic criterion and try to estimate on the basis of past experience what the effects of the proposed alternatives would be and thus which of these alternatives would be right or wrong.

What now are we to think of Toulmin's approach? One early difficulty stems from his treatment of the notion of ethics. For although ethics and morality are certainly concerned to some extent with the elimination of social conflicts, it is clear that we use these terms to cover a much broader range of problems than that. For instance, lusting in one's heart of itself does not bring about social conflict, but it is obviously considered a moral matter. As a method though, the good reasons approach is clearly an improvement over those of Stevenson and Hare. For, first of all, it brings out the rational character of ethics more adequately. The insistence that right conduct is to be determined on grounds that are relevant and true is clearly necessary if one is to have a theory of moral conduct that is rational and effective. Contrary to Stevenson's, Toulmin's approach enables one to reject many considerations as irrelevant. Toulmin's approach is also superior to Hare's because it shows more clearly how moral rules are based on and reflect objective conditions, a situation which Hare tended to ignore because of his interest in the logical and linguistic aspects of moral discourse. However, what especially makes Toulmin's approach better is its clear recognition of the teleological aspects of the moral life. Moral codes, he points out, develop under social conditions as a result of the fact that people are always seeking various ends, and there has to be some means of reducing the ensuing conflicts and achieving a harmony of goals.[14] In this way Toulmin is bringing analytic ethics back to face up to the essentially practical nature of moral theory: the basic reason men engage in ethical thinking is to guide their conduct, but conduct is determined primarily by the goods and the ends which they seek. Perhaps the most telling and frequent objection raised against analytic ethics as developed by Moore, the emotivists and the prescriptivists, was that it was useless for most practical purposes. The good reasons approach was an obvious and necessary step to take to render that objection invalid. But Toulmin's version of this approach still has certain deficiencies. For instance, he summarizes his work on the logic of moral reasoning in this way: "I have simply tried to describe the occasions, on which we are in fact prepared to call judgments 'ethical' and decisions 'moral', and the part reasoning plays on such occasions. This description has led us to see how, in <u>particular types</u> of ethical question and argument, good reasoning is distinguished from bad, and valid argument from invalid--to be specific, by applying to individual judgements the test of principle, and to principles the test of general fecundity."[15] Thus, what he has done is to <u>describe</u> what he has found people doing when they engage in moral reasoning. He then accepts this description of accepted procedures as his norm. But this clearly will not do. You cannot conclude simply from the fact that men do something that they ought to do it. This particular difficulty is tied in with another. Toulmin argues that we can give good reasons and thus justify individual judgments and principles, but that the way of life within which these principles are formulated is not susceptible to moral evaluation. But now, since the validity of any set of moral rules will obviously be a function of the validity of the way of life which gives rise to them, if no way of life is morally justifiable, then basically there are no moral rules that are justifiable. Thus, for Toulmin, as for Hare and Stevenson, ethics is ultimately arational, a matter of personal choice and preference.

There were some analytic philosophers also who were bothered by Toulmin's inability to show how a way of life as such could be validated. Paul Taylor made a noteworthy attempt to remedy this failure. In his <u>Normative Discourse</u> he discussed at length various aspects of moral reasoning and language. In general Taylor's approach to moral thinking is similar to Toulmin's. Thus, he would say too that moral rules are justified only in terms of the way of life we have adopted. But he insisted that one's way of life can also be rationally justified. He argued this to be the case by pointing out various criteria that would have to be met for one to make a rational choice between various ways of life. In sum, these criteria concern conditions of freedom, of enlightenment and of impartiality. Anyone choosing a way of life on the basis of these criteria would then be rationally justified in doing so.

While we can admit that Taylor's position here represents a distinct advance over Toulmin's, it also is not completely satisfactory. The basic problem is that Taylor's criteria are all of a formal sort. They are certainly necessary conditions for a rational choice of a way of life, but they provide no indication of what it is specifically on the basis of which one can determine what constitutes a rational way of life. Thus, we can also raise against Taylor the objection which has frequently been raised against analytic ethics in general, that it is so much concerned with logical and formal aspects that it has lost sight of the basic concrete purpose of ethics.

Such considerations led to attempts to develop a good reasons approach in a more practical manner. One such attempt was made by John Wilson in his <u>Reason and Morals</u>. He proposes here a method of morals. The task of the philosopher, he points out, is to help clarify our thinking by showing how to use concepts, language, etc. One obvious fact about human life, however, is that we use criteria of various sorts in every sphere of our activities. Moreover, after we have accepted a certain set of criteria, they determine to a large extent how we think and act. Thus, the philosophical moralist tries to find out how we establish criteria and how we know which ones we ought to accept. The answer is simple and clear enough. We do it in terms of our goals. Man is a purposive animal. He is always seeking one end or another. To achieve these various ends he tries out various means and on the basis of the experience gained thereby he gradually develops criteria whereby he can evaluate these ends and means. But, is it ever possible that men can agree on ultimate ethical criteria? Yes, providing we overcome obstacles such as the difficulty of getting enough relevant facts--about man's nature, the ends that truly satisfy him and what means are necessary to achieve that satisfaction. We have indeed already achieved unanimity in regard to many ethical criteria, e. g., in regard to those relevant to stealing, killing and rape. When we find that the ends of different men conflict, we have in the same way only to develop mechanisms, moral, legal or other which will allow us to achieve together the most satisfactory lives possible. Thus, moral judgments are true or false and they are established rationally by working out criteria based on our experience. Because however knowledge is not ever completely adequate, we cannot expect to achieve logical necessity in regard to the acceptance of every ethical standard, but we can expect to continue to achieve a greater unanimity of ends as our knowledge of ourselves becomes more adequate and full.

Looking back over the range of analytic philosophers that we have seen, Wilson's methodology clearly seems to be more to the point than those of the others. It seems also to both reflect and illuminate more adequately how people do and should function. Wilson also starts off with a more adequate and realistic idea of what ethics is all about. Nevertheless, there are a couple deficiencies in his approach that we must note. Even if we agree with him that a moral theory and code should be based on an understanding of man's nature and ends, we must still acknowledge that this does not go far enough. For there is a wide variety of views as to what are man's nature and ends. So, to develop a valid theory and code a moralist has first of all to know which of those views to accept. The second difficulty is that Wilson admits that men seek many different and frequently conflicting ends, but he provides no criteria whereby we could rank those ends.

## Critique

Analytic moralists in general have a very explicit interest in methodology. This has been very helpful to us here, since this is precisely the aspect that we have been concerned with. But now we must try to summarize and extend the critique that their approach seems to require.

As in any developing tradition, there was, as we have seen, much internal discussion and criticism among analytic moralists. Thus, Moore's ethics attracted a good deal of attention even though few accepted his view that goodness was a non-natural, intuitively known property. The issue then became, if goodness does not refer to either a natural or a non-natural property, what does it mean? The emotivist answer of Ayer and Stevenson seemed for a time to many to be definitive. But it was not long before other analysts pointed out that when you call an action good, you are doing more than merely giving vent to your approval. Moreover, Stevenson's views entailed that little of moral thinking could be rationally justifiable, a conclusion that most analysts came to consider unacceptable. So, Hare wanted to show how it was possible to make rational moral choices, but he thought this was possible only within the framework of the ultimate values we have chosen for ourselves. Similarly, Toulmin argued that it was possible to distinguish good and bad reasons for different types of action in terms of what will make for an harmonious society, although it is up to us to choose which kind of society we shall remain a part of. But to other analysts both Hare and Toulmin seemed to stop unnecessarily short of the total rationality possible for ethics since they hold, both of them, that the ultimate foundation of morality depends simply upon what we choose. So, more recently Taylor has argued that although we have to choose what way of life we shall follow we should base that choice on rational criteria. Wilson has gone even further, holding that we can make ethics a rational discipline by basing it on experience, our knowledge of human nature and the relevant rational criteria.

Looking back over this train of developments, we

notice that while analytic philosophers started from and have kept to an empiricist, Humean outlook, their moral theory has generally become more and more Aristotelian. Thus, Aristotle had held that "practical wisdom, then, must be a reasoned and true state of capacity to act with regard to human goods"[16] and that in the moral syllogism one premiss is a universal judgment about what kind of act should be done and the second premiss is a judgment that a particular act is of that sort.[17] Similarly, Hare argued that moral reasoning is deductive and either true or false, explicitly concurring with Aristotle's analysis of it.[18] In the beginning of his Ethics, Aristotle pointed out that in all their activities men aim at an end and that we can determine empirically which are the ones we ought to seek. Wilson, as we have seen, insists also that man is a purposive animal and that it is only through experience that we learn what are man's nature and the ends that truly satisfy him. In the first paragraph of his Politics Aristotle argued that the state is the highest community because it seeks the highest good. Hare, Toulmin and Wilson all emphasize the harmony of society as being a basic criterion of morality. Aristotle repeatedly made the point that ethics is a discipline both empirical and rational. Wilson is equally emphatic on the matter.

Although this conversion to Aristotelian views was an improvement, nevertheless the root defect remains. Language analysis by itself is not sufficient as a method for ethics. There are several reasons. While it is true that language to some degree epitomizes the experience of past generations, there is no reason to suppose that those past generations necessarily interpreted correctly what they experienced. Nor can we assume that those past generations worked out an adequate and complete analysis or that language adequately and completely reflects what they knew. But even if such an analysis had been made and encapsulated in language, there is no guarantee that in the course of time this analysis did not get distorted or lost to any extent. Another difficulty is that analysts generally seem to take it as necessary that only what they derive through their analytical approach is of any value or even is real. But we cannot analyze out of our terms and linguistic usages anything that men did not previously put there as a result of what they intellectually grasped in their relations with each other and with the things of this world. And so, though some language analysis certainly has its place, to establish a moral theory we should take the more direct course of dealing with all

125

things in their concrete interrelatedness rather than depend on such an indirect approach as the analysts employ. To use the language of Plato, the analysts are concerning themselves with images of reality rather than with reality itself. Another point is that, like any other method, linguistic analysis is based on certain metaphysical views that determine to some extent at least its direction, limits and adequacy. Thus, the validity and usefulness of any method is a function of its metaphysical basis. Now, linguistic analyis has developed from an outlook of Humean empiricism. If one sticks to such Humean views, he will then find it difficult if not impossible to accept also the trend to Aristotelian positions which analysis has taken. But if one finds this Humean outlook an unjustifiable interpretation of reality, then he certainly may want to use the method of linguistic analysis, but he will have to base it on his own type of metaphysics and in all likelihood he will grant this method a much lesser role in the development of philosophy and ethics than have our contemporary analysts, because with their Humean notion of reality they have nothing like the notions of substance, nature or teleology to explain regularity and order, and all they have to fall back on is language and logic. This brings us to another difficulty. A common theme among analysts nowadays is that the criterion for the validity of a proposed moral rule is its universalizability. That is, if everyone lived according to such a rule and the results would be desirable, then the rule is valid. On the other hand, if everybody followed the rule and the consequences would be disastrous, then the rule is invalid. It is clear though that universalizability is justified as a criterion only in reference to a more basic criterion, that of the consequences of acts. But how do we know if the consequences of our acts are good or bad? We can make universal and necesary judgments in regard to that, only if all men have fundamentally the same nature, ends and needs and if the same acts always and necessarily produce the same results. It will not do to say that universalizability is simply a necessary result of the logic of moral discourse, because the realm of thought and its expression is distinct from the realm of physical acts, and unless one holds that the former reflects the conditions of the latter objectively and necessarily, the necessary logical relations of the former will not necessarily correspond to anything in the latter. Thus, the principle of universalizability, which is so commonly accepted by analysts today, is not compatible with the Humean metaphysics on which they base their method. And that, from a methodological point of view, is monstrous.

What the analytic approach needs then is a more solid ontological basis.[19] As we have seen, the analytic moralists have moved towards positions that were Aristotelian but without wanting, it seems, to also accept the metaphysical underpinnings of those positions, while without wanting either to give up Hume. Consistency however is a prime requisite of a valid method. If we cannot make sense of our moral experience in terms of a Humean metaphysics, then we should give it up. If analytic moralists have found it necessary to adopt so many of the same positions as Aristotle did, then the conclusion suggests itself that they should perhaps also accept some of his other philosophical positions too. Let us note briefly what might be some of the consequences of such a move. If with Aristotle we hold all men to be rational, free substances, capable of understanding their situation and needs, then there is no difficulty in seeing how men would want and would make for themselves a rational theory and code of conduct. If we hold with Aristotle that all men are essentially the same, having the same needs, inclinations and ends, then we can see without too much trouble why moral rules have to be universal. If we hold with Aristotle that this world, though complex, is orderly, and that we can to some extent at least understand what this order is, we can then also understand why moral judgments can be objectively true or false. We do not mean here that we ought to take a Kantian turn and try to establish our metaphysics on the basis of what we believe is required by the moral life. What we are suggesting is a dialectical argument: a metaphysics that is compatible with our moral experience is more likely to be correct than one that is not.

From the very beginning, analytic philosophers emphasized the need to clarify what is meant by goodness and other moral terms. The need still remains, which is a bit disconcerting when we remember Moore's optimism about how such difficulties could be resolved if only philosophers would adopt the analytic method. But let us focus on one particular issue: to what extent did analysis clarify the meaning of "good"? Moore insisted that goodness is not a property in the same way that for instance redness is. Now this, we might all agree, is quite true, but it is also something which philosophers have generally admitted since antiquity. To further clarify the meaning of goodness, Moore indicated that it was a non-natural property. This idea has struck most of his readers as being decidedly odd.

However, Moore went on to further describe goodness as a supervenient quality, one, that is, which an object has because it possesses certain other properties. Here, Moore seems to be making more sense and the doctrine of the supervenience of goodness has become a commonplace in analytic texts, although the fashion more recently seems to be to eschew talk of supervenience and to say the same thing in another way: by talking about the "good-making" characteristics of things. Later on, Moore himself raised the question as to whether we should speak of goodness as being a property at all, but he did not pursue the matter. Unfortunately the other analysts have not seemed very interested either. It is unfortunate, we would suggest, because further analysis might have led them to an important discovery, namely that goodness is indeed not a property but rather a relation. To illustrate. When we say "X is a good act," what this means is that X is an act that has certain features or characteristics and that as a result of having these features this act is a means to achieving a given end, say, an harmonious society. The goodness of this act is not some feature or property which the act has along with the others, but is rather precisely the relationship which this act has, because of its various features, of being a means to an end we are seeking. Another important point which a further, more adequate analysis could have clarified was the analogical character of the term "good". We are here using the old distinction of traditional logic between terms that are univocal, equivocal and analogous. Contrary to Moore's view that goodness is a simple (and univocal?) property, if we consider how we use the term we find that it is attributed to widely disparate sorts of things. We can say that a diamond, a man and an act are all good, even though diamonds, men and acts are obviously quite different sorts of things. Goodness is not some single property which they all possess, rather, when we call all those different things good we are saying that they are similar in this way, that they are all means in some way to some end. Thus, the supervenience of goodness is just one aspect of its analogicity. And we see that here again with this whole matter of the meaning of goodness we have another instance of the need for any methodology to be used within a solid ontological framework.

In the light of all of this we can finally come now to our basic question: Is language analysis an adequate method for the development of ethics? There is no doubt of its usefulness, since already in antiquity we find Plato using it extensively and fruitfully. Then

too, besides its long history, our analytic philosophers have honed it into as sharp a condition as is
probably possible. This method is assuredly quite helpful in eliminating confusions and inconsistencies in
our use of language and our reasoning. It thus has a
large role to play in metaethics, since this is concerned precisely with the kinds of language and the
modes of reasoning used in ethics. Thus too, we can see
why analytic moral philosophers have used this method
so much: they have concerned themselves mainly with
metaethical questions which naturally require such a
method. But it is equally well the case that they have
been concerned more with metaethics than with ethics
because they were so enamoured with language analysis.
However, it cannot be the basic method of ethics, which
deals with far more substantive issues. We cannot establish by linguistic analysis what are men's ends, by
what criteria we can rank these ends, what effects a
given kind of act has, or what are virtue, vice and
their various species. Ethics involves establishing
good, objective reasons for doing or not doing a wide
variety of acts. But the evolution of analytic ethics
has shown that we cannot do any of that just by linguistic analysis.

This evolution suggests also another conclusion.
It is possible to treat of metaethical issues apart
from ethical ones; Hare did it. And from the point of
view of academic scholarship, that may be justifiable.
We would judge however that it is a methodological error for a moralist to try in general to separate ethical and metaethical issues. Rather, what the moralist
should do is to address himself to moral problems and
depending on what his general philosophical orientation
is, he will try to resolve those issues along the lines
that are the most compatible with his <u>Weltanschauung</u>.
As he addresses himself to individual questions, he
will note on reflection that besides the substantive
issue that he is working on, there arise others as a
result of his need to use language to work out and com-
municate his thought. This is how metaethical questions
spontaneously and in an ad hoc fashion arise. They
should also, it would seem, be normally handled at that
same time, because it is only in their genetic context
that they can be best understood and so resolved. Just
as we can study logic by itself, so if we wish we can
study metaethics by itself. But Aristotle could never
have developed the science of logic unless he had, as a
basis to work on, the attempts of mathematicians, philosophers, politicians and others to think logically.
Similarly, we can work out a metaethics only by obser-

ving what moralists do and meet up with in doing ethics. So, as the moralist is working out a theory and a code, he will need language analysis to deal with metaethical issues as they arise, but then analysis will be only a secondary, ancillary method.

To sum up and to close, a more positive conclusion that we can draw from the evolution of analytic ethics is that the proper method of developing a moral theory will have to be ontologically realist, teleological and empirical. It has to be ontologically realist, as opposed to ontologically Humean, because as moral agents we experience ourselves actively and responsibly producing various acts and thus too their consequences, and so we cannot make sense out of our moral experience if we hold to a causeless, agentless metaphysics. It will have to be teleological because, as so many analysts have noted, the only way that we can make sense out of morality is in terms of how our acts bring us to the fulfillment of certain ends. It has to be empirical because it is only on the basis of our common, everyday experience of ourselves, along with the further additions and refinements of scientific and philosophical studies, that we can know what we are, what our common, basic needs and inclinations are and through what means we can best achieve them. With such a method ethics can be established as a thoroughly rational discipline that will in turn be able to help all men achieve a more rational and effective morality.

# CHAPTER SEVEN

## THE PRAGMATIC AND SITUATIONIST APPROACHES TO ETHICS

Dewey frequently pointed out that the ways in which men had in the past attempted to achieve certainty were no longer accepted. Nevertheless, he argued that a certain sort of practical certitude was possible for us if we applied the scientific or pragmatic method to our problems. In the last fifteen years Joseph Fletcher, with his situation ethics, has reinvigorated pragmatic ethics with his new version of it. Our concern and purpose here remain methodological: to analyze and evaluate the pragmatic-situationist views on how we should proceed in developing moral theories.

We shall first point out the salient aspects in the development of the pragmatic approach to working out an ethics, with a special emphasis on Dewey and Fletcher. Then, we shall consider the main strengths and weaknesses of such an approach. In conclusion, we shall summarize our findings.

## The Pragmatic Method in Ethics

Pragmatism is basically a form of positivism, but one that is indigenous to the United States. We may reckon its birth as a philosophical movement to have been the publication by Charles Sanders Peirce of an essay entitled "How to Make Our Ideas Clear."[1] In it he proposed a theory of meaning which has proved to be the cornerstone of the whole pragmatic approach. Disillusioned by what he believed to be the murky distinction made by logicians between clear and obscure ideas, Peirce sought to clarify the meaning of these terms by attending to the effects which a concept has, instead of to its denotation. "It appears, then, that the rule for attaining the third grade of clearness of apprehension is as follows: Consider what effects, that might conceivably have practical bearings, we conceive the object of our conception to have. Then, our conception of these effects is the whole of our conception of the object."[2] He bases this view on the observation "that the whole function of thought is to produce habits of action; and that whatever there is connected

131

with a thought, but irrelevant to its purpose, is an accretion to it, but no part of it. . . To develop its meaning, we have, therefore, simply to determine what habits it produces, for what a thing means is simply what habits it involves. . . . Thus, we come down to what is tangible and conceivably practical as the root of every distinction of thought, no matter how subtile it may be; and there is no distinction of meaning so fine as to consist in anything but a possible difference in practice."[3] This, he observed, is merely an extension of Jesus' statement that we know things by their fruits.

Pragmaticism, as Peirce later preferred to call it, was thus from the very beginning primarily a means of clarifying one's ideas. That is, it was a method of resolving problems. As such, it was not, except for its formulation, anything new and, more importantly, it could thus be used in combination with different sorts of metaphysics. Peirce himself worked from a viewpoint close to Scotistic realism and argued vociferously against the nominalism which he felt infected most of modern philosophy.

At the turn of the century, William James took up, with some modifications and considerable amplification, the suggestions of Peirce and made pragmatism the object of lively and international discussion. Like Peirce, James held pragmatism to be, not a doctrine, but a method. He held that it does not stand for any special results but is the use of any and all ideas and theories as instruments to change existing reality. It is thus characterized by an attitude, "The attitude of looking away from first things, principles, categories, supposed necessities; and of looking towards last things, fruits, consequences, facts."[4]

For James, pragmatism is also a theory of truth. It accepts the dictionary definition of truth as the agreement of an idea with reality. However, it denies that this agreement consists of copying reality, which would result only in stagnancy. Applying the pragmatist test then, a true idea is one which we can assimilate and verify. We verify a theory when we successfully use it to manipulate nature. Thus, "To 'agree' in the widest sense with a reality can only mean to be guided either straight up to it or into its surroundings, or to be put into such working touch with it as to handle either it or something connected with it better than if we disagreed. Better either intellectually or practically! . . . The essential thing is the process of be-

132

ing guided. Any idea that helps us to deal, whether practically or intellectually, with either the reality or its belongings, that doesn't entangle our progress in frustrations, that fits, in fact, and adapts our life to the reality's whole setting, will agree sufficiently to meet the requirement. It will hold true of that reality."[5] Thus, truth is only an expedient way of thinking,[6] for, "True ideas lead us into useful verbal and conceptual quarters as well as directly up to useful sensible termini. They lead to consistency, stability and flowing human intercourse. They lead away from excentricity and isolation, from foiled and barren thinking."[7] Hence, they also involve a painless assimilation. For they will disrupt previous beliefs as little as possible. "Truth in science is what gives us the maximum possible sum of satisfactions, taste included, but consistency both with previous truth and with novel fact is always the most imperious claimant."[8]

In metaphysics James espoused both nominalism and phenomenalism, doctrines which Peirce detested. From that base, he used his pragmatic approach to support and reinterpret traditional religious beliefs, the value of which he thought tough-minded empiricists had lost sight of. He likewise thought that traditional moral values, though always subject to revision, should be presumed to be valid until proven otherwise. However, he never worked out a comprehensive moral theory. It was John Dewey who developed what we generally think of as the ethics of pragmatism.

As a result of his university training Dewey was initially an idealist. He soon however converted to naturalism and pragmatism, the combination of which he preferred to call instrumentalism or experimental empiricism. From then on, he continually repeated his criticisms of other methods and philosophies. Renouncing the extra-empirical, he rejected all supernaturalism and dogmatism. He also argued that rationalism, though necessarily founded in some way on experience, ignored many essential aspects of it. He considered earlier empirical philosophies on the right track and attributed their failure to their lack of scientific methods of discovery and testing.[9]

Just as the success of modern science is due to its adoption of experimental and operational methods, so to succeed, ethics, claimed Dewey, will have to accept the same procedures. The old empirical morality merely cataloged those acts which men enjoyed and called them good. The new will not consider an act good simply because it is enjoyed. It counts an act as morally good only if the subject foresees his enjoyment of it on the basis of past experience and can define it as the result of certain other acts and conditions, therefore controlling it. "Operational thinking needs to be applied to the judgment of values just as it has now finally been applied in conceptions of physical objects. . . . The scientific revolution came about when material of direct and uncontrolled experience was taken as problematic; as supplying material to be transformed by reflective operations into known objects. . . . Consequences of operations became the important thing. The suggestion almost imperatively follows that escape from the defects of transcendental absolutism is not to be had by setting up as values enjoyments that happen anyhow, but in defining values by enjoyments which are the consequences of intelligent action. Without the intervention of thought, enjoyments are not values but problematic goods, becoming values when they reissue in a changed form from intelligent behavior."[10]

Dewey not only claimed that it was possible and desirable to use the methods of the positive sciences in ethics, but he also maintained that they were the only valid and useful ones. "The method we term 'scientific' forms for the modern man (and a man is not modern merely because he lives in 1939) the sole dependable means of disclosing the realities of existence. It is the sole authentic mode of revelation."[11] In short, Dewey is a positivist.

As an experimental empiriricist, to use his preferred designation, Dewey held that a scientific ethics would be in some way verifiable. He found the possibility thereof in a pragmatic test, in examining the way in which moral theory grows.

Dewey, it seems, would have admitted the dialectical character of ethics,[12] but he emphasized mainly the steps an individual takes in solving the problems confronting him. His ethics is more a study of how concrete problems are solved rather than a generalized theory of conduct. For him, moral ideas are an outgrowth of experience and indications of human potentialities. They result when the smooth course of one's life is broken by the conflict of two contrary purposes. "But let the value of one proposed end be felt to be really incompatible with that of another, let it be felt to be so opposed as to appeal to a different kind of interest and choice, in other words, to different kinds of disposition and agency, and we have a moral situation. . . . There is no longer one end, nor two ends so homogeneous that they may be reconciled by both being used as means to some more general end of undisputed worth. We have alternative ends so heterogeneous that choice has to be made; an end has to be developed out of conflict. The problem now becomes what is really valuable. It is the nature of the valuable, of the desirable, that the individual has to pass upon."[13]

Thus, for Dewey moral conflicts take place on two levels. On the simpler, a need makes itself felt and the problem is simply to determine what will satisfy this need. "Wherever there is a appraisal involving rules as to better or as to needed actions, there is an end to be reached: the appraisal is a valuation of things with respect to their serviceability or needfulness."[14] On the more complex level, the conflict is between ends, and the problem is to appraise the ends themselves. Dewey answers that "ends are appraised in the same evaluations in which things as means are weighed,"[15] because "the object finally valued as an end to be reached is determined in its concrete make-up by appraisal of existing conditions as means."[16] And again, "the end-in-view is formed and projected as that which, if acted upon, will supply the existing need or lack and resolve the existing conflict."[17] "It follows from this that the difference in different desires and their correlative ends-in-view depends upon two things. The first is the adequacy with which inquiry into the lacks and conflicts of the existing situation has been carried on. The second is the adequacy of the inquiry into the likelihood that the particular end-in-view which is set up will, if acted upon, actually fill the existing need, satisfy the requirements constituted by what is needed, and do away with conflict by directing activity so as to institute a unified state of affairs."[18]

In this view, there is such an intimate continuity of ends and means that, contrary to the traditional theory, the latter determine the former. "Things can be anticipated or foreseen as ends or outcomes only in terms of the conditions by which they are brought into existence." Hence, "propositions in which things (acts and materials) are appraised as means enter necessarily into desires and interests that determine end-values."[19]

Such end-values are ultimate only in the sense that they conclude one's appraisal of a particular

135

case. "The quality or property of value that is corre-
lated with the last desire formed in the process of
valuation is, tautologically, ultimate for that particular situation."[20]

Ends have no hierarchy or values. One will be
preferred to another only to the extent to which it
promises to better resolve a conflict. "The 'value' of
different ends that suggest themselves is estimated or
measured by the capacity they exhibit to guide action
in making good, satisfying, in its literal sense, existing lacks."[21]

The quest for really ultimate values is not only
fruitless but actually harmful. "Search for a single,
inclusive good is doomed to failure. Such happiness as
life is capable of comes from the full participation of
our powers in the endeavor to wrest from each changing
situation of experience its own full and unique meaning. Faith in the varied possibilities of diversified
experience is attended with the joy of constant discovery and of constant growing. Such a joy is possible
even in the midst of trouble and defeat, whenever
life-experiences are treated as potential disclosures
of meanings and values that are to be used as means to
a fuller and more significant future experience. Belief
in a single purpose distracts thought and wastes energy
that would help make the world better if it were directed to attainable ends."[22]

End-values, such as he understands them, says
Dewey, are empirically verifiable.[23] For if we act on
them and they satisfy our desires, they are valid;
otherwise, not.

Due to the influence of Dewey, most pragmatists
have been naturalists and have seemed to be areligious,
if not antireligious. It is thus somewhat surprising to
find pragmatic ethics in the sixties becoming again the
center of much attention and study as a result of being
advocated by a moral theologian. Joseph Fletcher, who
is one of the main proponents of "situation ethics",
explicitly grounds his version of it on Dewey.

Just as Peirce and James had held that pragmatism
is only a method, so Fletcher insists that situationism
too is not a system of moral concepts and rules, but
only an approach or method of making moral decisions.
He considers all moral systems to be straight jackets.
To act in a sufficiently flexible manner to be moral,
we have to have a way of making decisions which are not

hamstrung by any unchanging notions or rules.

According to Fletcher, there are methodologically only three alternatives for the moralist. The first is legalism, in which the letter, not the spirit, of the law reigns supreme; codified rules provide preset solutions, which must be followed, for all problems. The second is antinomianism, according to which decision making should be purely spontaneous, ad hoc and without principles or rules. Typical examples of it are the Gnostics and Sartrean existentialists. The third is situation ethics which uses traditional moral laws as maxims and guideposts but does not shrink from going contrary to them if in the situation love seems to require it.[24]

Christian situationism, says Fletcher, is a method that involves three moments. In the first, we recognize the only absolute law: to love. In the second, we take note of the general rules of morality, which represent the accumulated wisdom of the ages. In the third, we decide as responsibly as we can whether, in the given situation we face, conventional wisdom really serves love and so should be followed or not.[25]

Fletcher points out four presuppositions of the situationist approach to moral problems. The first is pragmatism, which, however, he notes, "of itself yields none of the norms we need to measure or verify the very success that pragmatism call for! To be correct or right a thing--a thought or an action--must work. Yes. But work to what end, for what purpose, to satisfy what standard or ideals or norm? Like any other method, pragmatism as such is utterly without any way of answering this question. Yet this is the decisive question."[26] The second is relativism, the rejection of any system of absolute, objective values. Nevertheless, he notes, to be relative means being relative to something, and so true relativity involves an absolute of some sort. The third is positivism, by which he means that by a free decision we determine in an a-rational but not ir-rational way what our fundamental principles and values are to be. Thus, a Christian situationist posits the existence of God without being able to prove it, while a hedonist will similarly posit pleasure as the supreme good. The fourth is personalism: all values are relative to persons, that is, to free, responsible beings interacting together in society.

Fletcher reduces his situationism to six basic propositions: 1. "Only one 'thing' is intrinsically

137

good; namely, love: nothing else." 2. "The ruling norm of Christian decision is love: nothing else." 3. "Love and justice are the same, for justice is love distributed, nothing else." 4. "Love wills the neighbor's good whether we like him or not." 5. "Only the end justifies the means; nothing else." 6. "Love's decisions are made situationally, not prescriptively."

In sum, then, Fletcher's method of resolving moral problems consists of determining on the basis of experience the result that would be achieved by different courses of action and then choosing the one that involves the most loving response. "Love, unlike law, sets no carefully calculated limits on obligation; it seeks the most good possible in every situation. It maximizes obligation."[27]

There are several points of comparison between Fletcher and the earlier pragmatists that are of interest to consider.

Take the role that Fletcher assigns in our moral life to love. His view is not unlike Peirce's, who wrote, "The moral stand-point from which every man with a christian training sets out, even if he be a dogmatic atheist, is pretty nearly the same. . . . He is also more or less touched with the spirit of christian love, which he believes should be his beacon . . . . such a person, if he have a clear head, will at once reply, right and wrong are nothing to me except so far as they are connected with certain rules of living by which I am enabled to satisfy a real impulse which works in my heart; and this impulse is the love of my neighbor elevated into a love of an ideal and divine humanity which I identify with the providence that governs the world."[28] Fletcher however holds that the acceptance of moral ultimates is a matter of choosing. Peirce goes much further. The ordinary christian, which he seems to consider himself to be, feels, he says, "that every man may come to the same passion which animates him by a mere enlargement of his horizon, and that his is the only sentiment in which all others may be reconciled."[29]

Similarly, Fletcher's antipathy to moral systems and abstract, absolute rules and his maximalist view of conduct explicitly repeat positions expressed by James: "They <intuitional moralists> do much to spoil this merit on the whole, hoever, by mixing with it that dogmatic temper which, by absolute distinctions and unconditional 'thou shalt nots,' changes a growing, elastic,

138

and continuous life into a superstitious system of rel-
ics and dead bones. In point of fact, there are no absolute evils, and there are no non-moral goods; and the
highest ethical life--however few may be called to bear
its burdens--consists at all times in the breaking of
rules which have grown too narrow for the actual case.
There is but one unconditional commandment, which is
that we should seek incessantly, with fear and trem-
bling, so to vote and act as to bring about the very
largest total universe of good which we can see. Abstract rules indeed can help; but they help the less in
proportion as our intuitions are more piercing, and our
vocation is the stronger for the moral life."[30]

Although they reject any and all sets of absolute
moral rules, pragmatists do allow for a principle of
universality and objectivity in ethics. It comes in the
form of a single ultimate goal which serves as a basic
moral criterion. Thus, even though Dewey explicitly
rejects any ultimate ends for men, when he analyzes the
process of resolving moral problems he nevertheless
introduces what amounts to the same. "The process of
growth, of improvement and progress, rather than the
static outcome and result, becomes the significant
thing. . . . The end is no longer a terminus or limit
to be reached. It is the active process of transforming
the existent situation. Not perfection as a final goal,
but the ever enduring process of perfecting, maturing,
refining is the aim in living. . . . Growth itself is
the only moral 'end'."[31] So what Dewey really wants to
reject is not an ultimate end for men, but only an ultimate that would be unchanging and therefore stifling.
And "growth" fits the bill. In a similar way, Fletcher
has stated, "This posture or perspective sets us over
against all 'intrinsicalist' ethics, against all 'giv-
en' or 'natural' or 'objectively valid' laws and maxims, whether of the natural law or the Scriptural law
varieties. It means, too, that there are no universals
of any kind." But then he immediately brings in his own
single ultimate and absolute: "Only love is objectively
valid, only love is universal."[32] As Fletcher himself
has pointed out, the pragmatic method as such does not
entail the acceptance of any ultimate value in particular. Thus it is that Fletcher derives his from his
Christian faith, while Dewey's results from his naturalism.

Critique

Now that we have considered in some detail the
pragmatic and situationist approach to ethics, we need

139

to try to determine how effective their methodology is and the extent to which we should accept it.

The great emphasis which Dewey and Fletcher place on the consideration of the concrete situation within which we act is certainly valid. Though moralists have long been aware of the crucial importance of circumstances for morality, in our time people have tended to overlook it because the moral climate which we inherited from the nineteenth century did indeed have strong legalistic overtones. Besides that, there is the natural inclination to resolve our moral problems in the simplest and easiest fashion possible, namely, by doing so in terms of the moral categories and stereotypes we have become accustomed to. So, we always need to be reminded occasionally that we cannot be moral mechanically. The moral life is the examined life; it requires thoughtful attention and analysis. It does not follow from this however that the means by themselves determine the moral end or that the situation by itself determines morality. What it does point out is simply that the situation within which we act may affect the results of our act, and so the situation and its results are factors which we must consider in determining what moral rule we should follow. For even though our goals may remain the same, we cannot always achieve them in the same way. As Fletcher himself notes, it is the ends which determine the means. But it is equally clear that the means at our disposal limit us as to the ends we can achieve.

What is even more important is that such an approach does much to increase moral sensitivity. By requiring the analysis and evaluation of every moral situation it forces and habituates one to pay close attention to whatever is of ethical relevance. Its practice would thus tend to bring about a fuller awareness of the implications and potentialities of our conduct. Indeed, in Dewey's view this is precisely what constitutes growth in moral freedom and perfection.

On the other hand, we must note that from Peirce on up, pragmatists have claimed pragmatism to be not a philosophy but only a method of philosophizing. When then they set about to develop an ethical theory and code, they have to combine their pragmatic method with a metaphysics or worldview of one sort or another in order to make their moral philosophy sufficiently concrete and relevant. Thus, as we have seen, Peirce and Fletcher base themselves on Christian notions while Dewey works from a humanistic naturalism. What this brings out is that their ethical method is not simply a clear-cut pragmatic testing but involves and includes as a determinant part certain metaphysical and/or religious views. The reason for this is clear. The pragmatic appeal to consequences is fine as far as it goes but as Fletcher himself points out we can judge consequences only in terms of ultimate ends, which the pragmatic method as such does not provide. It is then necessary to take them from some other source. It follows that the validity of the method which an individual pragmatist uses to develop his moral theory will depend on the validity of the ultimate goal he accepts, which in turn will depend on the adequacy of his world view. It would then be quite possible to accept without any inconsistency the moral methodology of one pragmatist while rejecting that of the others. It would however bring us too far afield if we tried to evaluate them on the basis of a detailed study of their metaphysics. We shall therefore limit ourselves to a consideration of some of the more salient aspects of the approaches of Dewey and Fletcher.

One striking difference between Dewey and Fletcher is found in the role they assign scientific method in ethics. Dewey explicitly identifies scientific and ethical methodology. Fletcher however is little concerned with science or the scientific method. As a pragmatist, he would certainly admit that the consequences of many acts may and should be determined in a rigorously empirical manner. But he considered it obvious, as Dewey did not, that neither a scientific nor a pragmatic method can of itself establish the fundamental criteria of morality, which can only be the ultimate ends to which we tend. For Fletcher, acceptance of these is a result of a personal commitment based on faith or intuition and they are thus hardly susceptible of scientific validation; thus, when Dewey holds that growth is what all men should always strive for and that growth is the bedrock of any valid moral decision, he is making a claim and establishing a principle that results from an intuitive interpretation of life experience. It is not an experimentally established conclusion, which is the sort we usually mean by "scientific." It is simply a formulation of what he found to work well, and chose, as a guide to living. Similarly, when Fletcher accepts God as love for his basis of all moral values it is because he makes a decision to choose this as his life-option. Dewey of course did not claim ethics to be an experimental science. For him, all rational inquiry was scientific and it did not have to be experimental. This broad sense of "scientific" conforms to the older usage which goes back to the Greeks, but Dewey's employment of it is frequently confusing. Fletcher however insists that values are decisions, not rationally established conclusions, and hence not scientific, even in the broad sense. For Dewey, even the ultimate moral values are experientially and rationally validated. In short, in regard to ultimate moral values Dewey is a rationalist and Fletcher, a voluntarist. Thus, we see here again how the validity of their approach depends on the acceptability of their metaphysical stance.

The basic cause of Dewey's difficulties concerning scientific method is that like all positivists he tends to think of method in a univocal manner, whereas in actuality it is an analogous concept. Because he would like to unify all knowledge and because he considers scientific knowledge to be clearly warranted, he frequently argues that all warranted knowledge has to be achieved through the scientific method. But then, since the "scientific method," taken in its usual sense of experimental method, is clearly not applicable in many areas, he has to extend its meaning to include any sort of rational inquiry. Thus, he would say that mathematicians, biologists and moralists all use the scientific method. But it is clear that their methods are radically different, so such a statement makes sense only inasmuch as "method" and "scientific method" are understood to be analogical notions, that is, to refer to things which are essentially different from one another but similar in some manner. But once we acknowledge "science" and "method" to be analogical terms, we can avoid much thinking and talking that is both confused and confusing.

For Dewey the ultimate criterion of morality is growth; for Fletcher, it is love. One basic methodological issue here is whether or not such criteria can be expected to work. It does not seem that they will, for while they are certainly important values, there are many moral problems that cannot be resolved simply by an appeal to them. This is more obvious in Dewey's case, since most moral problems are social ones to which the criterion of growth will apply at most in many cases only obliquely. For instance, if I am faced with the moral isssue of whether or not I should stop to help a stranded motorist, considerations of growth would not seem too relevant. Now, it could be argued that they are relevant, on the grounds that stopping would serve my growth inasmuch as it makes me a more altruistic person and that it would help the growth of the stranded motorist inasmuch as he will then be able to go about his business. While such a line of thinking is not implausible, it is not really conclusive. For what may help to make me more altruistic could at the same time interfere with my task at hand, thus directly disrupting my ordinary course of moral development, and even interfere with the altruistic mission I was already engaged in. Besides that, I really would have no way of knowing that the motorist was indeed intending to do what was in line with his growth. He may have been on his way home to murder his wife. Hence, if growth is my sole and ultimate criterion I have no really good reason for helping him. To arrive at a valid and firm moral decision, we would need, not one basic value, but a set of values which could be hierarchized and which would be broad enough to enable us to rationally resolve whatever moral problems we may encounter.

A similar argument can be raised against Fletcher. To hold, as he does, that love is the sole "absolute" value and that it suffices to resolve every moral conflict is methodologically untenable because it is inconsistent with his pragmatic principle that the good is what works. For love, like growth, is by itself not an objective and effectively consistent guide to moral judgment. The Grand Inquisitor loved. So does a "Jewish mother". Thus, even though Fletcher says love is to be guided by wisdom and knowledge, this does not really work, unless he subordinates love as a moral criterion to wisdom and knowledge. But this would bring him back to the sort of objective morality which he refuses to allow. Yet, it will not work if we try to reach a moral decision simply by judging a situation in reference to love. We have to look at what the consequences of our various acts may be, which we usually have to determine on the basis of past experience and generalizations from it. Then we can formulate a general moral rule which will mediate between love and our decision. But to try to do otherwise will mean that in every problematic situation we ought to revert to antinomianism, which Fletcher rightly rejects as breeding chaos.

There is another difficulty which arises if one accepts growth or love as one's "absolute" value or end. For despite what Dewey may say about the life-fulfilling satisfaction of continuous growth, it remains the case that change is not satisfying unless it fulfills certain objective needs and criteria. We cannot determine whether our behavior really does constitute growth except in terms of our innate needs and natural tendencies. Activity, that is, constitutes growth and is valuable only because of the good achieved through it. The relative value of such goods in turn is determined by how well they fulfill the ends we seek, but also by how well they satisfy the various needs and drives that we have--especially those that are common to all men--and by the extent they do so in a manner that is compatible and complementary. Thus, the only way we can really judge whether growth is occurring is in terms of the goods achieved: we are growing only if we are continuing to achieve a more deep and/or a more variegated range of goods which satisfy our inborn inclinations and needs. Growth is then a great good, but only an instrumental one, not the ultimate one. Similarly, love is certainly one of our very greatest goods. But its value is a function of what is loved. Since Fletcher thinks of love as being directed to an all-perfect God, he logically considers it to be the highest state possible to man, since it unites us to the highest good and is the source of whatever can be considered right action. Nevertheless, love and the loved are distinct and we can love things other than God. Our society is not theocentric like it used to be and the love of power, of status or of pleasure is the dominant feature of the lives of many men. But it is doubtful that Fletcher would consider the resulting life-styles to be of the proper sort. He can consider theocentric love as the ultimate value because he holds God to be the ground of all goodness and value. But this love then has its value only as a result of what it is ordered to. Thus, love too is only an instrumental good and not the ultimate one.

Methodologically, then, the pragmatic ethics of Dewey and Fletcher are untenable because they do not work, that is, they do not meet the pragmatic test. To work, they would have to provide ultimate moral criteria that, as ultimate, would not be derived from any other. But neither growth nor love are really ultimate goals or values. They are established as having value by showing that they are necessary to achieve a life that is full and satisfying. But what it is that will constitute a full and satisfying life is not itself established pragmatically, but is rather a necessary precondition to the application of the pragmatic test. We have to empirically determine what needs and drives are characteristic of men and what consequences are characteristic of different kinds of actions in respect to the satisfaction of those needs and drives. Having done this, we will be in position to pragmatically test the value of growth and love, should we feel that that is necessary. However, a pragmatic test of such a point would clearly be unnecessary under such conditions. If we can empirically establish that we have various inborn needs and drives and if we grant that the moral life consists at least to some extent of satisfying them, then it patently follows that growth and love are moral values since they are necessary aspects of the achievement of that satisfaction. But it is equally clear that they are specified and valued by us only in reference to what has traditionally been called human nature. A pragmatic test will be required only for specific kinds of acts, to determine whether they really do conduce to growth or are expressive of love, and whether they are then means to our basic ultimate goals.

We find in Fletcher another inconsistency related to this. He continually enjoins his reader not to absolutize moral principles but always to make his moral decisions according to the context. "We don't have to be either legalists who absolutize ethical principles, or extemporists who make decisions without any principles at all. We can choose (and I would urge it) to be situationist, acknowledging our heritage of canonical and civil principles of right and wrong but remaining free to decide for ourselves responsibly in all situations which principles are to be followed, or in some cases to decide that the 'relevant' principles are to be rejected because they would result in more evil than good."[33] There are two points to note here. First, he admits the validity of traditional ethical principles, the rules of behavior whose wisdom and value centuries of experience have established. He would not deny that these rules have been empirically and pragmatically vindicated. We would say their validity can indeed be so established and is a result of the fact that certain acts have as their natural effects the satisfaction of one or another inborn need or drive. Secondly, he proposes here the situationists' alternative to other moral approaches, but this turns out upon examination to be in fact only another moral rule, which has also been traditional since at least the thirteenth century. Aquinas, for instance, following other moralists, held that in the consideration of concrete cases, the circumstances are one of the determinants of morality we should always pay attention to and that they can make right or wrong an act which in other circumstances would have just the opposite moral quality. This traditional moral rule, which is Fletcher's situationist principle, we can formulate as "Always take into consideration the circumstances." The rationale in part of this rule in traditional moral theory was to enable one to determine whether a specific moral rule was relevant, that is, was to be applied. The purpose in general of moral rules is to guide us to our proper ultimate ends. If however, because of the circumstances, following a specific rule would lead us away from those ends, such a rule would not in these circumstances be relevant. We would have to act in another way, one in accord with an actually or potentially established rule, which would help us achieve our ends. It is then possible, if not necessary, to hold moral principles to be absolute and to simultaneously insist that they have to be applied with reference to one's situation. Thus, the classification of moral approaches into legalistic, antinomian and situationist, of which Fletcher makes so much, is in the abstract correct. Historically, however, it is invalid. Although some moralists may have applied their moral theory legalistically, few if any held to legalism as their basic theory. On the other hand, what Fletcher describes as situationism is a rather inconsistent combination of traditional moral and Christian ideas and the philosophy of Dewey.

From a methodological point of view, the main source of the difficulties of situationism is Fletcher's nominalism. This is one of the basic presuppositions he explicitly adopts. The moralist, he says, has to subordinate principles to circumstances, the general to the particular, the "natural" to the personal, the theoretical to the actual.[34] The purpose of this is to ensure that morality be really relevant and adequately flexible.

One problem with this is linguistic. Such a manner of speaking is ambiguous and confused. To simplify matters we can limit our consideration to the relation of the theoretical to the actual. We might all agree that the theoretical is subordinate to the actual in the sense that theory should be based on the facts, and so any theory that is incompatible with the facts should be revised or dropped. The theoretical is also subordinate to the actual in the sense that the actual is of greater value, inasmuch as theory is of worth only to the extent that it illuminates the actual or enables us to control it. There is however a crucial difference between theories set up to explain the actual and theories set up to guide behavior. It makes sense to say of the former that theory is subordinated to the actual, but not of the latter, which is the kind of theory moralists provide. It is certainly the case that moral theories should be based on the facts and should take into consideration all the relevant facts. But once the moralist has done this and provided an adequate theory of how we ought to act, it does not make sense to say that the theory should be subordinate to the actual. For, the whole purpose of a moral theory is to shape the actual, i. e., what we shall actually do. Fletcher might riposte that what he means is that no theory can be expected to be adequate in each and every case and so we have to be ready always to give up our theories. But that does not follow. Although we certainly should give up a theory we have discovered to be inadequate, acting contrary to or without theory is not the only alternative that remains. Rather, the sensible course in such a situation is to work out another theory, however tentative, that does seem adequate and to act in accord with it.

A more basic problem with Fletcher's nominalism is metaphysical. He is denying the possibility in principle of arriving at generalizations and theories that are known to be true. He would say all we can do is to form constructions that are more or less plausible and useful; we can never hold them to be definitively established and certainly and universally correct. Hence, Fletcher concludes, in any situation in which our usual moral theories would require an act contrary to love, we should put them aside and do what is loving. We cannot here undertake a full-blown discussion of nominalism, but we shall make a couple of methodological observations. First, as Fletcher himself has pointed out, his situationism is based on a nominalist view. Hence, if nominalism is untenable--and its difficulties have frequently been pointed out--situationism is unacceptable. Secondly, there is a serious inconsistency here in Fletcher's position. According to nominalism we cannot grasp intellectually the nature of things or make certain, universal and necessary statements about them. But if this is so, then he has no grounds for affirming, as he does, that we should always act in a loving way. For, to apply such a general rule we would have to understand the nature and consequences of love and other acts. Thus, if a moralist accepts nominalism, he logically has no way of showing how we can live in a rational, unified and effective manner. So, if the pragmatic test is warranted, nominalism and situationism are not.

To buttress his position, Fletcher also holds to "positivism", by which he means that every one establishes his ultimate values by a personal choice and decision, and not by discovering them through rational or empirical inquiry. Thus, he says, his acceptance of love as the basic value results from his own choice and faith, while the hedonist similarly chooses pleasure as his. First of all we must note that there is an inconsistency between Fletcher's positivism and his Deweyite pragmatism. For, Dewey always insisted that values are the result of rational inquiry. Secondly, we see too that this way of establishing an ethics has the advantage of ease and simplicity. However, it is clear that it also involves a certain arbitrariness. The question that has to be raised then is whether or not there is a more factual and adequate alternative. Like Dewey, we would say that what is called for is that we use our intelligence to rationally establish all our values on the basis of experience. But we would go yet further and affirm that we are pragmatically justified in holding that all men have in common various needs, that these can be satisfied only in certain empirically ascertainable ways, and that we can thus establish a hierarchy of factual values.

## Conclusions

In conclusion we may sum up our findings in this way. The pragmatists and the situationists give some very good advice as far as the application of a moral theory and code are concerned: Do not apply them in a narrow and legalistic fashion; Pay close attention to the changing circumstances; Be flexible and relevant in your principles; Value an act on the basis of its consequences; Let growth and love serve as your ideals in life. Even though this is excellent advice, giving it is a quite different matter from providing a method to develop a moral theory and code. Our analysis of the various pragmatists shows that their moral theories are the result not so much of the pragmatic method itself as of the different metaphysical stances which they adopt. So, one conclusion we draw is that moralists need a solid metaphysics from which to work. Another related conclusion is that moralists should make clear and explicit how their moral theories derive from their metaphysics.

As Fletcher has implicitly indicated, Dewey's rejection of ultimate ends and his theory of the continuity of the means and ends are unpragmatic and unacceptable, since it is always and only the ends which determine the means. Nevertheless, it is true that we frequently become aware of possible new ends for ourselves by examining our situation and the means at our disposal. The means however only limit us as to the ends we seek; they do not determine these ends for us.

In regard to the difficulties which both Dewey and Fletcher have in providing unified and consistent guidelines for conduct, they show the need for a comprehensive hierarchy of factually based goals and values, which neither man provides. So, situationism too, as a method for developing ethics, is not effective or pragmatic, and hence is unacceptable.

If we take pragmatism in its narrow sense, as an approach which judges theories and acts on the basis of their effectiveness, it cannot serve as their principal method either but is valid and has long been used in an ancillary role of verification. The degree to which it can be used will vary according to the type of judgment involved. In the case of judgments concerned about which means are possible, useful and best in achieving an end, instrumentalism, we must admit, has great value. However, it should be noted that such judgments are usually borrowed by ethicians from other disciplines, such as political science, psychology or sociology, or simply from men's general fund of experience. In the case of those more basic ethical judgments which deal with whether or not an end is morally right, here pragmatic verification will hardly be possible, because in fact it requires as already established a higher end, in terms of which the value of lower ends may be determined.

Pragmatists and situationists at least implicitly accept the dialectical nature of the growth of moral theory. We can now see how pragmatism and situationism may function as a secondary method within a dialectical framework. Indeed, this has been perhaps best pointed out by James himself. "The observable process which Schiller and Dewey particularly singled out for generalization is the familiar one by which any individual settles into new opinions. The process here is always the same. The individual has a stock of opinions already, but he meets a new experience that puts them to a strain. Somebody contradicts them; or in a reflective moment he discovers that they contradict each other; or desires arise in him which they cease to satisfy. The result is an inward trouble to which his mind till then had been a stranger, and from which he seeks to escape by modifying his previous mass of opinions. He saves as much of it as he can, for in the matter of belief we are all extreme conservatives. So he tries to change first this opinion, and then that (for they resist change very variously), until at last some new idea comes up which he can graft upon the ancient stock with a minimum of disturbance of the latter, some idea that mediates between the stock and the new experience and runs them into one another most felicitously and expediently."[35]

# CHAPTER EIGHT

## THE IDEALIST APPROACH TO ETHICS

Though idealism has patently fallen far from the dominating position it had a century ago, it is far from being moribund. Though now relatively few, idealists still have among their number some of the most outstanding thinkers alive. Even if this were not so, however, it would still be worth while to study idealist moral theories and how they were developed. Since they have worked out such distinctive viewpoints and approaches, even though one may in general reject their views, one can still learn from their mistakes and adapt their insights.

Idealists seem to use two quite different methods in developing their ethical views. One is the self-realization approach. This was used by Green and Hill in the nineteenth century and also among our contemporaries by Bertocci. Fundamentally, this methodology is Aristotelian. The second one is more Kantian, starting off with a consideration of how men know and function and deriving from this analysis theories as to how we ought to act. This was the kind of approach used by Fichte and in our own century by Paton. Since this approach seems to be more in the character of idealism, we shall concern ourselves only with it.

Since every philosopher has his own way of applying a method, we can make our treatment more simple and concrete by focusing on how a particular idealist has done it. We have chosen for our paradigm Georges Bastide. His writings have been for the most part in the field of moral philosophy[1] and he is counted among the most outstanding idealist thinkers of this century. In his philosophy he seeks to maintain and to develop further the tradition of Descartes, Maine de Biran, Brunschvicq and Le Senne. Although he is little known in English-speaking countries and did not succeed in rebuilding a strong following for idealism in France, he has been recognized even by non-idealists as a moralist of originality and power.

Since we are concerned here primarily with methodology, we shall first of all describe in some detail how Bastide applied his idealist method to the working out of a moral theory. In doing this we shall refer mostly to his main work, the Traité de l'action morale, and shall bring in points from other works only when necessary for clarity. In a second section we shall then try to point out the main strengths and deficiencies of such an approach.

## Bastide's Methodology

It will help us to understand Bastide's method if we first of all consider his notions of philosophy and ethics. For him, philosophy's Copernican revolution occurred with Descartes. In antiquity and the Middle Ages philosophers approached their task in a spirit of naive realism which necessarily resulted in inconsistencies and dead ends. Despite his own many inadequacies, Descartes understood this and found the only valid solution: he turned within himself and found in his Cogito a solid foundation for, and the first principle of, truth and certainty. What we find however when we look within ourselves is not a human nature whose structure we can analyze into patterns of atoms or sets of substantial and accidental forms, but rather only a human condition, characterized by doubts, tensions, discordant tendencies and inconsistencies. Philosophy thus becomes a metaphysical drama in which we take stock of our condition and can will to rectify it or to continue as we have. Kant then was right in according primacy to the practical intellect. As we reflect on how we act, we discover two levels and kinds of values that we may follow, the empirical and the spiritual. We thus become aware of the possibility of adding by our free choices a vertical dimension to our lives. We do this by freely choosing to create and to follow values of a spiritual sort, which are characterized by unity and consistency, and thus transfigure our world. So from this purview ethics is no longer seen as a static discipline which establishes universal rules that we must follow in order to achieve happiness. It is rather a dynamic and reflexive critique in which we investigate the human condition and discover the sources of its tortuous and tragic tensions and through our free and insightful choices give new, fulfilling and transfiguring directions to our lives.

The reflexive method, Bastide tells us, goes back to Socrates. At the turn of the modern era it was practiced by Descartes and Spinoza and has since inspired a variety of technical and popular works. It has especially influenced French philosophers, who have maintained it in the present century as a living tradition through their university teaching. In general we could contrast the reflexive with the realist or ontological method. The latter considers what is given to us in our experience to be real, classifies it in terms of substance and attribute and tries to explain it through causal and telic relations. The reflexive method is often mistakenly taken to mean a sort of introspection by which we observe ourselves in an interior mirror. But this is incorrect, for in this case we would be simply again playing realist games with the images therein and mystifying ourselves. Rather, the reflexive method is based on the direct and immediate presence of ourselves as persons to ourselves. By drawing out and analyzing the implications of this presence, we can build up an objective and certain grasp of what we and the world are. With his analysis of the a priori conditions of knowledge, Kant was going in the right direction but nevertheless ended in a sterile formalism because we cannot know our spirit from the outside, from a position of exteriority. The spirit is present to us only from a position of interiority, in which we grasp it in its life, its acts and its becoming. Thus we correct the deficiencies of the Kantian approach by combining it with those of Maine de Biran and Bergson. In this way the reflexive method establishes the unity of the empirical self and the pure self and at the same time avoids the rationalism, formalism, fideism and impersonalism to which Kant and the classical idealists tended.

Bastide also refers to his approach as an axiological idealism, in order to underline one of its crucial aspects. On the basis of his analysis of experience he rejects as unsatisfactory any realist view of the world. Only an idealist view, he finds, accords with that experience. An adequate idealism however can be developed only through the reflexive method. Kant had shown that our knowldge and the objects of our knowledge are only possible through, and thus depend on, the activity of the subject, but he had also held to the necessity of the thing-in-itself to provide the sensory experience that initiates knowledge. Idealism arose with the denial of the thing-in-itself. For French idealists like Brunschvicq and Bastide, this creative life results from the limitations inherent in the spirit itself. As it becomes conscious of its limitations, it seeks to transcend them and thus creates for itself an ever evolving world. Moreover, Bastide argues, this activity is free, on both the theoretical and the practical level; both my thinking and my willing are undetermined. As a result, the world I create depends on the values I choose for myself. Metaphysics thus merges with ethics. Faced with a variety of options as to how I may act, I am free to choose either an authentic or an inauthentic mode of life. As I reflect on my condition and activities, it is my values which I first create, then in terms of those values I seek to understand and explain my world. I thus have, as foreshadowed by Plato and Kant, an idealism that is axiological, in which the good is prior to being and the practical to the theoretical.

Let us now consider in some detail how Bastide worked out and applied his method. Initially, he distinguishes four main possible approaches to moral activity, since this is necessary to grasp their dialectical relations. He refers to these four methods as doctrinal edification, mystical exaltation, technical intervention and reflexive provocation.

The method of doctrinal edification is the most widely used because it is in a sense the most natural. A doctrine is a body of knowledge that can be taught to others. If a doctrine is considered capable of providing us with the elements necessary to orientate, regulate and motivate our lives, it starts to be used for the moral uplifting of people. Such a doctrine is arrived at in this manner. We start off with a naive realist epistemology, which both leads us to and guarantees a certain view of the world, so that moral goodness is conceived as living in conformity with these views. The epistemological stance involved here tends to succumb to two equally disastrous inclinations: the first is to give a privileged status to one kind of knowledge over the others and the second is to try to resolve problems by an eclecticism which is no more than a verbal conciliation. Thus, it is argued, to ground morality means to give certain rules of action and to justify these rules through certain basic principles, hence providing a rational set of reasons that justify and legitimatize our acts. But, Bastide objects, this does not work, because when we try to establish the reasons which explain our activities, we do so by appealing either to causality or to teleology or to both. Such a procedure however manifests a fundamental misunderstanding of the moral life. For, the more we try to explain human activity by demonstrating its necessity, the less is it possible to grasp the interior conditions which give our activity their moral value, namely, liberty, responsibility and merit. Another difficulty with the method of doctrinal edification is that it eventually results in attitudes of either dogmatism or scepticism. It tends to produce dogmatic consciences bscause it depends on maintaining people in a relationship of disciples to master. As the self-confidence or just the decisiveness of the master meets with any docility or even passivity on the part of a disciple, doctrine becomes dogma for both of them and the magisterial revelations turn into hermetic seals. As generations go by, the dogmas lose their power to persuade and become simply an instrument of social pressure in the hands of an authority, whom no one believes any more. Thus does scepticism grow out of dogmatism. To avoid this, the dogmatic society vigilantly seeks to conserve its traditions of orthodoxy through such practices, when necessary, as excommunication and intolerance. And more positively, it will adopt in science pragmatism, calling truth whatever is useful to its doctrine; in aesthetics, academicism, calling whatever exemplifies orthodox standards beautiful; in the moral life, conformism, calling any action supposedly inspired by the dogma heroism. But morality and civilization require a certain pluralism and tension, which is why dogmatic societies always finish by breaking down. But a sceptical society is not any more healthy, for scepticism is really just a negative and multiple dogmatism. Being based not on liberty but on license, it responds to dogmatic rigidities with a desire for novelty and originality at any cost, thereby totally disfiguring any values it may invoke.

A second method of establishing the direction of our moral life is that of mystical exaltation. By mysticism Bastide means the phenomena connected with man's achieving a direct and intimate union with God, a union which, though momentary, is beyond and superior to the normal relations that one may commonly have with God. Consequently, when a mystic is recognized as such, he can become an heroic moral leader. Just as a mystic has reformed his own life, so now he may want to reform his society. He will protest against its values and seek to transfigure them. Because however mystical experience and knowledge are by their nature ineffable and non-discursive, the mystic hero can reform and lead his society only by exalting the emotions of his fellowmen through his words or by bringing them by his example to imitate himself. Since however the claims of the mystic cannot be rationally demonstrated, the only way to evaluate this method of moral guidance is to look at its results. It turns out to be deficient, even if we admit the objectivity of the claims of the mystic. One reason for this is that most of the mystic's hearers will react to his words emotionally and will distort their sense, using them to justify their own feelings and desires, whatever they are. Besides this, the mystic reformer will need helpers in his task and among the volunteers there will always be the clever opportunists who know how to turn any situation to their own advantage. Such difficulties are unavoidable whenever one intends to unify and direct society in terms of a personal, non-rational insight. And of course there is in every case the fundamental issue of whether the seer who has arisen is truly a mystic or not. Prime examples of the users of this approach are the Hebrew prophets and the Christian saints, but more recently Nietzsche, Berdyaev, Heidegger and Hitler have followed an analogous line. The common defect of all such approaches is that they seek to unite men together in a community of non-rational immediacy. Even though such a union may be possible between certain individuals, the moral value of human communities does not come from that but from working together for values whose objectivity is known. It is only a rational love which is respectful of the autonomy of others that can base an authentic community. A mystical community often will be without freedom, since it will be ruled by passions, not reason.

The method of technological intervention is a result of the positivistic and pragmatic interpretations of modern science. Thus, it is relatively new, only about a hundred years old. It starts off with a Baconian view of science as being fundamentally utilitarian. It conceives of science as seeking to understand nature in order to be able to predict what nature will do, so that it will be able to control it. It is this notion of science which is behind our present technological civilization with its emphasis on controlling all phenomena and which has also inspired this methodology. It takes on different forms depending in part on which science is taken as a point of reference. Thus, if one starts from biology, one derives from the biological notions of adaptation and equilibrium the concepts of the normal and natural, which then serve as the criteria of morality. Or, if one prefers to begin from the social sciences, one can oppose to eschatological ethics and to metaphysical utopianism a scientific knowledge of the moral, that is, the social and historical, reality. Through sociology and history we can determine what is normal and natural at a given stage of man's development and on this basis work out the moral science that will provide man with the rational guidance that he needs to free himself from encumbering anachronisms and to get rid of any impediments to normal evolution. Alternatively, one could start from the science of psychology from which one can borrow the idea of a normal and natural state of psychological equilibrium and psychopedagogical techniques that will assure to mankind a correct growth. It is beyond doubt that these various sciences have provided men with an imposing arsenal of techniques to reshape the world and have therewith provided man with a level of power far beyond what was previously available. To this kind of approach Bastide objects that we have only to consider some of the latest features of technological progress, such as pharmacological interrogations and artificial insemination, to start having doubts about the extent to which these technological results of science are really effective and worthwhile as far as human morality is concerned. For, we cannot let our awe of modern technology make us forget what are the nature and function of technology in general. Technology is simply a set of means that are rationally organized to achieve a given end. We have to return here to the old scholastic adage that efficient causes depend on final causes. It is clear that any technological development presumes as given and valid a certain end or final cause to achieve. It is thus equally clear that technology of itself cannot tell us what are the ends we ought to seek. Since however morality has to do with the ends which man ought to want, technology cannot be our moral guide. Similarly, the technicist claim to moral self-sufficiency resulting from the way it establishes what are normal and natural conditions and evolution is unfounded. On a strictly empirical basis, the notions of "normal" and "natural" are used in two different senses. In one, they refer to a banal mathematical average, in which case both Socrates and Caligula are equally abnormal. In a second sense, they are taken so broadly as to include a wide range of contraries. So, for the sociologist crime and its repression are equally normal and natural since they are found in all societies. Thus, the only reason a normative function can be claimed for such notions is that they are shored up with some unannounced metaphysical presuppositions and some implicitly accepted moral ideals. But this does not make for a solid, rational ethics. Technological ethics also is based on a confusion of totality and unity. The sociologist can describe the various conflicting segments which make up the totality of a society and which may have even over long periods of time a certain equilibrium. But that need not be, and frequently is not, an ethical unity. Technological ethics also confuses the natural, the social and the moral orders. We certainly should accept whatever scientific knowledge we can have concerning the necessary effects produced by natural and social forces, but morality has to do with something quite different: the exercise of, and the growth in, personal autonomy.

The inadequacy of these methods is seen in the results that they lead to, such as the view that virtue can in effect be funneled from those who have it into those who do not, or that virtue is something that we can achieve simply by ourselves, apart from any social intercourse. The root of such misconceptions is physical realism. This conceives of moral subjects as though they were the same kind of things that we experience in the world and to which apply such notions as substance and quality. Thus, if you transfer enough good qualities from one person to another, the latter will eventually also be virtuous. But, since the moral worth of an agent comes from what is in the strongest sense within him, these methods of exteriority will not do. We need one which focuses primarily on the moral agent himself. Such is the method of reflexive provocation.

Moral reflexivity develops in three phases. The first is purification. Here a person lays aside all that comes to him from the outside as having of itself no positive value. He must dam out everything he gets from his passive faculties: all sensations, images, habits and customs, since these are the causes of prejudice and hasty judgments. All that is produced in him but without him is then alien and imposed. When therefore he inquires concerning his authentic self and his freedom, the negative characteristics for which he repudiates the experiential given unveil to him the positive characteristics that will identify himself to himself: the multiplicity that imposes itself on his consciousness has varying degrees of obscurity and so lures him into contradictions and error, hence it is clarity in knowledge and unity in volition that will permit him to recognize his true inner self. The second phase consists in the growth of self-knowledge in such a way that a person will be able to substitute voluntary action for behavior arising simply from the results of passivity. By finding what is truly objective and universal within ourselves, we can make practical judgments that we know to be correct and which thus justify us in acting one way rather than another. The third phase consists of the construction of the self by the self. What rules here is the radical necessity for unity. A moral agent cannot really be unless he is an unity. So, by willing only what fits in with a truly unitary mobilization of the whole person, which is what we mean by goodness, we shape ourselves into morally good persons.

What Bastide means by the method of reflexive provocation is an approach in which a moralist who has achieved a reflexive conscience seeks to have others, who do not have it, achieve it. In it there corresponds to the purification phase the use of Socratic irony and other procedures inspired by it. The goal here is to take an unreflective person and to show him how his moral actions lead him into obvious contradictions, so that he will himself become aware of his inconsistency. What is to be especially noted though is that this inconsistency is not merely a matter of logic but of morality; there is a diffraction between what the person says, believes and does. He is thus forced to recognize that his conscience is not a unity. This revelation will usually then cause anguish, anger and anxiety, all of which however is simply an indication that purification and wisdom are starting to develop. The provocation to self-knowledge involves, to put it in Socratic terms, maieutic processes. It consists in helping a person discover the truth that he has within him. Taking possession of this truth makes possible a unification of what one believes and what one says. This clear and certain knowledge thus produces autonomy and also makes one able on his own to fecundate other consciences. All this provokes further the construction of the self. Spinoza expressed it perfectly when he said that any affection which is a passion ceases to be one as soon as we form a clear and distinct idea of it. As a person gets rid of his prejudices and becomes aware of the truth of his condition, he ceases to be the plaything of impersonal forces and becomes the lucid artificer of his own morality. In this way he can achieve a total integration of what he says, of what he believes and of what he does, thus eliminating his initial painful doubts and inconsistencies.

In Bastide's view, the indisputable advantage of the reflexive method over the others is that it respects the fundamental condition of any authentic morality, namely, that it emanate from within a conscience that is master of itself. The power of the reflexive method comes precisely from this that, when properly used, it is identical with the moral life of the agent, it is what makes his action moral, and it is the indubitable source of moral authenticity. We must however be careful not to confuse true reflection with any of its counterfeits. It is not autism: it is not a repudiation of the real world in order to bask in an illusory and subjective self-sufficiency. It is not a wholesale discrediting of all sorts of motives and acts under the guise of thereby purifying one's conscience. It is not a mere lazy curiosity about one's self. It is not a precipitate attempt to forge one's self anew without going through an initial purification and without submission to the claims of objectivity. But, of course, objectivity should not be taken in its usual, naive, realist sense.

One of the central aspects and results of the reflexive method is what Bastide calls spiritual conversion. Although we can and should study man from the point of view of the different sciences, it is even more important that we study him philosophically, as a person. It is however only through reflection on ourselves that we grasp what it is to be a person: a subject who reflexively inquires into his reasons for existing and who is continuously giving shape to his daily life by the direction and meaning which he gives to his existence. So, we have to give up trying to explain what persons are in terms of ontological structure and particularly in terms of an Aristotelian substantialism. Rather, we must admit with Pascal that we do not know what is in us nature and what is habit. Nevertheless, we are all born with what we may call an innate (but not natural) faith. This innate faith is unreflective and spontaneously dogmatic. By this faith we believe that the world has the precise qualitative and quantitative determinations that we perceive it to have. Through it we believe in a cosmic power which has planned and caused this world. Through it we believe in the intrinsic value of each of the things that make up the world, according to their place in its hierarchical order. This faith is thus a realism of exteriority; it sees everything in the world as exterior to everything else. Thus, atomism represents it in its purest form. This faith has its source in an egocentrism that is unreflective and antinomical. Since however it is afraid of its antinomies, it masks them with verbalisms, circular reasonings and arbitrary judgments. When then an individual starts to take stock of this situation, these antinomies start to tear him apart. He experiences frustration because he cannot anymore believe in the meaning of the world; he despairingly recognizes how totally and radically in error he has been; he feels guilty because he sees that he has filled the world with the debris of his monstrous attempts to remake nature as though he were a God.

These experiences of frustration, error and guilt can bring man to despair. When this disturbed conscience recognizes that the source of his problem is the exteriority of his primitive faith, he can find the antidote to his despair by a reflexive conversion to his inner self. With it opens up the possibility of transcending the frustrating dead end of the world of exteriority by entering the life of the spirit. For, the inner self is spiritual, that is, it is endowed with intelligence and freedom. Thus, when the spirit recognizes itself as intelligent, i. e., as always able to move on further, it refuses to think of itself any more as a passive thing. It thus also experiences itself as Freedom, but also and simultaneously as Duty. In this conversion we substitute for the experience of frustration and guilt the taking on of a responsibility for ourselves that is clear and total. For, through the spirit, "we are free to be free: we are free with the freedom of free choice to be free with the freedom of autonomy by accepting as our duty adherence to Wisdom."[2] This duty is not however a Kantian formal law. It is a duty to rectify what we did when acting on the basis of innate faith. Thus, it is always concrete and specific. The good we can do is defineable only in terms of the evil we have done.

Along with spiritual conversion comes the transfiguration of values. It is not the same thing as Nietzsche's transmutation of values, which was rather a rejection of transfigured values and a consequent desperate search for a return to empirical values. Nor is it the same as Freudian sublimation, which is a way of avoiding reality. Rather, it involves the substitution, as the subject of reference of values, of man inasmuch as he is open to a continual transcendence of himself, for the empirical and egocentric man of innate faith. It thus also involves two different orders of value: empirical values which diminish when people participate in them and the exclusive pursuit of which produces hatred and poverty, and spiritual values which increase when they are participated in. The same objects and acts can take on either an empirical or a spiritual value. Spiritual conversion and transfiguration occur when we substitute, for an empirical and pragmatic interest, an attitude of disinterestedness, by which is meant not an indifference to things but, on the contrary, a penetrating attention to them to determine what they have that is authentically (i. e., universally, objectively and eternally) of value. Thus, the converted conscience holds that by different sorts of disinterested activity it can undo the evil caused by the self-seeking conscience. Through science, art and morality it seeks to renew the world by establishing a network of comprehensive relations. That is why the converted conscience also believes in the "idea", the immanent law of the activity of spirit as constituting the world of tranfigured values. Thus, the converted conscience also believes in an infinite value-conferring power which is nothing else but the spirit itself. What grounds these beliefs is its experience in the transfiguration of values, which has shown that the spirit can, with difficulty of course, but always, win out over the will to power. For, the beliefs of the converted conscience produce a dialectic of promotion of human values which is just the opposite of the dialectic of dissolution brought about by the power-seeking, primitive conscience. The latter uses all the resources at its command to satisfy its uncontrolled desires. The spiritualized conscience on the contrary seeks to develop a culture in which it will become ever more adequate. The only acceptable viewpoint then is a personalistic spiritualism, which can only be grounded in a moral idealism.

Reflection has shown that the principal axis of the development of morality is autonomy, taken as the progressively more adequate conformity of our volition and our knowledge to each other. Further reflection uncovers the main criteria we need to determine if a conscience is developing authentically. Among the first things that an emerging reflection notices is that it has to distinguish in the temporal dimension between a heteronomous and alienating past, which it has to repudiate, and a future that it wants to make autonomous by its rational and responsible control. And this implies a second distinction which is, so to speak, perpendicular to the first. Such a transformation of the imposed past into a planned construct implies a distinction between those essences and existences in terms of which we describe what was, and a new set of essences and existences which are the result of our responsible acts. The axiological world of the conscience thus has a certain structure, whose other elements can now be considered. We find the axiological horizon of the reflexive conscience to have four cardinal types of values. The values of retrospection come from our imposed past and without them our conscience would not have any experience of frustration, error or guilt. The values of prospection are concerned with what we are constructing and without them our conscience would have no ideals or beliefs, which would be the same as being dead. The values of intelligibility are based on the

162

essence of things and without them the conscience would plunge into absurdity. Finally, the existential values are related to what is in fact and without them conscience would be like a light that illuminates nothing. The values of retrospection constitute the richness of conscience, since the function of reflexive retrospection is to provide grist for the conscience by analyzing the oceanic depths of the data of our experience. The prospective values are concerned with the unity of conscience as it manifests itself in its works. The values of intelligibility, the function of which is to so illuminate the conscience as to make it transparent to itself, give to conscience its clarity. The existential values give depth to the conscience since they make possible the vast network of experience. Richness, unity, clarity and depth are then the main criteria by which we can judge the level and the extent of the moral development of any person. And since too they have an indissoluble solidarity in the total act of reflection, we can formulate the fundamental law of their correlation, which is also the golden rule of the progress of the conscience: "A conscience is in general progressing every time that it simultaneously increases its richness, unity, clarity and depth in a dynamic equilibrium which cannot be obtained and preserved except to the extent that this conscience puts into operation the conversion that turns it away from dispersing itself in empirical interests in order to consecrate itself to the common and universal values of the spirit.[3]

At different points as he proceeded, Bastide indicated various characteristics of his method. First of all, it is objective.[4] The whole point of purification of the self is to lay aside the causes of hasty and prejudiced judgments, so that when one turns to discover his inner self, he may with a calm and clear mind distinguish what is particular and universal within him and concentrate on grasping the latter just as it is. His method is also fundamentally critical.[5] For Bastide, however, being critical does not mean mere negativity, which would be sterile. It consists rather in grasping data in such a way as not to be enslaved by them and of understanding them so well and thoroughly that we rightly distinguish authentic from inauthentic values. The reflective conscience is also characterized by involvement, not of course in the sense of immersing ourselves in the flow of events and taking up every new fad, but rather it means resolutely following through on whatever we have decided to be right in the light of our norms of clarity and unity.[6] Thus, the involvement of the reflective conscience does not produce frenetic and pell mell action. It manifests itself as calm, far-sighted and effective, although limited, activity. The reflexive method is also social, because it aims at helping everyone achieve autonomy and the full develop-ment of their personality, but this can be done only by men interacting and working together to understand and achieve their common ideals and good. Indeed, you have to say that, in the concrete, moral activity is social activity. Finally, the method of ethics is dialec-tical, but not in a Hegelian sense in which human an-tagonisms are transformed into a metaphysical law.[7] Rather, for Bastide morality, and human history too, are dialectical inasmuch as when we work out a solution to a problem, this solution itself gives rise to anoth-er problem that, though different, is of the same order as the preceding one. Consequently, morality involves two different forms of dialectic. There is a dialectic of dissolution which takes place when an unconverted conscience seeks its happiness in empirical values in accord with its egocentric, pragmatic drives. There is also a dialectic of promotion in which the reflective conscience seeks through science, art, philosophy and religion to exist more authentically. Dialectic, then, is not synonymous with progress, since these two dia-lectics tend in opposite directions and since there is in us all the time a tension between them. In each and every one of our acts we have to make a choice as to which to follow.

To understand more adequately what the reflexive method is, let us consider how Bastide applies it to one specific area. Among the moral problems that he discusses at some length are alienation, war, the fami-ly, economic life and the state. From this wide range of problems let us look at his treament of the family. Since he holds that the only good activities open to us consist of repairing the evil we have previously com-mitted, he takes up first of all the breakdown of fami-ly life and from that moves on to consider what we should do to bring about a more adequate family life. For, the dialectic of dissolution provides the seeds for the dialectic of promotion.

We can start off with the former by turning to historical studies. In the West and since the Greeks, the family has undergone a certain number of crises, an historical study of which allows us to enumerate a va-riety of features that are characteristic of them, such as easy access to and the increase of divorce and the progressive acceptance of perversion. From these and from a philosophical analysis of the structure, forms and functions of the family, Bastide infers that there are two main causes of the dissolution of the family: the one is eroticism, whose devotees make their sexuality the dominant concern of all their activities, and the rule of material interests, which excites and is pervaded by a variety of emotions, such as avarice and parental autocracy. Each of these sources of disintegration are powerfully corrosive by themselves, but when they appear together as they frequently do in our urban civilization, they produce contradictory inclinations which tear families and individuals apart. An example: a woman who has to choose between being a mother who can cleverly calculate her family's position in the far future, or being a passionate lover fervently engaged in the exaltation of the present or imminent encounter. Such tensions show clearly that one is involved in a phase of dissolution. The disruption of family life can also arise because of the variety of functions it has to fulfill. When the biological, economic, educational and spiritual functions of the family can be achieved in an integrated way, family life is productive and without tension, But this is not what is usuallly happening in our families nowadays. In multifarious ways the fulfilling of one function can make it extremely difficult to fulfill another, as when a couple would like to have several children but can barely afford to support one, or when the daily difficulties of raising a family and earning a living produce such frayed nerves and tension that the parents cannot control their tempers or give clear, consistent guidance to their children. As such conditions spread, the attitudes and characters of people deteriorate. This has a threefold source. First, there is the alienation which arises in a family because one confuses autonomy with the absence of law. Thus, we do nothing to rid women of their alienation if we are satisfied merely with informing them that their bodies are their own and how they can use them to achieve the ideal sensuality. Nor do we help men to achieve true liberty by simply making available to them a greater variety of enticements for their libidos. Nor are we liberating adolescents by just teaching them at length about how instinctive drives and complexes are highly powerful forces, without also making clear the overriding need for self-mastery. Secondly, mistaken notions of justice lead to a false kind of egalitarianism. For, while women are neither inferior nor superior to men, they are different. The misunderstanding of this difference is what very often kills an initial and loving generosity, so that marriage becomes a rather boring game whose only goal is a hedonistic or a utilitarian sharing in a community of goods, which in this way becomes the causes of arguments and dissension. Thirdly, the family is the source of the worst forms of hate, anger and cruelty. This is because there is initially love in the family, and a love which gets turned into hate is far deeper than one which arises otherwise. Thus is it that as license and egalitarianism erode the bonds of a marriage, it turns into "a nest of vipers." Besides these various factors already pointed out, we find in our culture a build-up of others which also militate against the biological and educational functions of marriage: our industrial economy, inflation, expensive and inadequate housing, etc. Another central aspect of the crisis of today's family is the tremendous increase in the number of divorces. These may of course solve certain problems, but this does not alter the indubitable fact that the majority of disturbed and/or delinquent children are the product of homes that are broken up or threatening to. And thus the dissolution of family life increases.

Such an analysis of that process has positive results in that it helps to make clear the values and criteria that should be used in the dialectic of promotion of family life. Thus, since one of the main causes of marital dissolution is eroticism, one of our main tasks is to determine how to achieve the spiritual promotion of our biological nature. Love is the motive force behind every fruitful and generous enterprise of man. However, love is not likely of and by itself to establish a rational order. The divorce statistics manifest the fragility of unions based only on love. The foundation of a home has to be an effective, personal commitment for both good and bad times. Such a constancy requires that people have submitted their emotions to a rational discipline. From the initial, loving commitment to the final, habitual serenity of a life in common, one needs the continual guidance of a will always illuminated by the supreme familial value, the moral value of the children. But we should not forget here the social aspect. It is one's culture that separates nature from spirit. And if our culture is erotic and/or utilitarian, it will pervert family life. But conversely, if a culture is orientated to the correct values, it will illuminate and give depth to the conscience of men, enabling them to progress individually and as a group. Thus, the increasing concern for demographic planning is certainly well-founded, but its ends cannot be achieved merely through technological manipulations. Of themselves, these lead only to dehumanization.[8] A valid solution will necessarily involve the establishment of a familial morality pervaded by a rational and voluntary discipline of our inclinations.

Both the moral and biological progress of man depend on his recognition of the primacy of the educational function in the family. For, animals have the function of reproducing, whereas men have the duty of procreating. The conventional terms used here reflect the experience of generations, that the basic criterion of family morality has to include both reproduction and education. For, we have to choose, not between morality and animality, but between a morality of spiritual values and a monstrous, "natural" immorality. And there is no possibility of dissociating the biological future of our species from its moral evolution. Hence, it is its educational function that gives the family its <u>raison d'être</u>, that is, its value and its unifying principle, as it is the only means through which a child can get a fully integrated and effective education. That is, it is only the family that can give a child fully personal guidance by a continuous, vigilant, sensitive, concerned and affectionate attention. For this, parents have to become confidence-inspiring authorities. Authority, which is spiritually transformed power, does not work through coercion but through rational appeals based on the values of the personality and through the quality of its love, and it seeks thus to set the youngsters on the path of an objective autonomy. Of course, to so spiritualize their children parents have to also make use of the wealth of resources offered by their traditions and culture. This however entails that family life educates not only the children but also the parents, who have to be continually trying to understand better themselves, their children and the world, so that they will be able to point out to their children the snares and delusions of false values and of counterfeit forms of liberty.

This primacy of the educational function is what can give the family the unity of structure and functions that will make it open to a dynamic promotion in spirituality. Thus, for instance, our industrial economy has menaced the family with dissolution in various ways. Nevertheless, many families have been able, through a lucid grasp of their functions, to maintain themselves and to adapt themselves to new and very different conditions. Moreover, they have forced the state to lay aside its individualism and to regulate the economy in such a way as to favor the family. In our complex society, the family has also given up to other institutions certain tasks for which it is not too well suited, such as training in a trade. Thus too, the open family is now more concerned with housing than with owning land; despite inflation, it continues to try to build up its savings, but of course in new forms. By working further along these lines, the open family requires and will give birth to a new economic order that will evade both the individualist and the collectivist entrapments which are so destructive of the family. Hence, Bastide concludes, it is in and through the family especially that we learn both to transcend ourselves and to live together, and it is for this twofold reason that we achieve our salvation primarily in the family.

## Critique

Having seen in some detail what Bastide means by the reflexive method and how he applies it to the problem of domestic morality, we are now in a position to determine if such a method is a valid and/or effective method for developing a moral theory.

First of all, we should note that Bastide's is an imposing achievement. Even if we consider only his Treatise, he covers a wide range or problems, from a general and theoretical sort like the meaning of liberty and autonomy to concrete issues like that of the moral use of technology. Along with this moreover, we encounter a great wealth of ideas and of bibliographic references for further elaboration. Besides this, Bastide has a way with words; he piles image upon image and contrast upon contrast, so that the reader, even if not persuaded, is at least beguiled. What is perhaps most striking however, is the synoptic sweep and grandeur of his thought. His variety of themes forms a network that covers every kind of moral problem. Despite all this, we still have to say that Bastide's method is defective in various ways and for different reasons.

First of all, let us look at the question of how the reflexive method is tied in with idealism. Bastide, as we have seen, holds that there is a necessary connection between them. This however is questionable. For although idealist philosophy certainly may have a special affinity to the reflexive method, there have been many idealists, such as Werkmeister and Bertocci, who prefer not to use it. Nor is the reflexive method itself necessarily idealist, since it has been used by phenomenologists like Nabert, Thomists like Lonergan and Rahner, spiritualist thinkers like Lavelle, and an Augustinian like Blondel.

In Bastide's view most of our moral difficulties are the result of interpreting the world from the point of view of a physical realism, and more specifically of an Aristotelian realism. Methodologically, this is a matter of some importance, because the kind of metaphysics we start off with determines to a large extent our moral views and success. When however we analyze Bastide's objections, it becomes clear that he misinterprets at least the Aristotelian view and we can even doubt that he really understands it. For instance, he argues that in the realist view moral subjects are thought of as beings to which are applied the notions of substance and quality, which, being derived from the world of things, have been improperly applied to persons, who are then divided into moral and immoral in the same way that bodies are classified as heavy or light, so that morality is then thought of as a quality that can be poured from one conscience into another; it is the old dream of the alchemists.[9] In regard to this, we would point out that even though men are persons, they are also physical beings and so may quite reasonably be interpreted as substances having qualities of various sorts, both physical and mental. Thus, it does not follow that classifying men into moral and immoral entails that moral and immoral are physical qualities like heavy and light. Consequently, it does not follow either that a realist would have to think goodness to be a quality that can be funneled from one container to another like water. Nor then does realism logically entail the acceptance of an alchemy of morality. Indeed, it is most doubtful that a search through the history of moral philosophy could dredge up any moralist who has held such a view. Bastide also argues that for realists the moral subject is a substance that receives from various outside sources its "accidents", which can never change his essence, and as a result the realists are always faced with a dilemma: if morality is communicable, it is only an accident and hence unimportant, but if morality is an essential characteristic, it is not communicable.[10] Here again we see how Bastide misinterprets at least Aristotelian realism, according to which some accidents have extrinsic sources but others (including the most important) are necessary attributes, e. g., the intellect is an accident in the sense of inhering in a substance, but it is what differentiates men from beasts. Furthermore, for Aristotelians virtues are moral qualities and thus accidents, but they are of the greatest importance. They are also communicable and transferrable but of course, not like water or money, but through example, imitation and exhortation. Bastide argues further that it is this sort of realism which, when spontaneously adopted by people, leads them to think of the world as made up entirely of isolated things, thus grounding their egocentrism and anthropomorphism, which results in an innate faith that is always vacillating in its choices and is philosophically antinomical. Then, afraid of its own chaos, it masks it with all sorts of rationalizations and mystificatory language.[11] While we have to agree with Bastide that rationalizations, anthropomorphism, egocentrism and an isolationist atomism are unfortunately common enough and not conducive to morality, these nevertheless have no logical or necessary connection with an Aristotelian realism, whose proponents also have long objected to them. We have to say then that Bastide has laid his finger with considerable panache on some very real problems but he is quite mistaken in his diagnosis of their causes. Methodologically, this has serious consequences for his position, since he holds that moral theory develops dialectically but is from the very start misconstruing elements and relations of that dialectic.

We have to agree with Bastide that the proper working out of a moral theory requires a solid metaphysical foundation from which to start. The question that arises here however is whether an idealism like Bastide's provides it. Since our primary concern here is with methodology, it would take us too far afield to discuss in any detail the adequacy of an idealist metaphysics. Let us simply note the following. In advocating idealism, Bastide stresses especially the various problematic aspects of realism, concluding to its inadequacy and the need to accept its opposite, idealism. Although he does this with flair, we have just seen how he often misinterprets and distorts the object of his criticism. In a more positive vein, he argues that to the extent that we are passively receptive in our experience we cannot really be sure of it; we can know with certainty only what depends upon and results from our own acts. By ourselves positing the values in terms of which we shall act, we give meaning to our acts and to the things of this world in which we act. Clearly, we are here meeting with the most crucial issues of epistemology and metaphysics. However, a proper methodology requires, for the solution of such problems, that we start off with whatever relevant facts we can establish. One such fact is that human knowledge involves both passivity and creativity. Any theory that involves a rejection of either aspect is methodologically questionable. Bastide admits that there is a given and a passivity in our experience, but he argues that it gets its value(s) and meaning(s) from us. But we cannot accept this. We experience the things of the world as having a variety of determinations and of relations that they impose on us, not we on them.

A related problem that comes up is this. Although he does not discuss it at any length and is not very explicit about it, Bastide indicates that the world is in some sense an obstacle for us. It is a stimulus and a foil to our activity. He also admits that it is at least to some extent independent of us, since it obtrudes itself on our consciousness. Consequently, the difficulty is this. Even if it is unknowable to us, the world has to have some determinate characteristics which make it other than us. Since Bastide explicitly rejects solipsism, how can he expect merely by reflexive interiority to ever adequately cope with that external, impinging force? Nor will it work to say that the world is simply what we interpret it to be. Apart from the conflict of interpretations, the world, as Bastide himself admits, is not only an obstacle but also an obtruding force. Both moral rules and moral theories then will have to be based on and to some extent be determined by the nature of that obtruding reality, if a rational and effective ethics is to be possible.

The matter of the passivity and creative agency of the mind is of such central importance to Bastide's method that we must examine it more closely. For him, certainty can be had only of what results from our sole activity; we cannot have any sure knowledge of what is imposed on us, of what we are passive recipients. And so, by inventing our own values, we give meaning and fulfillment to the world and to our lives. His favorite paradigm of our passivity is the qualitative and quantitative determinations of our sensory perceptions. Our self-initiated activity is experienced in our efforts to see the world in a consistent, unified way and to make ourselves be the kind of person we freely choose. When a man takes stock of the results of his naive, realist faith in things, he becomes aware that he does not have to accept such discordant and frustrating situations and that, if he chooses, he can create and follow a set of unified values what will give him an authentic and fulfilling existence. We can now see a crucial inconsistency in Bastide's approach here. Why does the converted conscience choose to follow through with its transfiguration of values? Is it simply a matter of deciding to choose a set of values that are in no way imposed on us? That cannot be, for then there would be no point to Bastide's lengthy discussions of the authentic solution to the problems of war, the state and the family. Then too, and more directly, he holds that it is <u>necessary</u>, in order to achieve authenticity, to choose values that meet certain criteria. These criteria are then themselves values and they impose themselves upon us. Granted, we are free to either accept or reject them and authenticity. All that this means though is that we have to distinguish between the natural necessity with which our perceptions impose themselves on us and the moral or spiritual necessity whereby values require our acceptance of them. But both impose themselves on us, though in different ways.

Another difficulty with Bastide's view arises in regard to the objectivity of values. According to him, the world and what is given to us in experience do not of themselves have value. So, he argues further that we do not discover values, we invent them. Finding ourselves in an ever-changing, problematic situation, we posit our different values in terms of which we try to make sense out of things. Depending on how we do it, we are involved in a dialectic either of dissolution or promotion, that is, we develop into alienated, frustrated beings or we achieve an authentic existence. The latter we accomplish through spiritual conversion, by organizing our lives to achieve unity, richness, depth and clarity. Clearly then, we can object that from this point of view values are not objective. Bastide would agree that values cannot be objective--in the usual realist sense of the term, but that, he would aver, is irrelevant since he has shown that the realist position is untenable and that values are simply posited. Can it really be said though that this is a proper method of establishing our values? Again we see that the solution we accept to the problem will depend upon our metaphysics. Prescinding from metaphysical considerations however, we can judge Bastide's method here again in terms of its consistency. He holds that values are not objective and discovered, but created by us and also that there are both authentic and inauthentic values. The latter however makes sense only inasmuch as our values will either perfect or deteriorate our nature. It is only if we all share in a certain persistent potentiality for a given kind of existence that our values and our acts can either fulfill or thwart such capabilities. Unless we all participate in a common nature and can to some extent know what that nature is, there are no grounds for saying that any values are authentic,

172

valid or true. Or, for that matter, inauthentic and destructive. Thus, Bastide's approach involves here an inconsistency; he explicitly holds that values are not objective (in the realist sense) but implicitly he has to admit the objectivity (in the realist sense) of what he holds to be authentic values.

Other difficulties arise in regard to the criteria that Bastide uses for the direction of the moral life: richness, unity, clarity and depth. One obvious problem here is that these criteria, although unexceptionable in themselves, are too broad and formal to provide adequate moral guidance. We would readily agree that the moral life requires unity, but the moralist also has to specify what it is around which the moral life ought to be centered. We could not deny that the greater variety of experience we have, the more fulfilling and adequate can our lives be, but only if that experience and variety are of the right sort and are correctly interpreted: for which we need other criteria. We find it equally obvious that the increasing clarity of our knowledge can help us live better lives, but only if the objects of our clear knowledge are those factors that are really relevant to living a good life. We would likewise have to concur that the mature conscience requires an awareness of the different levels of existence and activity, but it needs even more to be able to evaluate them objectively, which also requires more specific criteria. In other words, it is quite insufficient for adequate moral guidance of people, even though it is perfectly true, to tell them that they have to develop consciences that are characterized by richness, clarity, unity and depth.

Another problem with these criteria results from the manner in which they were derived. Having been established by a reflexive analysis of the moral agent, they reflect primarily his subjective requirements for moral action: the moral agent must be consistent, lucid, possessed of the relevant facts and of a broad background. By itself however this is not enough. For, the moral agent is functioning in a continuously changing world and so has to continuously perform new kinds of acts. He must then have not only subjective criteria; he needs theories and standards concerned with the various things and actions he has to deal with. Clearly, however, this is possible only if we can to some extent grasp the nature of those things, how they are interrelated and how our actions will necessarily affect them in certain ways. In other words, such objective criteria as we also need can only be based on some ontology, some metaphysical version of the world. But an objective ontology of this sort Bastide holds to be impossible. His method then leads to an impasse. It can provide some general, subjective criteria but has closed itself off from the necessary means to deriving objective standards. Of course, Bastide would retort that our objection fails because it is the moral subject who establishes the meaning of objects through the values he imposes. To this we would note the following. If Bastide's axiological idealism is correct, then his method is valid and perhaps the only possible one. But if this is the case, then morality will be completely relative to the values we choose and it would not seem possible then to establish any universal moral standards such as Bastide holds to. But if Bastide's metaphysics is wrong and the realists are right, then his ethical methodology has to be deficient.

Another inconsistency can be seen in Bastide's treatment of retrospection. By analyzing past moral activities and values, the conscience achieves the necessary richness of data that it needs for its prospective synthesis. Now, from the point of view of a realist, dialectical method, such a procedure is not only defensible but necessary. It is however quite questionable if taken from the point of view of Bastide's axiological idealism. For, the data of retrospection were generally elaborated within a realist matrix. The values developed in that framework consequently reflect and depend on a realist ontology. Bastide claims that such values can be transfigured by his reflexive axiology, but this leads him into a dilemma. If empirical values can be transfigured as he says, then the realist metaphysics whence they come cannot be as inadequate and destructive as he claims. On the other hand, if, as Bastide claims, the things of the world have no ontological structures of their own and if realism is such a complete and gross error as he makes out, then it is illogical for him to try to transfigure its values. In this case the obvious alternative would be to invent new and authentic values.

This brings us to what is perhaps the major problem in Bastide's approach. He bases his position on the notion that neither man nor things have a knowable, objective, ontological structure and telic cause. But then, in developing his positive theory, he analyzes what he calls the fundamental forces, structures and functions encountered in human life and here he works out what is essentially a teleological account, which of course also and necessarily involves some sort of ontological structure. To establish and illustrate this, we shall for brevity's sake quote only from his treatment of the family. The emphases are his:

> There is then incontestably a <u>natural function</u> of the family. It is the one that a biologist could place, from his perspective, in continuity with the analogous biological functions in the species that we habitually say are next to ours. It is a matter here of everything that gravitates around the species' continuity, taken biologically: biological relations of the sexes for the procreation of a line; protection and bringing up of the progeny by the parents through a more or less sharp division of labor by sex. . . .
>
> . . . . . . . . . . . . . . . . . . . . . . . . . . .
> There is then an <u>economic function</u> of the family, in the sense that the family is always, with more or less stability, a center of production, consumption and circulation of wealth. . . . It remains however that around the functional biological core of the couple, and gravitating around its normal goal which is the social advancement of the children, there necessarily constitutes itself an economic communal life that has conditions of equilibrium in itself and in its relations with the other functions.
>
> As to the <u>moral function</u> of the family, it necessarily takes the stance of the educational function with its precise point of application on the child. Even in the conjugal love that is the most attentive to itself, in the willing of the reciprocal perfectioning of the spouses, the draining of the moral function into the education of the child is inevitable. The thing is that the moral function grafts itself there directly onto the biological function, through which it takes root in the depths of the vital. And thus is it through it that a direct link, so to speak, establishes itself between nature and the spirit--so much so that it is certainly along the length of this axis of the educational function that the moral destiny of the family will play itself out.[12]

Bastide's analysis here takes its data, as he indicates, from sociology, psychology and philosophical studies and though it is good, it is thoroughly structuralist and teleological, as indicated by the continual use of such terms as "incontestably", "natural", "function", "always", "normal" and "necessarily". Later on he use it to discuss with considerable insight the dialectic of the dissolution of the western family. But he cannot have it both ways; he cannot continually deny the existence of natural ends and relations and at the same time develop his theories in terms of them. What is wrong, we would say, is not his teleological analysis, which is one of the better and more useful parts of his work, but his metaphysics which led him to deny the possibility of any natural teleology.

Another problematic aspect of Bastide's method is the practice of reflexive provocation. When an individual moralist has achieved authentic existence through reflexive analysis, he then has to provoke others who have not achieved it into doing so. Firstly, we would object that this is methodologically invalid for the simple reason that it will not work. As Bastide himself has pointed out, the general run of men spontaneously react to the world in realist terms and it seems quite unlikely that any sizable number of them will ever be persuaded to reject as unobjective what they experience of the world, which rejection is for Bastide a necessary initial purificatory step. Then too, there is the matter of his position's intellectual complexity and difficulty. Complexity and difficulty are not per se grounds for rejecting a theory, but Bastide is not here just proposing a theory. He is presenting a method of achieving moral authenticity, which all men should therefore accept and practise. It strikes us that we have to invoke here Bergson's distinction between open and closed morality. Although an open morality is admittedly more adequate, for many and perhaps the majority of men however a closed morality of a reasonably enlightened sort seems to be a practical necessity and one that is from the point of view of its moral results usually quite adequate. Secondly, we rather fear that in practice Bastide's method would have to involve a reversion to mystical exaltation. For, few would ever become highly proficient at it, as he himself admits. Thirdly, we would object to Bastide's attempt to identify Socrates' method with his own. While we certainly would not object to Bastide's incorporation of Socrates' method into his own, we cannot admit that Socrates practised Bastide's method, not even in a primitive form. For, it seem clear to us that Socrates accepted the existence of an independent natural order which we can to some extent at least understand, through the correct interpretation of the data of experience. Socrates was an axiological realist and would therefore have rejected Bastide's axiological idealism and also therefore different aspects of his methodology, such as his explicit rejection of a natural teleology.

In light of all this, we have to conclude that the reflexive method cannot be the proper one to develop a moral theory or to provide moral guidance. It is simply too limited. It can legitimately provide only moral criteria of a very broad and formal sort, and it is capable of determining only those conditions of morality that are implied by the nature of the moral agent. Moreover, as Bastide uses this method, he is inconsistent, largely because of the metaphysical positions which he tries to tie in with it. Such inconsistencies then are not a necessary result of the reflexive method itself. But even if used with other types of metaphysics, the method of its nature has a very restricted scope. Thus, we have to say that the very real power and value of his ethics derive not from his reflexive method but rather from the empirical richness of his data, his teleological analysis of them and his dialectical confrontation with, and his assimilation of, other moralists.

Nevertheless, the reflexive approach can be used to help clarify certain points. One obvious example would be the conditions of moral agency. It is of course through reflexion that we primarily become aware of ourselves in our spirituality, that is, as rational and free agents. Bastide's criteria of unity, richness, clarity and depth are criteria precisely because they are seen to be necessary conditions for effective and rational action. That is, granting causality, we can achieve our ends only if they are consistent one with another, and the ends we seek will be and be known as the proper ones only if we accept them as a result of a deep and rich experience of the world and ourselves, which experience has been at least to some degree assimilated and interpreted to form a reasonably clear and unified Weltanschauung.

A second instance would be its help in elucidating the meaning of moral perfection. Here again his four reflexively determined criteria will come into play. The more fully a person meets these criteria, the greater will be his moral perfection. To the extent that a person has achieved knowledge that is rich, deep and clear, i. e., to the extent that he is wise, he will be the more able to determine for himself a set of moral ends that are not only consistent but reflect our objective condition and form a hierarchical unity well suited to guide us into an existence that will be proper and fulfilling. In other words and in brief, moral perfection consists of the unity of wisdom and autonomy whereby we can fulfill our duty. It is, as Bastide liked to say, being able to say what we believe and to do what we believe right.

# CHAPTER NINE

## THE NEOTHOMISTIC APPROACH TO ETHICS

The Thomists, or, more accurately, the neo-Thomists, have exercised a wide-ranging influence in the last hundred years, especially in moral and social philosophy. Their views on methodology, although inadequate, are interesting and useful.

At this point it would be helpful to take a quick look at the origins and development of neo-Thomism. In its initial phases scholastic philosophy was predominantly Platonic. Thomas Aquinas helped to revolutionize it in the thirteenth century by his adoption of an Aristotelian approach. Nevertheless, although Aquinas was well known and respected, his philosophy was never the dominant one in the pluralistic Middle Ages. With the rise of modern philosophy, the influence of scholasticism and of Thomism declined, although they remained strong in Spain and Italy. Their decline continued in the eighteenth and nineteenth centuries as they attempted to absorb from both rationalists and empiricists more and more notions that were inconsonant with their traditional realism. This situation started to be reversed around 1850 when a few Italian scholars urged a return to the texts and ideas of Aquinas. Eventually this move got the support of the papacy. The result was that the twentieth century saw a powerful revival of scholastic philosophy, which took the form largely of a neo-Thomism. Because it was used as the basis for the teaching of philosophy in Catholic institutions throughout the world, it produced a proliferation of textbooks which naturally tended to emphasize those points on which there was a consensus. Such a manualist tradition manifested itself perhaps most clearly in logic and moral philosophy.

### Thomistic Theory

Thomists, and indeed neoscholastic moralists in general, are in fairly general agreement as to how ethics is to be developed. They formulate it in different ways but the basic notion remains the same. Moral philosophy requires a double-stage approach, a combined process, consisting, as they say, of analysis and synthesis, or of induction and deduction, or of empirical and rational procedures. Their fundamental argument is that moralists should first of all determine empirically what man and the world are, and from there they can reason out how he should act. Thus, one recent Thomist summed up the position in these words: "Its method is a mixture of induction and deduction, rising from the experience of human behavior to a knowledge of human nature, and then applying its general laws to particular cases.[1] That such has been the usual neoscholastic view becomes evident as we survey the literature.[2]

As may be expected, this theory has a basis in Thomas Aquinas. He holds that we have two ways of reaching truth: resolution and composition (the medieval terms for analysis and synthesis). "There are however two ways of achieving knowledge of truth. One is through a process of resolution, in which we go from a composite to its elements, or from a whole to a part, as it is said in Book I of the Physics, because our first perceptions are of confused wholes. In this process our knowledge of truth is perfected when we arrive at a distinct knowledge of the individual parts. The other way is that of composition, in which we go from the elements to the composites. Here our knowledge of truth is perfected when we grasp the whole."[3] However, he seems to contradict the modern Thomistic doctrine that the method of ethics is a combination of analysis and synthesis when he states in his Commentary on the Nichomachean Ethics that in every practical science it is necessary to proceed in a compositive, i. e., synthetic, manner.[4] The reason ethics is a compositive science is that it proceeds from man's end to how he should act, which are as cause to effect. "For, to proceed from causes to effects is a compositive process, inasmuch as causes are simpler than effects."[5] It is only a seeming contradiction however, as he also admits the need in all activity to resolve the goal into its various means. "For when we want to deliberate about what has to be done, we first posit an end and then we proceed in an orderly way to determine the means which lead to the end, always going from what is posterior to what is prior, all the way to what first has to be done."[6] Thus, both analysis and synthesis are required in developing moral theory, as he elsewhere explicitly stated. "What is true concerning other matters is likewise true in regard to these. Concerning this statement of the Philosopher however, it should be noted that in order to know complex things it is necessary first of all to proceed by way of resolution, in order to divide the whole down to its individual parts. After that however, it is necessary to proceed by way of composition, in order to decide in the light of basic principles already known,[7] about the things which result from those principles." Thomas' statement that ethics is synthetic is thus to be taken as characterizing ethics at large, without excluding analysis.[8]

Of the modern scholastics, G. Sortais has perhaps dealt the most fully and clearly with methodological questions, so we shall take him as our paradigm, even though he is not a recent writer.

First of all, he notes that we speak of how we establish scientific explanations in two ways. Sometimes we say we arrive at them through analysis and synthesis; at other times, we speak of using induction and deduction. Thus, we have to ask ourselves what these mean and how they are related to each other. In synthesis we start off from principles, causes or conditions to descend to consequences, effects or the conditioned. But in analysis we do just the opposite.[9] Noting that these two terms seem to have different meanings depending on whether they are used in formal or empirical sciences, he argues that they really do not. "We can reduce these two types of analysis and synthesis to a unity. In effect, what characterizes synthesis in its geometric sense is to be a progressive process, since it goes from what is, in the order of logic, prior, to what is posterior, namely, from a principle to its consequence or from the condition to what is conditioned. Analysis, contrariwise, follows a regressive path; it is a procedure that goes backwards or back up (ana), for it starts off from a proposed issue and tries to relate it back to known principles out of which one can derive it as a consequence: it goes from what is posterior to what is prior, that is, from the consequence to the principle and from the conditioned to the condition."[10] Analysis and synthesis are thus each individual and autonomous methods which complement and control one another.[11] All induction is therefore analytic, because it is regressive. In the same way, all deduction is synthetic, because it is progressive.[12] All the other methods we use, observation, experimentation, hypotheses, classification, definition and analogy, are likewise reducible to analysis or synthesis.[13]

Rejecting as the method proper to ethics the purely empirical kind advocated by the positivists and the purely rational type used by Kant, Sortais con-

181

cludes that it must be empirico-rational:

This is the conclusion that comes out of the preceding considerations. The moral notions of good, duty, right, merit, etc., are not, as are the notion of mathematics, ideal constructions of the mind. On the other hand, they are not an object of direct observation. It is necessary then that the reason deduce them from the data gathered by the psychological sciences concerned with man.

A) Experience and reason: Since man is an animal that is reasonable, social and religious, to uncover the notions of the moral order, we must study anthropology, psychology, sociology and theodicy. But, relying on his personal experience and the experience of mankind, the moralist should especially concern himself with the analysis of moral judgments and attitudes. It is from the analysis of these psychological data and of the facts furnished by the other sciences which illuminate man's nature, that the mind through its reflection establishes the fundamental notions of the good, right, merit, etc. By then comparing these notions with each other, the reason discovers thereby relations that are absolute, necessary and universal and formulates them into judgments denominated the first principles of the moral and practical order. Examples: "Good is different from evil," " The superior has greater value than the inferior," "We should do good and avoid evil," "Good acts should be rewarded and evil acts punished," etc. . . .

B) Deduction: Starting off with these certain principles, with these necessary truths, the moralist deduces from them rigorous conclusions, which should serve as rules of conduct. In general, here is his procedure. In the formal part of ethics, he looks for man's sovereign good; then, in its material part, he determines for the totality of moral actions what is, in each individual case, the true good for man, in conformance with the absolute and general good previously established.

Conclusion: Law, end and nature are three notions that condition each other. Every being has an end in conformity with its nature; its

law is to tend towards it without cease; everything that turns it away from it is an evil.
Its relative perfection and happiness consist
in approaching ever closer to it; its absolute
perfection and happiness is to achieve it
fully. Thus, the law of a being is deduced from
its end and its end is deduced from its nature,
which we can know only through reflective observation: which is to say that the method of
ethics is deduction with a foundation in psychological experience.[14]

A terminological confusion might arise here,
which we can dispel immediately. Does Sortais mean by
an "empirico-rational method" what other scholastics
call an analytico-synthetic one? We must answer in the
affirmative. The trouble arises from that the former
term is more concrete and descriptive and thus seems to
have a wider connotation. Nevertheless, the core meaning is the same, as the scholastics refer by "analytic"
to the study of the relevant data provided be experience and the various sciences, and by "synthetic" to
the consequent deduction of what is right.

## Critique

Several objections against this theory, such as
we have found it in many scholastic works, seem licit.

In the first place it should be observed that
although present day Thomists identify their views with
those of Aquinas, we cannot ascribe to Thomas a very
burning interest in the theoretical aspects of methodology. Although he recognized its value, his remarks
concerning it are usually general and given in passing.
We must then be careful not to read more into them than
they actually contain. Thus, in speaking of resolution
and composition he states that they are in general the
ways by which we attain truth: "There are howevcer two
ways of achieving knowledge of truth."[15] This could
mean that they are either types or characteristics of
specific methods. Likewise, his statement that ethics
is synthetic is to be taken, as we have seen, to merely
describe as a whole the movement of moral discourse.

Since such is the case, we have to interpret what
Thomas has said in the light of what he has done. The
latter we have already examined in our second chapter,
where we saw that the characteristic feature of the
scholastic method was to be dialectical, that is, was
to proceed in the study of any problem by taking up one

by one, and by controlling by each other, all the opinions, viewpoints and data relevant to the problem..

Now, this control can take place only when one philosopher contradicts another, or when various conclusions which some thinker has reached contradict one another. The point in question then is whether Thomas actually thought that this dialectical control was of importance in the discovery of truth. The following text shows clearly enough that he did.

> Then where he says "not only" he shows how men help each other reflect upon the truth. For they do so in two ways, one directly and the other indirectly. One is helped directly by those who discover truth, for, as it has been said, when any of our predecessors has discovered any truth, as soon as it is related to the rest, he is bringing those born later to a greater knowledge of the truth. Indirectly however, those earlier men who erred in regard to the truth have helped by providing for later people an occasion to make the truth manifested more clearly through their diligent discussions.
>
> It is only proper that we thank those who have helped us to get so great a good as the knowledge of truth. That is why he says that "it is fitting to be thankful" not only to those whom we believe have discovered the truth and whose opinions we share by following them, but also to those who have spoken superficially in their investigations of truth, even if we do not follow their opinions. For these also give us something . . . We have to say the same sort of thing about philosophers who have formulated theories about the world. For we accept some of the opinions of some of our predecessors, when we believe they have spoken well, but we disregard the others. On the other hand, those whose opinions we accept had themselves predecessors from whom they got ideas and who helped advance their understanding.[16]

We should especially note the phrase, "to make the truth manifested more clearly through their diligent discussions." Although we would not go so far as to say, on the basis of this, that Aquinas held explicitly to a dialectical methodology, nevertheless it seems adequate proof that he would approve of it.

There is however another text which is even stronger, and which moreover was written only a few years before his death. "If then anyone wants to write against me on these matters, it will be most acceptable to me. For there is no better way to make truth clear and to refute error than to answer those who contradict us."[19] We need only observe here that "to answer those who contradict us" is a quite good description of the dialectical process, and that he says there is no better way of reaching truth. This leaves no doubt where he stands.

We have already noted a possible ambiguity in identifying the two couples analytic-synthetic and empirical-rational. The former seems an especially unfortunate choice of terms, for it tends to bring to mind the picture of a scholar busily at work in his university library, analyzing the latest sociological and psychological journals to synthesize the results in a new Summa Ethicae. This is admittedly a caricature, but it does make a point: these terms are too abstract to convey correctly the actual growth of ethics, which has often progressed as much in the concrete hurly-burly of life as in the thinker's study. For, many of the outstanding advances of moral insight have been the result of living dialectical experiences in which men, agonized by pressing problems, were forced to find solutions, as when Antigone formulated the principle of the natural law in defence of her life, as when Socrates developed the bases of ethics in his discussions with the youth of Athens, as when the Greeks worked out a popular theory of the cardinal virtues before its philosophical elaborations, as when the youth of Hungary, familiar only with communist doctrine, spontaneously developed and arose to defend ideals of justice and freedom.

From this point of view the terms empirical-rational are better, but their use by modern scholastics is still not satisfactory. For, ethics is empirical in a much deeper sense than they give it, as the moral dialectic is an integral part of every people's cultural life. Consider Sortais' explanation of moral method, and especially the sentence, "It is from the analysis of these psychological data and of the facts furnished by the other sciences which illuminate man's nature, that the mind through its reflection establishes the fundamental notions of the good, duty, right, merit, etc." This is clearly an example of excessive abstraction. For, Sortais would have us believe it is not within a culture as a whole that a moral theory develops but through a few scholarly spirits meditating on the data of their introspections and of sociology, anthropology, psychology and theodicy. On the contrary, ethics has in the past developed in a very different fashion, and we expect it to continue to evolve in the same way. For, as we have seen, the primary ethical concepts like the good, duty and right were not formulated by the first moralists but were found already made in the existing religious and social codes. These concepts have in the course of time been constantly reexamined and the concomitant principles reformulated. This has demanded considerable reflection. But this reflection has been the work not only of solitary scholars but also of various sorts of men actually pressed by the problems of life and seeking to solve them. Thus was it that Socrates was led to state the necessity of observing the law when he had occasion to save his life by disobeying it. Thus, again, Solzhenitzin's critique first of Soviet, then of western, morality is not an impersonal, professorial analysis, but a deeply emotional reaction to shared, agonizing experiences. The uprisings of untutored masses to overthrow the Shah in Iran and Somoza in Nicaragua were possible only with a consensus of their moral validity that developed after years of suffering, pondering and arguing. There are always some individuals who play more prominent roles than others in establishing a moral ideology and the better acquainted they are with moral theory, the more effective they can be. But in the development of ethics the work of the ethical scholar has been to some degree and for some time to state in technical language the insights of others, to place them in their historical and scientific context, to compare them, to criticize them and to pass them on to succeeding generations. Inventive moralists, those who developed these insights, did so in reacting against contemporary opinions about pressing issues. Some of them, like Aristotle, were both highly originative of new insights and involved in the academic, technical elaboration of the discipline. But now, since the main pioneering work in ethics has been done, the endeavors of the ethical scholars take on a relatively greater importance. Nevertheless, although the moral dialectic is now more frequently an academic matter, it still requires input and insights from moral agents functioning under ever changing conditions. In other words, the empiricism of ethics is dialectical.

The deductive function of reason in the elaboration of ethics, as usually explained by scholastics, is also inadequate, for they ordinarily say that the moral law is deduced from synderic principles, in the same way that a geometrician deduces his theorems from his definitions and postulates. Thus Sortais, as we have seen, says, "starting out with these certain principles, with these necessary truths, the moralist deduces from them rigorous conclusions, which should serve as rules of conduct." The actual establishment of a moral law does not follow such a rectilinear course. Take for example the morality of the right-to-work laws, which is at present being controverted. Whatever deduction the moralist makes regarding them will be quite short and simple. It will take the form either of

Avoid what is contrary to the common good.
Right-to-work laws are contrary to the common good.
Therefore, avoid right-to-work laws.

or

Pursue what advances the common good.
Right-to-work laws advance the common good.
Therefore, pursue right-to-work laws.

No one will object to the formal validity of these deductions. However, either of them will crown a vast number of inferences, which will not be deductive. For, all the disagreement will center on the minor premisses, which the antagonists will be able to posit only by establishing inductively the actual results of these laws where they are followed or analogically the possible results from similar situations. Thus, although the final reasoning in stating a moral law is deductive, it is unseemly to designate the whole procedure as deductive without making the pertinent qualifications.

To state it in another way, no moralist will ever be able to logically deduce a right-to-work law from only the scholastic first principles of morality. For, the means men use to reach their ultimate ends are determined dialectically, as is also the morality of those means. What happens is this. In the course of his life a person determines for himself an ideal or set of general goals, which is largely a result of his immediate and cultural environment. In a given situation, he finds himself confronted by certain objects which stimulate his desire. He thus has to make two quite different sorts of judgment. On the one hand, he has to decide if and how he can acquire those objects, and what would be the results if he did. On the other hand, he also has to make a moral judgment about the matter: Would such objects, acts and results be compatible with his ultimate goals? If they are, then they are morally licit. As many different people do this and compare their ideas and results, a consensus and practice may be established. Since however there is a great variety of ways in which one can work one's way towards his ideal--and also botch the job--, there is a corresponding variety of practices that may be established. It is this multiformity of human potentialities which lies at the root of the necessity of the dialectical emergence of their morality.

Saying that ethics uses the analytico-synthetic or empirico-rational method leaves the scholastics open to another objection, namely, that such a specification is insufficiently distinct. Although all other methods may be ultimately reducible, as Sortais claims, to analysis and synthesis, all that this can mean is that these are the general bases on which specific sciences build their particular methods. It seems rather strange that ethics should be the only discipline that has not developed specific procedures, so that its method can be characterized by only the most general and vague terms.

These considerations lead us to think that the only valid sense in which we can say that ethics is empirical and rational is not in specifying its method, but only in designating two necessary characteristics which its method, whatever it will be, will have to have. Since such is the case, it follows that the empirico-rational is not the method of invention of ethics, which also follows from what we have seen already here, and that the terms analytic and synthetic do not adequately describe how moralists have actually developed their science.

A further question here suggests itself. Why do neo-Thomists disregard so completely dialectics as the method of ethics? The reason seems to be that they considered moral philosophy primarily as a completed theory rather than a developing one. As they were more interested in proving the doctrines already discovered than in extending them, they were led to confuse the method they used in writing their textbooks of ethics with the method used by those who discovered and refined the theses expounded in these manuals. Once a theory of conduct has been worked out, it is only logical to avoid the meanderings which were necessary to its elaboration and to expose it in as simple a fashion as possible, which is as the result of a process of deduction based on evident principles and inductive data. Nevertheless, the method of one should not, in the interest of truth and accuracy, be called that of the other. A possible further explanation of this is the at least practical belief of many scholastics that their philosophy is capable of no essential improvement since it already possesses all the important truths. Thus, in one text we read, "The only complete, adequate, natural way of thought is scholastic philosophy. . . . There may be other non-scholastic ways of thought but none of them is complete and adequate, even supposing them sound."[18] If then scholastic ethics is complete and adequate, it cannot have a dynamic method, which pre-supposes radical improvement is always possible. To keep up with changing circumstances it has only to be sufficiently inductive to gather data on new situations; it can then deduce from its eternal and complete principles the needed practical rules.

## Conclusions

In conclusion then we may say, on the negative side, that neo-Thomistic ethics has generally been rather too rationalistic in its methodology. On the positive side, we may retain the capital point of its criticism of other systems, that moral theory can be neither purely empirical nor completely deductive, but must be a combination of both, while making the immediate reservation that such a description does not sufficiently circumscribe the evolution of ethical theory.

# CHAPTER TEN

## THE METHOD FOR ETHICS

From the beginning, our purpose has been to determine the proper, and some of the valid, methods of deriving moral theory. Accordingly, we presented in the second chapter an historical sketch of the methods used up to the nineteenth century, wherein we noted three major types of approaches to moral philosophy, the traditional, the rationalist and the empirical. In the following chapters we took up various contemporary representatives of each of these types and pointed out their various strong and weak facets, and in doing so were able to indicate to some extent the relative validity of each. We come now to the focal point of our work. We shall first review briefly the main characteristics of each type of approach; then we shall sketch out what we consider is the proper method of developing moral philosophy; and we shall conclude with a few reflections as to the results of our findings.

Characteristics of the Three Main Traditions

The traditional approach is first of all empirical. Aristotle, as we have seen, strongly emphasized the necessity to start off from the facts. But these facts are of many different kinds, and may vary in the certitude they offer. Some will be psychological, that is, will deal with the nature of man and with the type of acts he performs. Others will be metaphysical, referring to the structure and order of the universe. While yet others would regard the definitions and opinions which men have held of right and wrong acts. It is from these facts that the moralist derives both the general principles and the laws of morality.

Mere facts however are worse than useless unless they are understood, sifted and coordinated. Hence the stress which traditional philosophy lays on intuition. Its intuition, we would emphasize, is not that of the modern philosophers. It is not the intuition of Moore, by which, it is said, we perceive that elemental and ineffable quality called goodness; nor is it that of Ross or Hartmann, by which we would know an objective but intentional realm of values. Rather, it is an act of the intellect which, having pierced the phenomenal data, contemplates the underlying essences and their interrelations. It is by such acts that we know happiness to be our ultimate end, that we understand the primary moral principles, that we may view the moral life as a multitude of acts unified and directed to their ultimate end by the natural law.

This approach then is teleological, not merely in the sense that it recognizes that men seek ends, but in the fullest, to mean that it acknowledges an objective order of finality in the universe. This is of crucial importance for ethics, for in a practical science ends are first principles and if we can find in the world an innerly engraved design and order, then the moral life will in large part consist in conforming to them. It is a distinguishing characteristic of this approach that it does admit such a universal design and order and this is the basis of the natural law.

Although this approach upholds the natural law, it is not legalistic but is, rather, existential. There is, especially among the rationalists and the evangelical theologians, and to some extent among catholic moralists, a tendency to view goodness as consisting formally and exclusively in obedience to law. Thus, for Kant a moral act is one that is done purely out of respect for the moral law. But this is just the contrary of what we mean by the existential conception of goodness. According to it, a good action is indeed in conformity with the law, but this is not what makes it necessarily good. We call it good because the will, which is a rational appetite, accepts and cleaves unto that which the intellect presents to it as good and worthy of acceptance, and accepts it with the full and intimate response of the person's whole being. An act only in conformity with the law is only legal and materially good; a legal act is formally good when the agent commits himself to the object of this act in a loving and joyful union because he sees in it a means to reach his ultimate end. In other words the basic goodness of an action is not a result of its being prescribed by the law; on the contrary, the law prescribes it because it is good. Or, to put it another way, the law prohibits many actions because they are bad; but, on the other hand, some acts are evil only because the law prohibits them, e. g., driving on the left side of the road. Thus, the formal goodness of an act lies not in that it fulfills a prescription of the law, but rather in that the will chooses something which is really able to complete man's existence.[1]

Then again, the traditional method is integrative. On the basis of the unity of human nature and the consequent unity of our ultimate end and of the fundamental moral principles, we all have to follow essentially the same road to reach that end. Each step on this road can be described and explained in terms of the notions of traditional metaphysics, e. g., of act-potency and end-agent relationships. Primarily, however, this integration is the result of the application to the vast multitude of concrete and particular moral problems of the immutable laws of nature, which are all summed up in the unique, basic precept, "Do good and avoid evil." Such integration is impossible in other approaches where, on the one hand, man's nature and function are seen as continually emerging and changing, or, on the other, where man's nature and end are ignored and all is declared relative.

The final and perhaps most important characteristic of the traditional method is to be dialectical. For although it is, as we have seen, also empirical and intuitive, these do not indicate sufficiently the manner in which traditional moral philosophy developed. Experience gives the raw materials from which ethical theory is derived, but in the process these materials must be analysed, refined and sorted, and this is done dialectically. Countless generations have met essentially the same moral problems, every time in slightly different circumstances. They have passed on to their children their formulation of these problems, the definitions of their terms, and their solutions. However, as these are not always consistent and as they must also be applied to new varieties of problems, there is a continuous process of comparing the one with the others and with the new viewpoints forever emerging. Various traditions and schools form and they too criticize each others' doctrines and attempt to develop new insights into their own. This development of ethical theories over the centuries by their mutual criticism and reaction is necessary. Wherever over a long period of time controversy was squelched or was not possible, stagnation, then degeneration usually set in. The ages of greatest philosophic productivity were those rent by debate. As Adler has observed, "Controversy is essential to the philosophical enterprise as a whole. Engaging in controversy is not essential to the work of the individual philosopher. He can pursue in complete isolation his objective of knowing what is or should be the case. Conceivably, he might attain the truth he is seeking without paying the slightest attention to the thoughts of his fellow men. This possibility does not exclude the utility of philosophy as a collective endeavor. But it exists as a collective endeavor only to the extent that philosophers forsake their solitude and somehow confront one another in the light of their differences. To whatever extent the total philosophical diversity involves disagreement, controversy becomes an essential part of the philosophical enterprise as a whole."[2]

Such is the traditional method in ethics: empirical, intuitive, teleological, existential, integrative and dialectical.

As for the rationalist approach, perhaps its most striking characteristic in general is its persistent ond overriding demand for unity. This is also manifested in the manner in which it develops its ethical theory. It views moral philosophy as a statement of the necessary results, for man, of the evolution of the world, which can be understood only in the light of its (rationalism's) basic metaphysical intuitions. It is thus mathematical in spirit; it seeks to derive its whole theory from a few clear and simple definitions and principles. However, the complexity of its subject matter precludes the use of straightforward mathematical deduction; it relies therefore upon hypothetically deductive constructions. Since it cannot very easily question its own principles, the only way it can control its conclusions is by their logical consistency; whence the highly formal aspect of rationalist treatises; whence also a tendency to legalism.

The rationalist ethics is also concrete and dialectical, but here these terms have a very special meaning because of their particular metaphysical context. Dialectical here refers to the logically necessary evolution of a rational world by the thesis- antithesis-synthesis processes, or something analogous to them. It is thus quite dissimilar from the traditional dialectic, which is contingent and often deals with probabilities. Concrete here is more or less synonymous with empirical, but often it carries certain overtones from the usage of Hegel, for whom concreteness meant actuality, perfection.

A final, and striking, characteristic of rationalist ethics is its personalism. This of course derives from its metaphysics, in which mind and personality are the basic reality. So, in its moral philosophy the per-

194

son, rational and autonomous, retains the center of the
stage. This usually results in subjectivism, but the
dignity of man is its keynote and the foundation of its
theory of rights.

The empiricist approach to ethics is usually the
reflection of a materialist point of view. To be consistent with himself, the materialist can admit the
possibility and the validity only of sense knowledge,
whence his empiricism. But because the senses can know
only concrete singulars, that is, cannot form universal
concepts, he is also a nominalist. And this has important consequences, not only for ethics, but for the
whole of philosophy. For then metaphysics is impossible: impossible to know of God, to form a concept of
the universal good, to come to a realization of a
transcendent order of finality in the universe. Ethics
too as a practical science is impossible. If all that
we can know are concrete singulars, then these are all
that we can seek and we really have no free choice when
we seek those that we do. Hence, ethics is a theoretical science: a catalog of which things we seek, under
various possible circumstances. For these reasons empirical ethics are usually relativistic, anormative and
hedonistic. Since all we know are concrete singular
objects, we seek or flee them according to as they give
us either pleasure or pain. This however varies according to our upbringing, temperament and subjective
feelings. Hence, no universal norms for how we ought to
act can be set up.

The empirical approach is also scientistic. Because the positive sciences are empirical too, the empiricist moralist tries to adapt their methods and conclusions to his own subject, seeking in this way to
participate in their vogue and influence and to reach a
similar degree of exactness and certitude. He thus attempts to develop his moral theory inductively. His
ethics is in short essentially a list of those things
which men in general call either good or bad, and of
the reasons for which they denominate them so, be it
custom, utility, pain or pleasure; added to this are
considerations regarding what are the best means, as
shown by experience, of gaining or avoiding these same.
And finally, we see then that the empirical approach is
also univocal. It does not place any essential distinction between different types of beings, actions and
necessity, and so wants to use the same method all the
time to solve every kind of problem that arises.

Such is the empirical approach to ethics: materialistic, antimetaphysical, relativistic, anormative, hedonistic, scientistic, inductive and univocal.

## The Proper Method of Ethics

In regard to the relative value of these methods, our main conclusion is that the traditional or dialectical approach remains superior. For, it is the most objective, open and effective.

We shall then outline what we conceive the dialectical method at its present state of development to involve. We shall need to address ourselves to two major problems: first, the order of topics to follow in establishing ethics; second, the means used in establishing it.

## The Order of Development

As far as methodology is concerned, the question of the proper order of developing ethics is of the highest importance. This is generally admitted, but the fact remains that moralists differ greatly in the way in which they develop their theories. The reasons for this seem obvious enough. It is because they differ about the nature and function of ethics itself, about the nature of man, and about the nature of reality in general. So, as long as men hold to different kinds of philosophies they will necessarily have different views about ethics and methodology. Thus, depending on the general philosophy one holds to, he might use as his model of procedure the physical sciences, or the mathematical sciences, and so on, or he might alternatively consider ethics as requiring its own special approach.

From this it follows that in order to work out a moral system the first step should be to establish one's philosophical basis. We cannot develop a theory and code of conduct in a vacuum. Before any consideration can be given to what men ought to do, there are certain preliminary questions which must be answered. We have to resolve such issues as: What kind of being is man? How does he act, with freedom or according to a determined pattern? How does he as an individual come into existence and develop? Are there order and design in this universe? Is there a supreme being responsible for its existence and on whom everything in it is dependent? To what extent can we have an objective knowledge of our nature and of our situation in this world? These and similar related questions must be given a definite answer one way or another before a logical and adequate attempt can be made to guide man's conduct, for according to how we answer them, we shall arrive at respectively different views as to how man should act. All of which reduces itself to this, that ethics borrows, and necessarily, from psychology and metaphysics analyses and interpretations which function as the matrix of ethical thinking.

Even the most antimetaphysical thinkers confirm this through their practice. Thus, that antimetaphysician par excellence, A. J. Ayer, argued that ethical concepts are unanalyzable pseudo-concepts and that there is no way one can determine the validity of any objective moral values. Such views however clearly result from his particular nominalistic interpretation of nature and of our knowledge. With his different worldview, on the other hand, Dewey rejected such doctrines and held morality to be relative but objective.

Since his general philosophical position determines largely what his moral theories will be, every moralist has to take great care that he has an adequate and comprehensive metaphysics. Each one of course has to make his own decision about what kind of metaphysics satisfies best these criteria. Let me simply say that I have found the Aristotelian tradition of classical realism the most objective and useful. Viewing the world as made up of different kinds of beings, each with its own characteristic set of qualities, potentialities and tendencies but all forming together an orderly, intelligible universe, this tradition provides a solid basis for a rational morality. To the extent, then, that it provides a factual and reasonably complete interpretation of reality, the method implied by it for ethics will have to be given close attention by moralists of different mataphysical persuasions.

After assessing the adequacy of his general philosophical viewpoint, the moralist has first of all to take up the question of ends. The reason, as Aristotle noted, is that every act is done in order to achieve some good. Thus, every act has an end and the ends that we seek are what determine how we shall act. It will then be of crucial importance for the moralist to distinguish as well as he can, among the various ends which men do in fact seek, which are proper and improper, higher and lower, necessary and merely desirable, objective and subjective. Only in this way, by studying the whole range of possible ends and determining which ones men ought to follow, can the moralist provide valid and adequate guidelines for the conduct of his life. Of the various questions which arise here, the most important of all is whether or not men have any objective ends. For if it can be established that men do in fact have certain ends of their very nature, this will make possible a morality that is universal and objective.

On this matter also Aristotle provides an important insight. The main good and end of every kind of thing consists of performing its own characteristic functions. There is no reason to consider man an exception. Thus, by determining which actions and functions are characteristic both specifically and generically of man, we can thereby establish a certain number of objective ends. We have other ways too of determining objective ends. One is by determining the different sorts of innate tendencies we have; to each one there will correspond at least one objective end. Another would be to determine the different kinds and levels of needs that men have; the satisfying and the satisfaction of them would constitute natural ends. Yet another way is to study how men develop and to determine what are their potentialities and how they can achieve a broad and harmonious fulfilment of them. In all this,we should further note, scientific psychology, sociology and anthropology may supplement philosophical analysis considerably.

To achieve effectiveness in our lives, that is, to live morally, we have to integrate our acts into a coherent whole. In turn this is possible only inasmuch as all the ends which we seek can similarly form a unified coherent whole. This means then that we cannot just decide on various unrelated ends and then seek to achieve them. Rather, after we have established what are the main proper ends for man to seek, we must hierarchize them. This is a simple enough matter in regard to many, since those that are primarily means to others are clearly subordinate to them. A more difficult problem arises when we come to rank those various series of means-and-ends. Suffice it to note that in such cases our value rankings will be a function of our metaphysical vision of the universe.

Since the function of ethics is to guide conduct, after establishing the ends that we ought to seek and their hierarchy, the moralist must consider the means through which we achieve those ends, namely our acts. First, the moralist will have to have a clear analysis of how and why we act the way we do. For this he will rely largely on the work of the psychologists, both philosophical and scientific. To it he will add his own analysis of the effects of different sorts of circumstances on the agent's voluntariness, freedom and responsibility.

The hierarchy of ends having been established and the means to achieving them having been considered, the next logical step is to take up morality itself, the relation existing between our ends and our acts and whereby these acts are denominated good or evil. Here, the ethician will also have to make clear the distinction and the relations existing between moral, ontological and physical goods and evils. Another exceptionally important question that arises here concerns the difference between objective and subjective morality, which in turn leads to the issue about the degree to which objective morality is relative. In this way, we may further note, the moralist is laying the foundation for that art of ill-repute, which is nevertheless so necessary, which used to be known as casuistry.

Since we have various ends towards which we ought to tend, and since some acts are means to reaching these goals and others are not, the next problem for the moralist will be that of the moral laws or rules: the need for them, their nature, their functions, how they can be established and how they ought to be applied. Here let us simply remark firstly that despite the popularity nowadays of situationalism and of its denigration of moral rules, men still need a code of moral laws. It is a matter of psychological necessity. Even a professional moralist would have a hard time living a moral life from day to day if he had not learned a convenient summary of the main kinds of acts that should be performed and avoided. Secondly, the moral laws will have to be formulated in different degrees or on different levels of specification. The first and broadest of all moral rules, that we ought to do good and to avoid evil, is a self-evident precept that we derive simply by a consideration of the fact of ultimate ends and of the notions of good and evil. The other moral rules are simply applications and specifications of this general principle. We formulate them by analysis and interpretation of the various natural inclinations and ends which we have previously established.

To complete his theory on right living, the moralist will also have to discuss the various consequences that follow from what he has taken up: vice and virtue, conscience, guilt, responsibility and obligation, rights and duties. The development of these ideas will of course take place along with the others as it becomes possible, and needed.

Such, we hold, is the proper order of working out a general moral theory. It is the order made necessary by the nature of ethics and of human behavior. For, if man is a free, end-seeking, rational animal as he has traditionally been conceived, then to establish valid guidelines for his conduct we have to proceed as we have indicated by establishing the goods and ends that we ought to seek, and then determining how we achieve those ends through our acts. In the Aristotelian traadition the primacy of these notions of good and end has generally been admitted. Unfortunately, even in that tradition, the methodological implications of that primacy have frequently been ignored or overlooked. Perhaps the most outstanding illustration of this is the widespread use of the claim that "the end never justifies the means," just as though it were a literally true, self-evident proposition.

The central role which the notion of end has in the developing of moral theory has also been indirectly indicated by the practice of various modern moralists. Kant is a notable example of this. Thus, although he emphasized especially the formal aspect of morality, this, he says, "leads to a very fruitful concept, namely, that of a realm of ends."[3] As Kant sees it, this idea of the realm of ends has two important functions. First, it is the ideal in terms of which all activity should be guided. Second, it gives unity not only to the lives of individual people but also to the activities of all mankind. Thus, from this point of view, Kant and Aristotle agree. Then again, the Utilitarians, who along with Kant are among the most influential of modern moralists, also implicitly acknowledge the telic nature of morality. Explicitly, their approach is a consequentialist one: they determine morality on the basis of the consequences of one's acts or of the rules by which one guides one's acts. Acts that produce happiness are good; unhappiness, bad. However, such a consequentialism implies a teleological view of moral conduct: the good man is one who consistently chooses to do the sorts of acts that produce happines. Thus, there is a widespread, practical consensus among moralists on the need for a teleological structure for the development of ethical theory. Differences arise mainly in regard to the degree of relativity and objectivity of those ends.

The working out of a general theory is necessarily the first task of the moralist, since he has to establish some basic concepts and principles before he can adequately resolve any question of the morality of specific moral acts. However, a general theory by itself in insufficient. The general theory has to be applied to the whole range of possible human activities in order to ascertain which are morally acceptable and why. This second, more concrete and specific part of ethics can be developed in different ways. The older approach, favored by Aristotle and Aquinas, takes up one by one the various virtues and the corresponding vices. This has the advantage of continually emphasizing the fact that morality is not so much a matter of individual acts as it is of being a certain kind of person, of having a certain kind of character and of giving a certain direction to your whole life. A second approach, generally preferred by modern traditional moralists, takes up one by one the different kinds of acts, good and bad, that people commit. Its main advantage is that it makes possible a more logical articulation. We would suggest that a combination of the two, with the latter used first and followed up by the former, would give the best results.

Such is the order to follow in developing moral theory. We must next consider the means used in establishing it.

## The Dialectical Vehicles

Earlier we sketched the rise of the dialectical method in antiquity and the Middle Ages. By appropriate use of the developments of modern science and philosophy, we can now give a much more explicit, rich and adequate formulation of it in terms of the various means that the moralist can use to establish his theories.

The first and most obvious type of these means are facts. For here we must accept the position taken by Aristotle. We saw earlier how conscious and thoroughgoing was his empiricism in moral philosophy. This was not a mere bias, but a well-grounded perspective. As he pointed out, ethics deals with life and so must start off with the facts about it. Hence, even though it is not an exact science, we must still seek to make it as objective as possible, and we do this by first of all ascertaining as well as we can all the pertinent facts. These of course are of various sorts. Some will be borrowed from philosophical psychology and metaphysics; others will be more specifically ethical data, such as the moral principles which men apply when they find themselves in such and such circumstances; others yet will be the actual values and the opinions regarding values which men entertain, which can be ascertained through the polls and other research of sociologists and psychologists. In this area an analysis of literary works can frequently be of use too.

Common opinions about moral matters are also used by the moralist as means to establish his theory. Once he has established as a matter of fact that certain opinions are held, he then goes on to consider their validity. He cannot lay them aside as irrelevant, because their practical importance is great. His science is not the most precise; he cannot, like the mathematician, rely on clear deductions; nor can he, like the physical scientist, base himself on minute measurements; in many of his problems a multiplicity of factors create much confusion, so that the determination of the truth is often consequent to a certain flair, to insight, which may come at seemingly unlikely moments. Hence it is that the opinions of men may embody in various degrees the true solution of a problem. Whence also the necessity, for the moralist, to advert to these opinions, for even the most foolhardy of them reflect some smidgen of the truth, although in practice we can reject many of them after a brief examination.

Language analysis is a third means used to develop moral doctrine. It includes a wide variety of procedures. It may refer to searching through one's language to find the names of the virtues and vices, as Hume suggested. It may mean the study of how language is used, to determine thereby the meaning and definitions of ethical terms, in the manner of Hare. It may involve an analysis of the maxims and sayings current in a language, to uncover in that way the ethical principles accepted. The basis of all such analysis is the fact that language epitomizes in itself the experience of past generations, because it is our only practical medium of communicating that experience. Thus, whenever a new insight into reality is gained, a new term or a new use of an old term may be introduced into the language to tell others about it. If this insight has some validity, the use of the term expressing it may spread and become accepted. Later on, when these terms have thus become imbedded in the language, and so perpetuated, but usually also obscured, the moralist may then analyse this language to locate these various insights, which, when found, he can subject to a more philosophical type of analysis to make them sufficiently precise and useful.

The moralist also makes use of the positive sciences, but only as ancillary means. For he has at his disposal the philosophy of man and of being, and these, together with the data of ethics itself, provide an adequate base on which he can build a system which is complete as far as principles are concerned. However, as a practical philosopher he must apply these principles and laws, and it is here that the positive sciences are of use. First and mainly, they fill in or clarify many details which the moralist has to know to indicate the correct and full solution of many problems. Secondly, their studies may indicate to the moralist many specific problems which he either may not have suspected or which may have arisen with changing circumstances. Thus, anthropology provides much valuable information regarding the family, monogamous and polygamous. Psychology, by its study of personality structure and of reflexes, often renders clearer the etiology of much behavior which previously was either ignored or not too well understood. Sociology and political science determine more quickly and accurately for the moralist those conditions which are important factors in concrete problems of social ethics, such as the necessity for modern corporations to spend large sums to advertise their products; or again, the conditions which may create new problems of conscience for those individuals living in totalitarian societies: the citizens there face problems whose correct evaluation will depend to some extent on a knowledge of the sociological and political forces at work, for these determine how far co-existence and cooperation with the authorities are possible.

Moral philosophy also makes use of pragmatic verification. However, the legitimate employment of pragmatism in ethics cannot be along the lines laid out by Dewey, to wit, it cannot mean that the means determine the ends, that ethics should reject all ultimate ends, or that there is no objective hierarchy of values. Ethics nevertheless is pragmatic in two other senses. First, pragmatism is a corollary of ethics being teleological and empirical. After determining what are man's major objective purposes in life, ethics must then proceed pragmatically to discover which acts are good and which are evil, that is, it must establish on the basis of the experience of mankind which acts are means to these ends and which are not. Our traditional catalog of virtues and vices is thus quite pragmatic.

Moral philosophy is also pragmatic in its use of a secondary evaluative criterion of ethical systems. All moralists claim that application of their doctrines will make men happier; the degree then to which these doctrines achieve this, or make it possible, will be a measure of their truth, for we judge things by their fruits. On this basis, we can easily judge wrong such views as social Darwinism, individualistic capitalism and the various forms of totalitarianism. However, the pragmatic will necessarily be only a secondary criterion, since we often cannot determine with precision the efficacy of means to an end just from a consideration of concrete results, because there are uncontrolled factors also at work.

Consistency is another means of verifying and of developing ethical theory. As a manner of verification it is of particular importance in ethics, because pragmatic verification there is so often unsatisfactory and incomplete. The moralist then perforce judges theories by their logical consistency. For, as truth is necessarily one and cannot contradict itself, any doctrinal structure, once it has been set up, can be evaluated to some extent on this basis. This applies especially to ethics because of the large part which dialectic plays in its formulation. In this sense however, consistency is only an internal and formal type of verification. What is of greater importance is that it is used in a more material way in the actual development of moral theory. What ethics searches for is an integrated, harmonious and efficient set of means to the ultimate end. The moralist then must uncover which means objectively are consistent with this end and with each other. Thus, consistency under both these aspects is his necessary guide.

Extending, so to speak, the limits of consistency gives the moralist another means of making and evaluating theories, which we may designate as interdisciplinary compatibility. For, every ethical system is a function of a philosophy. In reference then to any philosophy, that moral theory is best which is the most compatible, the most consistent with that philosophy. But this indicates only a relative value of this moral theory. A more absolute evaluation will have to consider not only this, but also the compatibility and consistency of the ethics and the philosophy themselves with common experience and the other sciences. Thus, that moral theory will be best which will flow from the philosophy that is as a whole the most satisfactory explanation of the world, and which will also take into account most adequately all the pertinent data provided by the sciences of man, especially psychology, anthropology and sociology.

The formation and the consequent acceptance or rejection of hypotheses is yet another means of developing ethics, as necessary here as in the experimental sciences. Good examples of this may be found in Aristotle: his acceptance, as hypotheses, of the current opinions regarding happiness, the virtues and the vices. Thus, in regard to happiness he distinguished three arguable positions: that it consists of a life of pleasure, of honor or of contemplation; and he established the correct one both directly and indirectly, by showing that the first two were insufficient and that the third was the fulfillment of man's natural function.

Another characteristic means used in constructing moral theories is synthesis. Here, synthesis does not denote a mathematical deduction, nor is it merely a unified treatment of the problem. It signifies rather an organizing, an architectonic synthesis, an ordered systematization of human values. These cannot be deduced in the geometrical sense of the word, nor are they found as such in nature. They are the insights and opinions which men have in reference to what is good and evil. Ethical synthesis consists of defining, comparing and judging these values, in separating the real from the illusory, and in ordering these real values into a hierarchy, according to their usefulness and necessity. This is done by evaluating them in the light of the ultimate end, on the basis of their consistency and compatibility with it. Such a synthesis is thus deductive, but only in an analogical sense. It is not the strict mathematical type of deduction, for although its conclusions are necessary, they do not exclude the possibility of other equally good or bad acts. Consider what occurs. We know our ultimate end. Someone proposes some particular object as good. We investigate to see whether this object is in any way incompatible with the end or with the order of means to the end. If it is not, we say it is morally good and we relate it to other values in our hierarchy. If it is, we say it is evil and we exclude it from our system. We have gone from the end to the means for the end; these are related like cause and effect; we have then deduced, in an analogical sense, the morality of the proposed act from the end. Thus, because many different means lead to the end, it is possible to relate and order this wide variety of means into a comprehensive synthesis of values.

We come finally to the major means of developing ethics: dialectics. We have seen how it has been used since at least the time of Socrates and what we mean by it. It is that method of seeking truth which proceeds by comparing, criticizing and controlling by each other the various facts, theories and opinions which men have held in regard to each problem. It is especially necessary in ethics, which is a practical science and thus depends more for the solution of its problems on insight than on systematic deduction (as in mathematics) or on experimentation (as in the physical sciences). It is moreover the thread which binds and unifies the uses which the moralist makes of all these other means. Thus, he starts off in every problem by trying to ascertain the facts and here already he employs the dialectical method: by a continual comparison of these facts he is able to locate lacunae or errors in them by their lack of consistency. On the basis of these facts he is then in a position to criticize the various theories and opinions entertained for their interpretation. In so doing he may himself arrive at a new insight into the problem, which he may then propose as a new hypothesis, to be verified pragmatically if possible, to be checked by its consistency with the facts, with the more plausible theories and with the whole ethical system, and to be then in its turn inspected and criticised by the other moralists of the philosophical community. As this dialectical investigation continues, this insight may be either accepted or rejected, but ordinarily it will, by a greater emphasis on this point, by a deemphasis of another, by the discovery of new aspects of others, be subtly transformed and gradually incorporated into the tradition. Dialectics is thus a primary condition of progress. By it the ethical system remains open and hospitable to all new truth and growth. If all this is so, we are then justified in characterizing the whole procedure as dialectical.

We can now see why the traditional, dialectical method remains superior to all others. The basic reason is that it subsumes the other methods as aspects of itself. It thus has all their advantages and can transcend their inadequacies. It is also the most objective; that theory is the most objective whose bases and conclusions best agree with the facts, as well these may be ascertained; but the purely inductive and deductive methods arbitrarily predetermine that they will ignore certain whole areas of facts; the dialectical method on the contrary considers arguments drawn from any phase of experience and thus remains the closest to the whole of reality. In this way it is also the most open; based as it is on a foundation of insights into the nature of reality, it can readily absorb any new, founded insight into that same reality. It can do this because it respects the analogical character of reality and of our knowledge of it; for we must always vary our method according to the kind of objects we are studying, the viewpoint which we take and the type of necessity binding said objects; hence it is a methodological error in ethics to proceed inductively, as though we were studying completely determined physical phenomena, or deductively, as if living human beings were mere ideal constructs which never vary; the traditional moralists, seeing man as a free, end-seeking animal, developed a method, to determine how he should act, which allows full play to his ingenuity in discovering the indefinite variety of ways in which he can reach happiness, but which also takes into full account the limits imposed on him by reality. Thus, finally, the dialectical method is also normative, in a specific and adequate manner; ethics is the philosophical answer to man's most pressing problem: How should he act? The rationalists' answer, though highminded, is narrow and leaves many areas uncovered; the empiricists, if they do not simply deny the problem, cannot, with their assumptions, escape from the web of a relativism which makes impossible any real obligations and rights; but the supple and comprehensive method of dialectics provides us with what still remains the most complete and satisfying approach.

## Summary

Such then do we consider the proper methods of ethics to be. In regard to the order of development, there is a certain necessary minimum. The general directions, concepts and conditions of morality have to be established before one can determine the morality of particular acts. In regard to the means it uses, ethics must, because of the complexity and variety of its problems, employ a heterogeneous battery of them. It develops empirically, with a solid basis of principles from philosophy, common experience and the positive sciences, but deals initially to some extent also with opinions and approximative truths. Basing itself on an analysis of all of these, it arrives at many important intuitive insights, but more often must verify its theses by a pragmatic test, by their logical consistency, by their overall plausibility or by a demonstrative disjunctive hypothesis. It is then not so much deductive or inductive in the strict meanings of these terms, but rather is organizational, around the ultimate end, of an array of the possible means of reaching it. This synthesis is moreover established dialectically, through the continuous and mutual impregnation of their insights by the moralists.

The method of ethics, as we have described it, fulfills the conditions required by both the nature of ethics and the analogical character of all methods. As we have seen, the term "method" is analogical. For, what we call method varies with each science, because it must be modified and suited to every science, depending on the kind of objects with which it deals, the viewpoint from which it is applied and the type of necessity which binds said objects. Now, the objects which ethics deals with are man's free acts, with the view to direct him to his ultimate ends, in relation to which these acts are hypothetically necessary. Our proposed method answers these requirements. It is well suited to study human acts, because it bases itself on man's introspective testimony as to the acts he performs, and on the experience of the generations as to the effects of these acts. Being explicitly teleological, it respects the practical nature of ethics by determining with care the hierarchy of ends, in accordance with which man should order his acts. And finally, it allows for the fact that although every human has the same objective ends, which each can reach only by using essentially the same means, there is, within the limits of these means, a wide variety possible. Our methods thus avoids the error of those who would make ethics the study of acts which are extrinsically determined, and that of those who would allow no flexibility and diversity to man's moral life, but would cast it into a mold of universal conformity.

Finale

We have now in substance completed our study, having analyzed and criticized the various methods proposed for ethics and then presented what seemed to us the proper one. However, some further reflections as to the results of our findings suggest themselves.

An examination of this method brings out what seems to be another distinguishing characteristic: it is social in a way the methods of the other sciences are not. By social here we mean a dependence in the application of the method on the cooperation of a group, or to put it in another way, the degree of pos-

208

sibility of developing a science without the cooperation of a group. Descriptive sciences, like botany, and
deductive sciences, like geometry, are not social to
any great degree. The theoretical physical sciences,
especially in their present state, are quite social,
but this dependence on a group is limited, since the
group involved is the relatively small one of the community of scientists. Similar to them in this respect
are the speculative philosophical sciences. The social
sciences have a highly social method, as they depend on
the cooperation both of large teams of investigators,
and of the population who fill out questionaires, answer polls, etc. Ethics however is eminently social.
For, it develops only in the dialectical debates of
generations of moralists, who depend for their subject
matter on the whole of society, which creates the various axiological opinions which it is the task of the
moralists to evaluate. For, moral problems first present themselves in day-to-day life where they are given
tentative solutions, and are then brought to the attention of the ethical theorists, who are presumed better able to render a final and balanced decision. Thus,
what makes the method of ethics so social is its dialectical and practical nature.

It follows too that Aristotle's remarks to the
effect that wide experience is a prerequisite to the
study of ethics and that the young are thus not proper
students of it retain their validity. For, the dialectical nature of ethics makes necessary, to understand
its progression, a wide background in philosophy, the
positive sciences and the development of society, which
the young have ordinarily only in a spotty manner. Nevertheless, this does not mean that we ought not to
teach ethics to high school or college students. For,
they should have some knowledge of it and the time they
are in school is the most practical to present them to
it. For although at this time they may be incapable of
thinking ethics philosophically, they can learn what
the main problems and their solutions are. What is especially important at this stage is that they be made
aware that being moral consists fundamentally of living
according to reason. Having been thus provided with a
framework, they will in later life be able to build
around it. Thus, what is meant by calling the young not
proper students of ethics is that they are not in a
position to develop original solutions to moral problems or to evaluate on their own the theories of
others.

Along this same line, it would seem necessary,

when teaching ethics, to emphasize its dialectical nature and the fact that many of its arguments are not
apodictic. For otherwise, the students will get the
impression that ethics has evolved somewhat like the
positive sciences and mathematics, with proofs and certitude of the same order, and will tend to think that
ethics is a completed system, closed to any really new
problem or solution and thus not of any great interest.

In conclusion, we would also note that the dialectical character of the method of ethics manifests a
major reason for further and closer communication between philosophers of various schools. For even though
they may disagree on their basic principles, their particular viewpoint on a problem and their mutual criticisms often lead them to more adequate solutions.

# NOTES

## Notes to Chapter One

1. Novum Organon, I, 19.

2. Principles of Philosophy, III, 1 and 4.

3. Some Problems of Philosophy (New York, 1911), p. 23.

4. Idealism as a Philosophy (New York, 1927), p. 23.

5. Studies in Contemporary Metaphysics (New York, 1920), p. 27.

6. Cf. R. Carnap, "Logical Foundations of the Unity of Science," International Encyclopedia of Unified Science, v. I, no. 1, (Chicago, 1938).

7. Philosophy as a Science (New York, 1941), p. 223.

8. D. Mercier, Logique (Louvain, 1922), pp. 369-9.

9. Discourse on Method and Meditations. Tr. by L. G. LaFleur (New York, 1960), p. 15.

10. Cf. L.-M. Régis, "Analyse et synthèse dans l'oeuvre de Saint Thomas," in Studia Mediaevalia (Burges, 1948), pp. 303-330.

11. Cf. A. Lalande, Vocabulaire technique et critique de la philosophie.

12. For the medieval usage, see Thomas Aquinas, Summa Theologica, I-II, q. 14, a.5 ad corp.

13. Metaphysics 993b 20.

## Notes to Chapter Two

1. Cf. L. Robin, La morale antique (Paris, 1947), p. 1-2; L. Robin, La pensée grecque et les origines de l'esprit scientifique (Paris, 1948), ch. 1.

2. Nicomachean Ethics 114a 15.

3. <u>Discourses</u> 1. 9 and 3. 7.

4. <u>Nicomachean Ethics</u> 1144b 28.

5. <u>Protagoras</u> 352.

6. <u>Memorabilia</u> 4. 6. 1.

7. <u>Ibid</u>., 4. 6. 2ff.

8. <u>Metaphysics</u> 1078b 24-30.

9. Plato <u>Theaetetus</u> 150.

10. Xenophon <u>Memorabilia</u> 4. 5. 12.

11. Plato <u>Apology</u> 27.

12. Cf. L. Robin, <u>La morale antique</u>, 2nd ed. (Paris, 1947) p. 34-43 and J. Chevalier, <u>Histoire de la pensée</u> (Paris, 1955), v. I, ch. 3.

13. <u>Republic</u> 511.

14. <u>Philebus</u> 16.

15. <u>Sophist</u> 253.

16. <u>Republic</u> 511.

17. Cf. <u>idem</u>, as quoted in text.

18. <u>Parmenides</u> 136.

19. Cf. L. Robin, <u>La morale antique</u>, 2nd ed. (Paris, 1947), p. 36.

20. <u>Protagoras</u> 358.

21. <u>Meno</u> 88.

22. <u>Meno</u> 134.

23. Cf. our whole treatment of Aristotle with L. Robin, <u>Aristote</u> (Paris, 1944); O. Hamelin, <u>Le système d'Aristote</u> (Paris, 1920) and L.-M. Régis, <u>L'opinion selon Aristote</u> (Paris, 1935).

24. <u>Topics</u> 104a.

25. Cf. L. Robin, _Aristote_ (Paris, 1944), p. 41.

26. _Nicomachean Ethics_, Book 1, ch. 5.

27. _Posterior Analytics_ 71b 20.

28. _Ibid._, 72b 18.

29. _Ibid._, 100b 3.

30. _Ibid._, 100a 15.

31. _Topics_ 104b 13.

32. _Nicomachean Ethics_ 1094b 20.

33. _Ibid._, 1104a 3.

34. _Ibid._, 1095a 27.

35. _Ibid._, 1095a 16.

36. _Ibid._, 1095b 13- 1096a 10.

37. _Ibid._, 1097b 28.

38. _Ibid._, 1098b 9- 1099b 8.

39. _Ibid._, 1095a 30 ff.

40. _Ibid._, 1145b 1.

41. p. 10.

42. _Nicomachean Ethics_, Book 7.

43. _Magna Moralia_ 1182b 32.

44. _Nicomachean Ethics_ 1098b 9.

45. _Eudemian Ethics_ 1216b 26.

46. _Nicomachean Ethics_ 1179a 15.

47. _Ibid._, 1098a 16.

48. _Ibid._, 1104a 2.

49. _Ibid._, 1107a 1.

50. _Ibid._, 1145b 1.

51. Cicero _De Finibus_ 1. 9. Tr. by H. Rackham.

52. Diogenes Laertius _Lives of Eminent Philosophers_ 10. 128-9. Translation of the Loeb edition.

53. Epictetus _Discourses_ 1. 2.

54. _Ibid._, 2. 11. Cf. also Cicero _De Finibus_ 3. 9-10.

55. Cf. _Ibid._, 1. 22.

56. _Commentaria in Quattuor Libros Sententiarum Magistri Petri Lombardi_, I, d. 2, _divisio textus._ My translation.

57. _Quaestiones Quodlibetales_, 4, q. 9, a. 18. My translation.

58. Berengerius, _De Sacra Cena_, Vischer ed., p. 100.

59. M.-D. Chenu, _Toward Understanding Saint Thomas_ (Chicago, 1964), pp. 59-60.

60. _Ibid._, p. 157.

61. Cf., for example, H. V. Jaffa, _Thomism and Aristotelianism_ (Chicago, 1952).

62. Cf. _Commentary on Aristotle's Ethics_, I, l. 4.

63. "The Empiricism of Thomistic Ethics," _Proceedings of the American Catholic Philosophical Association_ 31 (1957): 13-20.

64. _Ibid._, p. 17-18.

65. _Summa Theologiae_, I, q. 58, a. 3. Translation by Kenelm Foster. (New York, 1968).

66. See _De Veritate_, q. 24, a. 1, ad 20.

67. Cf. _Summa Theologiae_, I, q. 2, a. 1 ad 1-2.

68. _Ibid._, I-II, q. 94, a. 2.

69. "Intuition in Thomistic Moral Philosophy," _Proceedings of the American Catholic Philosophical Association_ 31 (1957): 176. We have relied heavily on this whole article in our treatment of intuition.

70. J. Leclercq, Les grandes lignes de la philosophie morale (Louvain, 1947), p. 225. My translation.

71. Ibid., p. 225-6. My translation.

72. R. Descartes, Discours de la méthode, avec introduction et notes par Etienne Gilson (Paris, 1938), p. 23-7.

73. Cf. our treatment of Spinoza with P. Siwek, Spinoza et le panthéisme religieux (Paris, 1950).

74. Cf. I. Kant, Prolegomena to any Future Metaphysic, note to paragraph 5.

75. We were greatly helped in this section by J. Vialatoux, La morale de Kant (Paris, 1956); F. Sartiaux, Morale kantienne et morale humaine (Paris, (1917) and D. Ross, Kant's Ethical Theory (Oxford, 1954).

76. Cf. T. S. Jouffroy, Mélanges philosophiques, 3rd ed. (Paris, 1860), pp. 346-77.

77. Leviathan, ch. 6.

78. An Enquiry Concerning the Principles of Morals, end of section I.


Notes to Chapter Three


1. The Descent of Man, American ed. (1896), p. 97.

2. Touchstone for Ethics (New York, 1947), p. 58.

3. Ibid., p. 92.

4. Ibid., p. 66.

5. Ibid., p. 66.

6. Ibid., p. 166.

7. Ibid., p. 120.

8. Ibid., p. 30.

9. Ibid., pp. 32-5.

10. Ibid., p. 125.

11. Ibid., p. 131.

12. Ibid., p. 135.

13. Ibid., pp. 136-7.

14. The Ethical Animal (London, 1960).

15. Ibid., pp. 94-5.

16. Ibid., p. 137.

17. Ibid., p. 174.

18. The Meaning of Evolution (New Haven, 1949), p. 339.

19. Evolution after Darwin (Chicago, 1960), v. I, p. 542.

20. Ibid., pp. 523-4.

21. Op. cit., p. 193.

22. Op. cit., p. 203.

23. Op. cit., pp. 261-2.

24. Op. cit., p. 304 and p. 345.

25. Ethics (New York, 1960), p. 205.

Notes to Chapter Four

1. A Theoretical Basis of Human Behavior (Columbus, 1925), pp. 128-9.

2. Ibid., pp. 400-1.

3. Ibid., p. 401.

4. Ibid., p. 402.

5. Ibid., pp. 402-3.

6. Cf. What Life Should Mean to You (New York, 1931), p. 12.

7. A Preface to Morals (New York, 1929). Cf. especially pp. 155-191.

8. J. C. Flügel, Man, Morals and Society (New York, 1945).

9. E. Neumann, Depth Psychology and a New Ethic (New York, 1970). First German edition in 1949.

10. L. S. Feuer, Psychoanalysis and Ethics (Westport, Conn., 1973). First edition in 1975.

11. D. Skakow, "Ethics for a Scientific Age: Some Moral Aspects of Psychoanalysis," Psychoanalytic Review 52 (Fall, 1965): 5-18.

12. J. Wilder, "Psychoanalysis and Value" in Human Values and the Mind of Man. Proceedings of the Fourth Conference on Value Inquiry, 1970 (New York, 1971).

13. Cf. B. F. Skinner, Beyond Freedom and Dignity (New York, 1971), pp. 3-25 and pp. 102-3.

14. Cf. ibid., p. 101 and pp. 127-8.

15. Cf. ibid., pp. 103-8.

16. Cf. ibid., pp. 127-8.

17. Cf. ibid., pp. 127-43 and 164.

18. Cf. ibid., 145-53 and 180-3.

19. A helpful survey is Humanistic Viewpoints in Psychology (New York, 1965).

20. Ibid., p. 31.

21. B. F. Skinner, Beyond Freedom and Dignity (New York, 1971), p. 175.

22. Ibid., p. 181.

23. Ibid., p. 162.

24. Ibid., p. 183.

25. Ibid., p. 175.

26. Ibid., p. 173.

27. Ibid., p. 136 and p. 150.

28. Ibid., p. 164.

29. Cf. Joseph R. Royce, "Psychology in Mid-Twentieth Century," American Scientist 45, no. 1 (January 1957): 73.

30. Cf. Arthur Koestler, The Ghost in the Machine (Chicago, 1971), p. 352.


Notes to Chapter Five

1. Cf. J. de Maistre, The Pope (London, 1850), chs. 9-10.

2. (Paris, 1851).

3. Chateaubriand's The Genius of Christianity is a well known example of a more moderate use of this idea.

4. E. Durkheim, The Rules of Sociological Method, tr. by S. Solovay and J. Mueller (Glencoe, Ill, 1938), p. 14.

5. Ibid., p. 123.

6. This, we would note, constitutes in Durkheim a contradiction. For, health and disease are themselves normative concepts.

7. Traité de morale (Bruxelles, 1932), p. 290. See also pp. 262-3.

8. Ibid., pp. 280-1.

9. Ibid., see especially p. 220.

10. Ibid., pp. 286-7.

11. Ibid., p. 316.

12. Ibid., pp. 330-333.

13. Ibid., p. 325.

14. Ibid., p. 334.

15. Ibid., pp. 353-71.

16. Ibid., pp. 371-404.

17. Ibid., p. 527. See also pp. 438-40 and 521-30.

18. Ibid., pp. 531-2. See also pp. 514-21 and 530-2.

19. Ibid., pp. 684-7.

20. Ibid., p. 282.

21. Ibid., p. 280.

22. Ibid., p. 367. The emphases are his.

23. Ibid., p. 319.

24. Nicomachean Ethics, Book I, chs. 5-8.

25. M. Ginsberg, On the Diversity of Morals (London, 1956), pp. 119-20. The whole of chapters 7 and 8 are also especially pertinent here.

26. Op. Cit., p. 334.

27. Ibid., p. 687.

28. Ibid., pp. 286-7.

29. Here we must remember that he recognizes no specific difference between philosophy and science: he considers his philosophical principles to be necessary and integral parts of science.

30. Himalayan Village (New York, 1967).

31. P. Sorokin, Crisis of Our Age (New York, 1941).


Notes to Chapter Six

1. A. J. Ayer, Language, Truth and Logic (New York, 1952), p. 107.

2. C. L. Stevenson, Ethics and Language (New Haven, 1944), pp. 3-4.

3. Cf. ibidem, p. 14.

4. Ibid., p. 113.

5. Ibid., p. 138.

6. Ibid., p. 336.

7. Cf. ibidem, p. 4.

8. Ibid., p. 138.

9. Cf. W. D. Hudson, Modern Moral Philosophy (New York, 1970), pp. 231-9.

10. An Examination of the Place of Reason in Ethics (Cambridge, 1950), p. 61.

11. Ibid., p. 62.

12. Ibid., p. 137.

13. Ibid., p. 153.

14. Ibid., pp. 137-43.

15. Ibid., p. 160.

16. Nicomachean Ethics 1141b 20.

17. On the Soul 434a 16-22.

18. Op. Cit., p. 56.

19. This point is argued for at length by H. B. Veatch in his For an Ontology of Morals (Evanston, 1971).

Notes to Chapter Seven

1. Popular Science Monthly 12 (1878): 286-302.

2. Collected Works of Charles Sanders Peirce (Cambridge, Mass., 1931-58), 5.258.

3. Ibid., 5.356-7.

4. Pragmatism (London, 1908), p. 51.

5. Ibid., pp. 212-3.

6. Ibid., p.222.

7. Ibid., p. 215.

8. Ibid., p. 127.

9. Cf. "What I Believe," Forum 83, no. 3 (March, 1930): 176-182. Also Quest for Certainty (New York, 1929). p. 255-7.

10. Quest for Certainty (New York, 1929), p. 258-9. Cf. also "Logical Conditions of a Scientific Treatment of Morality," University of Chicago Decennial Publication 1st ser. 3: 115-6.

11. "What I believe," Forum 83, no. 3 (March, 1930): 177.

12. Cf. Ethics (New York, 1908), pp. 3-4.

13. Ethics (New York, 1908), p. 207.

14. "Theory of Valuation," International Encyclopedia of Unified Science (Chicago, 1939), p. 23.

15. Ibid., p. 24.

16. Ibid., p. 26.

17. Ibid., p. 34.

18. Ibid., pp. 34-5.

19. Ibid., p. 35.

20. Ibid., p. 45.

21. Ibid., p. 46.

22. "What I Believe," Forum 83, no. 3 (March, 1930): 179.

23. "Theory of Valuation," International Encyclopedia of Unified Science (Chicago, 1939), p. 58.

24. Cf. Situation Ethics (Philadelphia, 1966), pp. 18-31.

25. Ibid., p. 33.

26. Ibid., p. 42.

27. Ibid., p. 82.

28. Collected Papers of Charles Sanders Peirce

(Cambridge, Mass., 1931-58), 8.47.

29. Ibid., 8.49.

30. The Will to Believe and Other Essays in Popular Philosophy (New York, 1923), p. 209.

31. Reconstruction in Philosophy (New York, 1920), p. 177.

32. Loc. Cit., p. 64.

33. Moral Responsibility (Philadelphia, 1967), p. 33.

34. Ibid., pp. 34-45.

35. Pragmatism (London, 1908), pp. 59-60.


Notes for Chapter Eight


1. His books include : De la Condition humaine (Paris, 1939); Le moment historique de Socrate (Paris, 1939); Les grands thêmes moraux de la civilization occidentale (Paris, 1945); Méditations pour une éthique de la personne (Paris, 1953); Mirages et certitudes de la civilization (Paris, 1953); La conversion spirituelle (Paris, 1955) and his opus magnum, Traité de l'action morale (Paris, 1961), 2 vols.

2. Traité de l'action morale (Paris, 1961), v. I, p. 134.

3. Ibid., pp. 193-4.

4. Ibid., pp. 89-90.

5. Ibid., p. 106.

6. Ibid., pp. 102-5.

7. Ibid., pp. 440-1.

8. A good example of this would be the recent attempt of the Indian government to impose sterilization.

9. Op. Cit., p. 114.

10. Ibid., p. 114.

11. Ibid., p. 129.

12. Ibid., pp. 404-7.


Notes for Chapter Nine


1. A. Fagothey, Right and Reason, 2nd ed. (St. Louis, 1959), p. 28.

2. See D. Palmieri, Institutiones Philosophicae (Rome, 1874), v. I, pp. 174-85; L. Lehu, Philosophia Moralis et socialis (Paris, 1914), T. I, pp. 13-4; M. Cronin, The Science of Ethics (New York, 1930), v. I, pp. 20-1; H. Collin, Manuel de philosophie thomiste (Paris, 1927), v. I, p. 174 and 185; S. Lortie, Elementa Philosophiae Christianae, 6th ed. (Quebec, 1929), T. I, p. 278; J. Donat, Ethica generalis (Barcelona, 1944), p. 7; F. Thonnard, Précis de philosophie (Paris, 1950), p. 7; W. Wallace, The Role of Demonstration in Moral theology (Washington, 1962), pp.81-94.

3. In II Metaphysicorum, l. 1, n. 278.

4. In I Ethicorum, l. 3, n. 35.

5. Summa Theologica, I-II, q. 14, a. 5.

6. In III De Anima, l. 15, n. 821.

7. In I Politicorum, l. 1, n. 5.

8. Cf. E. Dolan, "Resolution and Composition in Speculative and Practical Discourse," Laval théologique et philosophique 6 (1950): 9-62.

9. G. Sortais, Traité de philosophie, Tome I: Psychologie-Logique (Paris, 1922), pp. 608-9.

10. Ibid., p. 614.

11. Ibid., pp. 615-6.

12. Ibid., p. 622.

13. Ibid., p. 623.

14. Ibid., pp. 759-60.

15. In II Metaphysicorum, l. 1, n. 278.

16. <u>Ibid.</u>, l. 1, n. 287-8.

17. <u>De Perfectione Vitae Spiritualis</u>, c. 26, n. 734.

18. J. D. Redden and F. A. Ryan, <u>A Catholic Philosophy of Education</u> (Milwaukee, 1942), p. vii-viii.

Notes to Chapter Ten

1. Cf. on this point I. Eschmann, "St. Thomas' Approach to Moral Philosophy," <u>Proceedings of the American Catholic Philosophical Association</u> 31 (1957): 25-33.

2. M. Adler, "Controversy in the Life and Teaching of Philosophy," <u>Proceedings of the American Philosophical Association</u> 31 (1956): 19.

3. <u>Foundations of the Metaphysics of Morals</u>, 433.

# BIBLIOGRAPHY

## Chapter One: The Problem of Philosophical Methodology

Buchler, Justus. The Concept of Method. New York, 1961.

Descartes, René. Discourse on Method and Meditations. Tr. by L. G. LaFleur. New York, 1960.

Dolan, E. "Resolution and Composition in Speculative and Practical Discourse," Laval théologique et philosophique 6 (1950): 9-62.

Donat, J. Ethica Generalis. 7th ed. Barcelona, 1944.

Ducasse, C. J. Philosophy as a Science. New York, 1941.

Edel, Abraham. Method in Ethical theory. New York, 1963.

Evans, J. D. G. Aristotle's Concept of Dialectic. Cambridge, 1977.

Mercier, D. J. Logique. Louvain, 1922.

Régis, L.-M. "Analyse et synthèse dans l'oeuvre de Saint Thomas." In Studia Mediaevalia, pp. 303-30. Bruges, 1948.

## Chapter Two: An Historical Sketch

Aristotle. Ethica Eudemia.

-----. Ethica Nicomachea.

-----. Magna Moralia.

Blanc, E. La philosophie traditionnelle et scolastique. Vol. I. 2nd ed. Paris, 1923.

Chenu, M.-D. Toward Understanding Saint Thomas. Chicago, 1964.

Chevalier, J. Histoire de la pensée, Vol. I: La pensée

antique. Paris, 1955.

Dittrich, C. Geschichte der Ethik. 3 vols. Leipzig, 1926.

Dürr, K. "Die Entwicklung der Dialectik von Platon bis Hegel." Dialectica 1 (1947): 46-61.

Eschmann, I. "St. Thomas' Approach to Moral Philosophy." Proceedings of the American Catholic Philosophical Association 31 (1957):25-33.

Gaudron, E. "L'expérience dans la morale aristotélicienne." Laval théologique et philosophique 3 (1947): 242-61.

Gillet, M.-S. La morale et les morales. Paris, 1925.

Goedeckemeyer, A. Aristoteles' praktische Philosophie. Leipzig, 1922.

Grabmann, M. Die Geschichte der scholastischen Methode. 2 vols. Freiburg, 1909-11.

Hamelin, O. Le système d'Aristote. Paris, 1920.

Hill, T. E. Contemporary Ethical theories. New York, 1950.

Isaac, J. "La notion de dialectique chez Saint Thomas." Revue des sciences philosophiques et théologiques 34 (1950): 481-506.

Lauer, Q. "The Phenomenological Ethics of Max Scheler." International Philosophical Quarterly 1 (1961): 273-300.

Masson-Oursel, P. La morale et l'histoire. Paris, 1955.

Régis, L.-M. L'opinion selon Aristote. Paris, 1935.

-----. "Origines psychologiques de la philosophie." Etudes et recherches 8 (1952): 111-35.

Robin, L. La morale antique. Paris, 1947.

-----. La pénsee grecque et les origines de l'esprit scientifique. Paris, 1948.

Ross, D. Kant's Ethical Theory. Oxford, 1954.

Sandor, P. Histoire de la dialectique. Paris, 1947.

Sartiaux, F. Morale kantienne et morale humaine. Paris, 1917.

Sidgwick, H. Methods of Ethics. 7th ed. London, 1907.

Thomas Aquinas. In Decem Libros Ethicorum Aristotelis ad Nicomachum Expositio. Rome, 1949.

----. Summa Theologica.

Tsanoff, R. The Moral Ideals of our Civilization. New York, 1942.

Vialatoux, J. La morale de Kant. Paris, 1956.

## Chapter Three: The Evolutionary Approach to Ethics

Deely, J. N. "Evolution and Ethics." Proceedings of the American Catholic Philosophical Association 43 (1968): 171-84.

Flew, A. Evolutionary Ethics. New York, 1967.

Hofstadter, R. Social Darwinism in American Thought (1860-1915). Philadelphia, 1944.

Huxley, J. and Huxley, T. H. Touchstone for Ethics, 1883-1943. New York, 1947.

Persons, S., ed. Evolutionary Thought in America. New York, 1966.

Platt, T. W. "Adaptation as a Normative Concept." Ethics 8 (1970): 230-5.

Quillian, W. The Moral Theory of Evolutionary Naturalism. New Haven, 1945.

Simpson, G. G. The Meaning of Evolution. New Haven, 1949.

Tax, Sol, ed. Evolution after Darwin. 3 vols. Chicago, 1960.

Teilhard de Chardin, P. The Divine Milieu. New York, 1960.

----. The Phenomenon of Man. New York, 1959.

Waddington, C. H. The Ethical Animal. London, 1960.

----. Science and Ethics. London, 1942.

Chapter Four: The Psychological Approach to Ethics

Adler, M. What Man Has Made of Man. New York, 1937.

Feuer, L. S. Psychoanalysis and Ethics. Westport, Conn., 1973.

Flügel, J. C. Man, Morals and Society. New York, 1945.

Fromm, E. Man for Himself. New York, 1947.

----. The Sane Society. New York, 1955.

Fulmer, G. "Skinner's Values." Journal for Value Inquiry 10 (1976): 106-18.

Hartmann, H. Psychoanalysis and Moral Values. New York, 1960.

Hinman, L. M. "How not to Naturalize Ethics: The Untenability of a Skinnerian Naturalistic Ethic." Ethics 89 (1979): 292-8.

Holt, E. B. The Freudian Wish and Its Place in Ethics. New York, 1913.

Krapfl, J. E. and Vargas, E. A. ed. Behaviorism and Ethics. Kalamazoo, 1977.

Lopez Castillon, E. Psicologia cientifica y etica actual. Madrid, 1972.

Maslow, A. H. "Psychological Data and Value Theory." In New Knowledge in Human Values, pp. 119-36. Chicago, 1959.

----. "A Theory of Metamotivation: The Biological Rooting of the Value-life." Journal of Humanistic Psychology 7 (1967): 93-127.

Neumann, E. Depth Psychology and a New Ethic. New York, 1970. First German edition in 1949.

Skakow, D. "Ethics for a Scientific Age: Some Moral Aspects of Psychoanalysis." Psychoanalytic Review 52 (1965): 5-18.

Skinner, B. F. Beyond Freedom and Dignity. New York, 1971.

Scribner, P. H. "Escape from Freedom and Dignity." Ethics 83 (1972): 13-36.

Smith, Richard L. "Essay on Personal Autonomy." Personalist 56 (1975): 47-54.

Weiss, A. P. A Theoretical Basis of Human Behavior. Columbus, 1925.

Wilder, J. "Psychoanalysis and Values." In Human Values and the Mind of Man. Proceedings of the Fourth Conference of Value Inquiry, 1970. New York, 1971.

Wolfe, David L. "The Behavior of Knowing: The Consequences of B. F. Skinner's Epistemology." Personalist 56 (1975): 233-41.

## Chapter Five: The Sociological Approach to Ethics

Deploige, S. The Conflict between Ethics and Sociology. Tr. by C. c. Miltner. St. Louis, 1938.

Dupréel, Eugène. Esquisse d'une philosophie des valeurs. Paris, 1939.

-----. Traité de morale. Brussels, 1932.

Durkheim, E. The Rules of Sociological Method. Tr. by S. Solovay and J. Mueller. Glencoe, Ill., 1938.

Ginsberg, M. On the Diversity of Morals. London, 1956.

Ossowska, M. "La contribution d'Eugène Dupréel à la sociologie de la morale." Revue internationale de philosophie 22 (1968): 84-94.

Paumen, J. "Eugène Dupréel et les deux philosophies." Revue internationale de philosophie 22 (1968): 66-83.

Petras, J. W. "Social-Psychological Theory as a Basis

for a Theory of Ethics." Journal of Value Inquiry
2 (1968): 9-21.


Chapter Six: Analytic Approaches to Ethics


Baier, K. The Moral Point of view. Ithaca, 1958.

Hampshire, S. Thought and Action. London, 1959.

Hare, R. M. The Language of Morals. New York, 1952.

Hudson, W. D. Modern Moral Philosophy. New York, 1970.

Kerner, G. C. The Revolution in Ethical Theory. New
York, 1966.

Lawler, R. Philosophical Analysis and Ethics.
Milwaukee, 1968.

Murphy, A. E. The Theory of Practical Reason. La Salle,
Ill., 1969.

Nowell-Smith, P. H. Ethics. Harmondsworth, England,
1954.

Sontag, F. "The Decline of British Ethical theory,
1903-1957." Philosophy and Phenomenological
Research 18 (1957): 219-26.

Stevenson, C. Ethics and Language. New Haven, 1944.

Taylor, P. W. Normative Discourse. Englewood Cliffs, N.
J., 1961.

Toulmin, S. An Examination of the Place of Reason in
Ethics. Cambridge, 1950.

Veatch, H. B. For an Ontology of Morals. Evanston,
Ill., 1971.

-----. "Language and Ethics: 'What's Hecuba to Him, or
He to Hecuba?' " Proceedings and Addresses of the
American Philosophical Association 44 (1970-71):
45-62.

Warnock, M. Ethics since 1900. London, 1960.

Wilson, John. Reason and Morals. Cambridge, 1961.

Chapter Seven: The Pragmatic and Situationist Approaches to Ethics

Bernstein, R. J. "Knowledge, Value and Freedom." In John Dewey and the Experimental Spirit in Philosophy, edited by C. W. Hendel, pp. 63-92. New York, 1959.

Blewett, J. E., ed. John Dewey: His thought and Influence. New York, 1960.

Cox, H. G., ed. The Situation Ethics Debate. Philadelphia, 1968.

Dewey, John. Ethics. New York, 1908.

-----. Quest for Certainty. New York, 1929.

-----. "Theory of Valuation." International Encyclopedia of Unified Science. Chicago, 1939.

Dougherty, J. "Recent Developments in Naturalistic Ethics." Proceedings of the American Catholic Philosophical Association 33 (1959): 97-108.

Fletcher, J. Moral Responsibility. Philadelphia, 1967.

-----. Situation Ethics. Philadelphia, 1966.

Hook, S. The Quest for Being. New York, 1961.

James, William. Pragmatism. London, 1908.

Peirce, C. S. Collected Papers of Charles Sanders Peirce. 8 vols. Cambridge, Mass., 1931-58.

Roth, R. J. John Dewey and Self-Realization. Englewood Cliffs, N. J., 1963.

Chapter Eight: The Idealist Approach to Ethics

Bastide, G. Traité de l'action morale. Paris, 1961.

Brightman, E. S. Nature and Values. New York, 1945.

-----. A Philosophy of Ideals. New York, 1928.

Le Senne, R. Traité de morale générale. Paris, 1949.

Paton, H. J. The Good Will. London, 1927.

Raich,M. Fichte, seine Ethik and seine Stellung zum Problem des Individualismus. Tubingen, 1903.

## Chapter Nine: The Neo-Thomistic Approach to Ethics

Calcagno, F. Philosophia Scholastica. Vol. I. Naples, 1946.

Gonseth, F., ed. Philosophie néo-scolastique et philosophie ouverte. Paris, 1954.

Johnson, D. H. "The Ground for a Scientific Ethics according to St. Thomas." Modern Schoolman 40 (1963): 347-72.

Lachance, Louis. L'humanisme politique de Saint Thomas. Paris, 1939.

Leclercq, J. Les grandes Lignes de la philosophie morale. Louvain, 1947.

-----. La philosophie morale de Saint Thomas devant la pensée contemporaine. Louvain, 1955.

Manser, G. M. Das Naturrecht in thomistischer Beleuchtung. Freiburg, 1944.

Rimaud, J. Thomisme et méthode. Paris, 1925.

Sertillanges, A. D. La philosophie morale de Saint Thomas d'Aquin. Paris, 1922.

Sortais, G. Traité de philosophie, Tome I: Psychologie-Logique. Paris, 1922.

Wallace, W. The Role of Demonstration in Moral Theology. Washington, 1962.

## Chapter Ten: The Method for Ethics

Adler, M. J. Dialectic. New York 1927.

-----. A Dialectic of Morals. Notre Dame, 1941.

Beis, R. H. "Some Contributions of Anthropology to Ethics." The Thomist 28 (1964): 174-224.

Edel, Abraham. Ethical Judgment. New York, 1964.

Edel, Abraham and Edel, May. Anthropology and Ethics. Springfield, Ill., 1959.

Krook, D. Three traditions of Moral Thought. Cambridge, 1959.

Maguire, D. C. The Moral Choice. New York, 1978.

Milhaven, J. G. "Towards an Epistemology of Ethics." Theological Studies 27 (1966): 228-41.

Noonan, J. T. The Scholastic theory of Usury. Cambridge, Mass., 1957.

# INDEX OF NAMES

# ABOUT THE AUTHOR

Gerard J. Dalcourt received his doctorate in philosophy from the University of Montreal and is now professor of philosophy at Seton Hall University. He edited (and translated in part) Yves Simon's <u>The Great Dialogue of Nature and Space</u>. Some dozen of his articles have come out in such publications as the <u>International Philosophical Quarterly</u>, <u>Metaphilosophy</u>, <u>America</u> and the <u>New Catholic Encyclopedia</u>. He has also published scores of reviews in such journals as <u>Choice</u> and <u>Catholic Library World</u>.